WHO KILLED JILL DANDO?

Executive Action

By Robert Rae

FOREWORD

This story will put into question the practices of a host of institutions. It is written to begin at the point when Robert Rae becomes certain the British Establishment are conducting a terror campaign in the West of Scotland with himself fully immersed in the ongoing bloody slaughter. Jill Dando is included in this episode; only survivors are rare in this situation. From Strathclyde in Scotland it goes on to give a reason for Jill Dando's murder as well as why Scotland, being one of the richest countries in the world today, had the highest emigration rate of any Western country, combined with other unsolved murders. It details how a democracy has been reduced to a dictatorship with a law that cannot address a single issue, a police force that behave above the law, an absence of human rights, government minister's involvement, and a media that behaves like a propaganda service to perpetuate the terror. Today they might see how shameful they really are because Jill Dando was their best example and had they acted with some conviction the lady might still be alive today. Her and hundreds of others...

1. THE WILD WEST

It was late Saturday morning, the 10th May 1997, when sitting at the kitchen table idly drinking a cup of tea I heard a vehicle approaching. The weather was dull and depressing and there was no reason for anyone to be about, let alone to create a disturbance. This vehicle pulled up and started manoeuvring outside. I glanced nervously through the frosted front door windows but all that could be discerned was that it was burgundy in colour. The house sits in a rural situation with no immediate neighbours on a single-track road, where opposite there is a rough farm track leading off into the distance.

The driver of the vehicle sounded his horn as if he/she was informing someone indoors that their lift had arrived. I thought that this was pretty odd because there was nobody here expecting to be picked up. So who could this stranger be? What was he/she doing here?

Immediately, I was worried. Having just recently survived an assassination attempt courtesy of the British Establishment, only an idiot was going to open the front door to a horn blast because the next blast might have come from the barrel of a gun. I kept calm and thought over what action I should take then rose and as a precaution turned the key to lock the front door and went upstairs. With a mixture of curiosity and fear, I looked out of the front bedroom window and was relieved to see that it was nothing more sinister than a stationery *Land Rover Discovery*. It was sitting quite peacefully at an awkward angle. The vehicle's front corner on the driver's side was nearest the house. The only occupant of the vehicle was a woman driver where both her and jeep were strangers to this locality. Then the thought struck me that others could have already left and approached the house with motives other than surveillance.

Fortunately, all remained quiet and so I reassured myself with the belief that this was the wrong time of day for them to make another hit on my life. Nevertheless, the woman sat at the wheel of the *Land Rover*, looking patiently to her right, with her eyes fixed upon the front door of the house. This was all very strange, and so, as a secondary precaution, I jotted down the registration number from the front plate. Then the woman appeared to be talking at one point, but, to whom was she speaking? Was she simply speaking to herself or to some other hitherto unseen occupant of the vehicle, or was she singing along to some music on the stereo?

Surveying the situation from an elevated vantage point meant my line of vision was directly down into the cab of the jeep. There, on her lap, was something of interest; a three inch blue circle. What was it? To me, it appeared to be a camera lens. Excited at this development, I peered even harder into the interior of the vehicle to see what other secrets it held, feeling the same expectations a child has on Christmas morning to see what Santa has brought. Hopefully, there would be no guns...

Eventually, another feature became apparent. Behind the two front seats, just below the driver's left elbow, there was the crown of a man's head. Wedged in where he was, obviously uncomfortable in that position, had the front door been opened, this cameraman was in a perfect position to take a photograph of anyone coming out. Now all the manoeuvring of the jeep to obtain the correct position made sense, as did the horn blast...

In this game of hard knocks, to be shot with something as mundane as a camera felt like a soft option, but it did raise one damning question. Someone was going to extreme lengths to get a picture of me. But; who? And, most importantly, why? Whatever the motives of this odd couple, they were going to wait a long hour before their quarry ventured outside. The man contorted into the backseat foot-well would begin to suffer from leg cramps sooner or later, and I reckoned that there is only so long any woman will remain fascinated by your front door before losing interest and driving off, so I decided to lay low. This reckoning proved accurate, as the jeep pulled away with the light-haired driver once again appearing to speak to her companion, who had slowly edged up onto the back seat as they departed. Little did they know that their adversary had been fully aware of their antics.

I found this experience both reassuring and puzzling. Relieved, of course, that I was still alive, but puzzled at why they had tried to shoot me with a Polaroid this time rather than with a firearm. I treated this experience as a warning, and decided to remain on full guard from that moment onwards. The next three days proved to be uneventful. However, there was no real preparation for the hammer blow their next attack was to be.

Having seen notices advertising that the murder of a local girl was to be reconstructed for the BBC *Crimewatch* programme for a second time, I immediately felt vulnerable. Interest in the case was high for a reason other than the fact that it was another on-your-doorstep incident. The second *Crimewatch* appeal was televised on Tuesday night on the 13th May, 1997, and the young woman in question was Jacqueline Gallacher. She had, unfortunately, turned to prostitution to fund her drug habit and, sadly, had become the fifth in a series of women murdered while working in Glasgow's red light district.

As I settled down to watch the programme, there was only one burning question on my mind, 'Who are they framing, tonight?' This may seem extreme to you for me to be thinking in this manner, but the word on these prostitute murders was both intriguing and damning.

NO MEAN CITY

Glasgow was once a sprawling city with a reputation for shipbuilding and for violence between rival gangs of youths. In recent years, the city's population has declined considerably along with its shipbuilding capacity and its 'hard man' image. However, in the 1990s, the city was plagued with a series of prostitute murders and an increasingly high number of drug-related deaths averaging over a hundred per year in Strathclyde, which have been given a high level of media coverage therefore frequently became a topic of conversation. Due to the absence of any convictions, the question of who was murdering the prostitutes in Glasgow remained unanswered. Was there a serial killer operating in the city? People were starting to speculate about a Glasgow Ripper. The police repeatedly dispelled any thought of this possibility by stressing that they did not believe there was a link between the deaths of any two of the murdered women. Such a statement thereby creates a question as to why these murders remain unsolved.

Thirty years previously, police believed that the murders of three women in Glasgow could be linked to the work of the same man, although it must be said, neither of these women were selling sex. In Glasgow's best gallows humour, the culprit was given the nickname, 'Bible John'. His physical description was well publicised by the media along with an artist's impression and information pertaining to how he operated. In spite of all this information being widely circulated Bible John was never captured.

It seems truly remarkable that the murder of five working girls can go completely unnoticed nowadays in Scotland's busiest urban centre in spite of the fact that an extensive network of CCTV security cameras cover Glasgow city centre, including the red light district. It is equally incredible that the police, armed as they are with all the advances that have been made in forensic science over the last thirty years, have such a lack of positive leads, accurate descriptions and eye witness accounts to follow up and these cases remain unsolved. This suggests that perhaps a more sinister answer lies lurking in the shadows.

Never ending speculation said that drug dealers and pimps were involved because both parties can be easily placed in the cauldron of sex, drugs and violence that exists in any inner city red light district. I would suggest that both these possibilities should be promptly ruled out by the fact that these people are unlikely to bite off the hand that feed them. The majority of women working in this notorious area are pressured into the vice trade to pay off debts created by drug habits, and likewise, pimps and drug dealers have a vested interest in their wellbeing in order to increase their own finances. No; there has to be more to all these deaths than simply to pass them off as purely random acts; the question is what?

The craic on the streets concerning these events was somewhat different to all the speculation and guesswork that was being circulated in the media, and, evil and outlandish as it sounded, it did have a ring of truth about it. Word was that the police were indirectly involved in the slaughter. Special Branch were allegedly going around systematically butchering prostitutes, junkies and down-and-outs and also those whom they had failed to frame for the prostitute murders and passing these deaths off as anything other than murder.

Backing this impression up was graffiti at the time reading, '*Police Murder Prostitutes*', or perhaps more accurately, '*Special Branch Murder Prostitutes*'. At least this provides an explanation for the lack of witnesses and why no accurate or positive sightings could be obtained from the CCTV and business security camera networks in the city centre. All along, the question has been not who was committing these murders, but who was covering them up? The answer to this dilemma will quickly reveal the culprits.

What aroused my suspicions most was the case of the prostitute who was drowned in the River Clyde when, over the spring and summer of 1995, several bodies were fished out of the water. Initially, her death was not classified as murder until another woman escaped the clutches of a man who tried to drown her in the river. Only after that happened, was the prostitute's case upgraded to a murder inquiry. No mention was ever made of the other victims drowned in the Clyde. I found it extremely strange that all these homeless people and others should decide to commit mass suicide over the same period of time. Further supporting this is anyone who has ever seen the murky water of this river, bordered by steep concrete walls covered in slime, will find this a horrific way to commit suicide. As far as the case of the woman who narrowly escaped her attacker is concerned, it would have been expected that the victim would have been able to supply the police with an accurate description of her attacker, thereby allowing them to compile a photo-fit of the culprit. Surely in the light of this evidence and the volume of suspicious deaths that had already occurred, a genuine investigation would have been relentlessly pursued. However, I remember waiting at the time for the description to be released and when it was revealed, it appeared that the police released it reluctantly and the description itself seemed extremely vague, and the entire episode quickly passed over.

People targeted as possible suspects for the prostitute murders then had a nasty habit of being found dead in varying circumstances. Brutal and callous as it sounds, what had been heard years ago as idle gossip, inevitably distorted by the telling by word of mouth, gradually began to gather credence. People like to solve mysteries, but this puzzle was different with frightening consequences for anyone caught up in it.

MURDER

The murder of Jacqueline Gallacher was on the 23rd June 1996, where shortly afterwards the BBC screened their first *Crimewatch* appeal concerning her death. On this programme, the investigation team specifically asked for information about a six-foot tall suspect driving a black *BMW* car. Her body was found twelve miles outside the city in a lay-by on the road that runs out towards the county of Argyll. The main suspect with the black *BMW* was a Mr McCall who lived out in the town of Helensburgh. His easiest and most logical route into Glasgow was along this same road. This suspect was never put up for trial but was later found dead, reported to have committed suicide. But, alternative rumours did circulate at the time concerning how Mr McCall met his untimely death!

With his demise, the Press reported that the police were no longer seeking anyone in connection with Jacqueline Gallacher's murder, which implies that they assumed he was responsible for what happened to her. At this point, one would expect that the Gallacher case should then be completed as quickly as possible in the given circumstances.

With the investigation supposedly brought to a conclusion; why was it deemed necessary to pursue a second *Crimewatch* appeal? Had some new evidence come to light, or was there some other more sinister reason for the resurrection of the investigation? Were police officers implicated in this man's death? Thereafter, was there then a need for them to cover their tracks?

The third way of viewing this affair fitted best with what was originally alleged concerning this series of prostitute murders. That is, that this dead man had had no contact whatsoever with Jacqueline Gallacher, and that the police having failed to frame him for the murder, then he was in fact murdered to look like the suicide of a guilty man.

Although details have been difficult to come by, Jacqueline Gallacher was found strangled after being last seen alive on a Sunday night as were the majority of other victims. Strangulation is a textbook form of execution. Sunday nights, from personal experience, is a favoured time for Special Branch operations. Both these details suggested, therefore, that Special Branch were most likely to be the perpetrators of this gruesome crime. The murder suspect was found dead *'in no suspicious circumstances'* according to news reports, but given the background to his death it all becomes questionable. If he was another victim of the alleged policy of mass murder being carried out in Strathclyde, it is imperative for the perpetrators to conceal the facts forever. No matter which way you view this matter, you will always be of the opinion this scenario is highly suspicious.

It was Jacqueline Gallacher's mother, Mrs Wilson, who was most vocal while the investigation was being conducted, always pressing for answers and frequently appearing on television concerning what happened to her daughter. Coincidentally, it was while the girl's mother was being visible that the police were putting the greatest effort into the investigation.

BEING FRAMED

Now you have the explanation of why I was asking, 'Who are they framing, tonight?' before the start of the screening of the second *Crimewatch* reconstruction. Curious as to why this was happening, I watched the programme in an inquisitive manner until the relevant subject came up. The appeal was presented by a female police officer from the Strathclyde force, where I thought that was a nice touch. After all, a female officer is able to display a more

compassionate and humane image than one of her male colleagues, and make the whole dastardly situation appear more believable. Watching the reconstruction unravel, my frame of mind changed from being one of scepticism to one of horror.
"Who's getting it in the neck, tonight?" I spluttered, "It's me!"

The black *BMW* car they had talked about in the first appeal had disappeared, and now they were seeking a small red *Citroen* type van with white lettering and a company logo in connection with this murder. The sense of horror and bewilderment multiplied the longer the programme continued. Did the death of the *BMW's* driver automatically eliminate this car from the inquiry? The new suspect vehicle is at the opposite end of the automotive spectrum in terms of specification. Could this really be a genuine investigation? Having been sceptical beforehand, this all compounded my deep mistrust of the process.

During the reconstruction, the above mentioned red van was stopped at the exact spot where Jacqueline Gallacher's body had been found, with a man matching my description apparently unloading a carpet out of the back door of the vehicle. This carpet fitted with the fact that Jacqueline Gallacher was found wrapped in a curtain in the undergrowth. The description of the original suspect had no features consistent with myself. The van was similar in appearance to a brother's van where, at that time, I had no transport and often drove his van. Their so-called new witness who made this new appeal possible was said to have come forward ten months after the murder was discovered.

Why was I certain the police were about to frame me, as opposed to any other innocent person with compatible features? My certainty about this arose not simply from the fact that I was convinced Special Branch were directly responsible for the spate of murders and covering up their acts with false allegations against innocent members of the public and wasting tax payers money conducting bogus investigations. I was expecting to be targeted by police when three men and two children, all of whom were personal acquaintances, were shot at in an incident at a flat in the neighbouring village.

Two nights before the shooting, the prime suspects drove past my house in a *Vauxhall Astra*. Upon passing each other at slow speed on the single-track road, I recognised the driver and the front seat passenger as being two well-known troublemakers. This passenger was moving around vigorously, to try to avoid being identified. I did not, however, recognise the third occupant sitting on the back seat. The driver wore a black commando type bonnet, which pulls down into a balaclava, the same as that used in the shooting. After the incident, the names of the persons alleged to be responsible did correspond with the two men in the front of the car, according to local gossip. The third name circulated was that of someone not known to myself. The get-away car, which was later found burned out, was a *Vauxhall Astra*. Therefore, it is clear that I could be an important witness who could identify the suspects as being inside such a car shortly before the attempted murder of five people.

At that time, my mother was ill with cancer, and given the past record of incompetence of the police in dealing with members of this family, I felt it would be pointless giving them a statement. I was afraid that by doing so would only lead to my victimization both by these men and the police. Then two weeks after this, the mother of the children shot begged me to give a statement to them about what had happened to her family. I told her that this would be pointless because of my suspicions about the police relationship with the family of the prime suspects but, realising that this dreadful shooting involved children, I reluctantly decided to come forward and give a statement. As I had expected, there was very little interest paid to what I had to say, which, I am sure you will agree, is odd considering my evidence could connect those alleged to be involved to the burned out vehicle. It appeared that the police were only going through the motions rather than conducting a proper investigation into this crime. For example, on the following Thursday night, there were roadblocks in the local village stopping motorists to ask them if they had seen anything suspicious on the night of the shooting. This may appear convincing as an investigation on the surface, but the basic information I had given in my statement, such like the colour of the vehicle used by the suspects, was never disclosed during this investigation. After all is said and done, there always remains a law of the jungle, although the Law at times can be inadequate where anything is acceptable except the abuse of children and the most depraved of crimes. However, to be framed for murder so as to conceal the background of a shooting involving children is never above board.

Long before the episode with the undercover man hidden in the back of the *Land Rover Discovery*, or this dubious appeal on *Crimewatch*, there was an amusing incident that signalled a warning for the future. My motorcycle had broken down and in an effort to try and get the engine running again, I decided to try and bump start it. I was pushing the bike along the wrong side of the road at a T-junction, having taken off my crash helmet not believing there was any need to wear it since I didn't think the engine would start. Anyway, to my complete surprise, the bike did fire up with a burst of acceleration and careered out of control on the right-hand side of the road towards the junction, dragging me behind it as I struggled to regain control. The situation came to a head right on the apex of the roads with a police van turning the corner right into my path. The bike screeched to a halt inches away from centre-punching this van thanks to the driver taking evasive action. Half relieved that the motorcycle had stopped short of leaving a massive dent in the side of the police van, I braced myself for the standard, "What do you think you're playing at, sonny?"
Coming to a standstill, I tried to regain some composure and glanced over to my left to find the police driver staring straight back. Then when the driver saw who it was, the van drove off, much to my bewilderment.
"Whatever happened to the Doc Martens to the rib cage?" I shouted after it in humour as it disappeared into the distance.

My personal opinion of the police wasn't always this low; it just deteriorated over the years with their constant persecution. It was obvious here that they had made alternative plans for this reckless soul, and from this point onwards a grotesque sequence of events began to unfold.

LIFE SENTENCE

Convinced my life was over after watching this television programme, I believed that the only two possible outcomes of this were certain death or life imprisonment, unless I could find a third outcome. Being sent to jail for such a length of time because of a blatant conspiracy to frame an innocent person amounts to torture and, as far as I am concerned, death would be a preferable option. The anxiety one suffers in the face of such persecution is unbearable. With a high level of intelligence, I could see that this was going to tax me to the limit because there was no obvious way out.

Although I lived out in the countryside, my knowledge of the ins and outs of these prostitute murders was superior to most and, as it transpired, better than they could possibly estimate. Even with some inside information, doubt remained as to whether or not I would remain a free man, because I knew full well how professional these people are with their limitless resources.

'What do they do next to frame someone?' This was the only burning question I asked myself from the 13th May 1997 onwards. Methodically thinking over the possibilities, I tried to recall examples of how other people had been fitted up. The brutal answer is they poison you prior to questioning, and by altering your well being to an ill state, with the purpose of making you easier to break down, therefore brainwash you into giving them the answers that they require.

Four days later on Saturday 17th May, sure enough, the tops of all six bottles of milk on the doorstep had been tampered with. It had been an eventful week, starting with the cameraman in the *Land Rover Discovery* and ending with this. This particular dirty trick was commonplace back in the 1980s in Northern Ireland. Using a syringe, a virus was injected into the milk of families suspected of terrorist activities before the suspect wanted by the authorities was arrested for questioning. When people eventually became aware of this kind of clandestine activity, it was rarely used. Any time it was referred to in the newspapers, it was called '*interfering with milk bottle tops*', but the reality of it was far more shocking and disgusting no matter how cosily it was couched in print.

When my father and I fell ill and had to go to the doctor after drinking some of the first pint of milk, it was clear that it contained more than just fat. On examination of the tin foil tops, which had various numbers and letters stamped on them, there was nothing more than the smallest speck of milk beside all the stamped number fives. So I turned the bottles upside down and watched to see if any more milk seeped out. It did, although the second time this was attempted, the fat from the milk had already sealed the minute hole. Only after holding the bottle upside down and depressing the top to pressurise the contents did any more milk seep out. Close inspection of the puncture holes revealed that the positioning of the holes was slightly different. This dismissed the possibility that it was a fault in the stamping machine. Any fault in the bottling process should create a hole at the exact same spot on the stamped number fives. This was convincing evidence that the bottles had been doctored where only a micro syringe could possibly create such a small hole and deposit anything inside the bottle. It was clear this was a highly professional operation involving specialists, and clearly outlined the peril of my position.

Having survived a recent assassination attempt by the SAS and avoided all kinds of other incidents, this was about as serious as their dirty tricks campaign could become. This doctoring of the milk bottles, coupled with five young women murdered mostly by strangulation (with all the expertise that requires) reinforced the conclusion Special Branch was directly responsible and that they were trying to cover up their crimes by framing me. It was clear that I would have to be constantly on my guard and take whatever chances were presented just to stay one step ahead of the game.

So, I decided to try and get the milk analysed. After discussing the situation with lawyers, doctors and the Health and Safety Executive I finally deposited a pint at the University for testing. Getting the answers required proved to be no easy task, because either people didn't want to know, were simply unable to help, or told me, somewhat naïvely, to take it to the police. The latter response was the answer given at the laboratory at the agricultural college where they examined bacteria present in the milk, where I found it impossible to explain to them that, in fact, it was the police who were the source of the problem.

In the meantime, the next delivery of milk was due on the Monday morning, and early, before the milkman arrived, we had other visitors. A white *Ford* car drove up and one of the two occupants got out and proceeded to break into the shed. The door wasn't secure so he was easily able to gain entry. However, my brother spotted this going on and phoned the police. Yet, in spite of all the attention I had been receiving, the police were surprisingly unable to find their way directly to the house. It was only after they had satisfied themselves that the occupants of the neighbouring farm hadn't seen anything suspicious going on that they turned up at our door. My suspicions about the actions of the police were increased when they claimed later that they had caught the culprits near Paisley. The plain white *Ford* car was transformed into an *XR2* and the number of occupants had increased from two to three, and yet they claimed that the three men they had arrested were all involved.

It was my belief that the two men who broke into the shed were lying in wait for the next delivery so that they could switch the bottles again. They had made a mistake with the dates on the tin foil tops on the first batch. One would have expected that Special Branch would have taken the matter of dates into account when planning their operation, but it transpired that the milk in the bottles was in fact fresher than that which the milkman had left. This evidence demonstrated that the milk bottles were not doctored on the doorstep but that the bottles delivered by the milkman were swapped with those which had been sabotaged beforehand by undercover agents.

Further scientific analysis of what was in the sabotaged milk baffled and intrigued the scientists at the university to the extent that they asked anyone who had consumed the doctored milk to provide samples of their stool for analysis. Excrement contains clues about the nature of a virus once it has passed through your system. At this point in time, the sample of milk was now developing elongated cavities in the culture, and although the scientists were unable to identify the bacteria present, it was clear that it was eating away at the souring rapidly solidifying milk. The analysis process also discovered another interesting element in the milk, which initially sounded like nonsense - oil. An explanation given for the presence of oil was that it provided the bacteria with a suitable environment in which it could thrive before injecting it into the milk. Now that I had this knowledge, the plot was disrupted and the police displayed conduct that was consistent with a cover-up.

Time rolled on, and now I was about to determine my fate by making the police aware that their scheme against me had failed. Something people queried later on was: why did I deposit the two and a half pints of the contaminated milk with the police? The prime reason for this was to avoid being questioned about Jacqueline Gallacher's murder and to escape the stigma of being associated with prostitution and the very real possibility of being branded as a serial killer.

So at just after 10:30pm on Saturday 24th May I walked into Kilbirnie police station carrying a polythene bag containing three milk bottles, two of which were full and unopened and a third which was half empty for it was the one that my father and I had been drinking. A solitary female officer was on duty at the reception desk. When she came forward, I presented her with the bag and informed her that the contents had been contaminated with a virus, which had been injected into the bottles by syringe, and that I was leaving the bottles with them for analysis. She started writing down the details and when she asked me who I was, I gave her my full name. On realising who was standing there she became very disgruntled in her mood. Having completed my mission, I left the police station and drove off up the main street. Although the station had not exactly been crawling with police officers to deal with my complaint, there was suddenly a tremendous rush to redress the situation. I continued on my way along the main street, past the row of shops and, as the van climbed up the hill from where you can look down on the River Garnock, I looked across over at the industrial estate to see a panda car racing at high speed with its blue light flashing along the low road leading back to the police station. Having expected this reaction, I chuckled, 'That's rattled them!'

I had, nevertheless, made a potentially serious error by not obtaining a receipt for the evidence just handed in. This was of no consideration because I was so convinced in my belief that I was to be their next victim that I wasn't going to argue the point in any case. But then, as luck would have it, they shot themselves in the foot once again. Upon arriving home that night I was met by my father. He said a Sergeant Webster was waiting to speak to me on the phone about the bottles of milk that had been left at the police station. In their panic they had given undeniable proof that I had left the milk with them. Switching off the engine, I ran into the house to answer the phone.

Sergeant Webster said, "I'm calling about the milk you left with us sometime today."

This struck me as being somewhat peculiar in his attempt to play down the situation.

"Sometime today!" I retorted, "I left it with you not much more than about five minutes ago!"

He then continued with a barrage of questions that centred on two points: Where had I gone to get the milk analysed?, and; what had happened to the rest of it? From his questioning Sergeant Webster knew that he was only in possession of half the milk. Although other questions were fired at me, he repeatedly returned to these two questions, each time subtly altering the context of the questions to try and throw me off balance and prise the answers he wanted. It was clear to me that this officer had no concern for the welfare of either my family or myself. Instead, he was intent on discrediting this important evidence in order to cover up what had really been going on. Becoming increasingly angry at his attempted line of questioning, I finally told him to stop wasting time and have the milk analysed. I slammed the receiver down and let rip with an obscenity; something I was not accustomed to doing in full earshot of my father. I just could not comprehend the gall of this man and felt disgusted that he could possibly have reached the rank of sergeant.

When the situation calmed down, I went to bed for quiet reflection. Thinking over these events, I was able to piece the following facts together: -

* The fact that the undercover jeep arrived to try and get a photograph of me three days before the *Crimewatch* appeal made me come to the conclusion that something underhand was occurring. I reckoned that this picture, if they had obtained it, would have been shown to a bogus witness prior to an identification parade and then the witness would have been told to, "pick him out";

* The fact that there was not just one *Crimewatch* reconstruction of this murder, but two, made me certain that Special Branch were responsible and that the murderer was known to them;

* The fact that the murder suspect's vehicle could change from a black *BMW* into a small red van with white writing sounded particularly dubious;

* The fact that it was commonly known that people who had managed to escape conviction for these prostitute murders were also being found dead, including the original murder suspect in the *BMW* car;

* The fact that the new witness who sparked off the second *Crimewatch* reconstruction took ten months to come forward suggests that this was a bogus witness planted by Special Branch as part of a cover up operation and that genuine witnesses were being excluded from the investigation;

* The fact that I had narrowly survived a major assassination attempt prior to being framed believing that the British Establishment lay behind it;

* The fact that there is no suggestion of these five unsolved murders being the work of a serial killer in spite of the fact that they were all very similar in nature;

* The fact that in opposition to the existence of hi-tech CCTV equipment in place in Glasgow city centre, the culprits were still able to kill in a phantom-like manner;

* The fact that this one murder out of the five received the most attention when it was the victim's mother who pressed hardest for answers;

* The fact that I knew that Special Branch had access to my home with a front door key;

* The fact that they had not only been caught out trying to frame me, but had tried to achieve this by poisoning our milk; a commonly known dirty trick employed by the intelligence services, which points the finger of accusation at those who are commonly believed

to be carrying out an on-going campaign of murder in the West of Scotland;
* The fact that several other incidents had occurred thick and fast prior to this;
* The fact that my unemployment benefit was stopped for no apparent reason and that no satisfactory answers were being given about why it was being ceased;
* The fact that I was informed that my benefit was being stopped in a provocative manner with a camera set up on a tripod in the office; and,
* The fact that I was being framed for murder, which would mean that if convicted, I would be discredited as a killer, should I stand as a witness in a case against the police where innocent children had been shot at.

All these thoughts were milling around my head as I lay awake all night. It was like being burned at the stake as flames tormented my soul with the discomfort increasing with the passage of time. It all served to form the opinion that the situation held only one conclusion: my life expectancy could be measured in minutes. Wherewith, I bolted out of the house that morning at exactly 4:20am. This was the time shown on the wall clock and it would prove important later on. With no clear destination planned, the only aim was to try to outrun the death squads. It was a scenario reminiscent of a futuristic action movie. The sports bag was packed with what few clothes or belongings could be found and I took the little money left in my possession to help me live a life on the run aboard a motorcycle. It might sound romantic to you, but I had no idea where this was going or that this adventure would be short-lived.

In the bitter cold of the early morning, I set off travelling southwards, getting as far as Ballantrae before stopping in the quietest location I could find on a back road beside the River Stincher, shivering quite violently due to the dampness which increased the uncomfortable conditions. In the end, it became a struggle to go any further, and so I set up camp by the riverside but, unable to get a fire going, I just got into the sleeping bag. Eventually, the sun began to rise slowly and the morning dew receded with the growing warmth, where this tranquil setting contrasted sharply with the turbulence I had fled from. The only disturbance to this newly found peace came from a passer-by, who looked over the hedge at the vagrant I had become. Now that my presence had been discovered, the motto I lived by - stay ahead: stay alive - raised its head, so once the sun was high in the sky, the time had come to leave. In the classic manoeuvre of the fugitive, I doubled back on the original route and headed north following the Clyde coast up as far as Greenock, where I pulled into a car park to get some food. Sufficiently at ease to eat quietly, I sat inconspicuously among the parked vehicles. Then a dark coloured vehicle came into the car park and then hastily drove back out again. I thought, 'Right, if I'm not mistaken, they've sighted me now, better get out of here.' Fears of the night before had not materialised yet, but this looked like the beginning of. I fired up the motorcycle and made a hasty exit and continued the journey northwards, hoping that I had been quick enough to escape before any trap could be laid. Speeding along the road, I came across another or quite possibly the same dark blue vehicle, which was parked in an unusual place. The driver seemed to be extremely interested in the rider of this motorcycle, and sure enough, the car pulled out onto the road in front of me. This was quite a relief, because the best way to knock a rider off a motorcycle is from behind, which was why I constantly checked both mirrors for any other pursuers who may have been lurking behind. As far as I could see, there was only this individual in front and so I followed with caution. As we approached a roundabout, the car in front went straight on, which was the direction I was intending to take, so as a precaution and also in a bid to try and confuse the driver, I decided to circle the roundabout. This continued until another motorcyclist was in front. If any ambush lay on the road ahead, this unfortunate biker would be the new victim.

The traffic police had established a stop-check in the next lay-by and if they were stopping motorcycles, the fellow in front was now the prime candidate. Like clockwork, the police officer stepped out into the road to pull him up, but, at the last second before he pulled up, the officer waved him through. Obviously, this rider did not fit the description of the person they were seeking with our two motorcycles being very different in appearance. The officer then gestured for me to pull over. The initial instinct was to try and run due to all the implications of why I was in this position; the decision not to do so was based on the fact that the dark blue car was further on down the road. Reluctantly, and very annoyed, I pulled the motorcycle over to the side of the road to be questioned and issued with a traffic ticket. The time was now two o'clock in the afternoon.

Later, when these two police officers were questioned in court about what time they started work, they gave two conflicting answers. One of them said that it had been 9am, the other earlier. They also claimed I had been the first motorcyclist they had stopped that day. When they were asked what they had been doing prior to making this detention, one replied that they had been putting out cones. When you think that at least five hours had elapsed, then the town of Greenock must have resembled a maze of cones if they were telling the truth. The claim that I was the first motorcyclist to be stopped showed that there was unequivocal evidence of the ongoing campaign of victimisation being conducted against myself. And so my best plan of action was to return home and confront this problem at the local police station, where I had left the milk the previous night, and take it from there. On the run for precisely nine hours and forty minutes and the story would be held in store for the court case for the next five and a half months.

I collected all the required documents and headed in to face my fate at the police station. Due to their skulduggery, I had committed a minor road traffic offence by being in charge of an illegal motorcycle. The Law governing the entitlement to ride motorcycles had changed on the licence. It was a Catch-22 situation, but at least I had made them work to catch such an inconsequential individual like me. Detained at the police station for exactly forty-five minutes; it all seemed very trivial with their childish actions. I was only facing a minor charge and was prepared to pay my fine on the spot but the Duty Officer held onto my documents. As far as he was concerned, this violation was going to court. This is exactly how they behave in a situation like this. Caught out by the poisoned milk the intention is to hold something over you, in this case minor motoring offences.

TIME FOR A SUNTAN

After waiting warily for nineteen days, it did not surprise me that the police failed to reply with the results of the tests on the doctored milk which had been handed into the police station. The only response was on the next Thursday morning. Again all six bottles had their tops punctured. This time it was over-obvious with white splodges of milk clearly visible on the tin foil. Having only informed professional bodies about the predicament this left the police, or sources close to them, as the most likely culprits here. This deduction was further supported by the presence of a police van that night that came racing along the single-track road to perform an emergency stop outside the house to exaggerate its appearance. A sole occupant jumped out to take a drink of water from the wishing well across the road and was then at his leisure to leave. How convenient this was, a second batch of sabotaged milk bottles followed by a police officer appearing hours later to address the problem. It was obviously all a deception so I shunned him and neither did I get this new batch of milk analysed. I decided the best next move was to leave the country, because it would only be a matter of time before the next pitfall appeared. Like generations of Scots before, feeling persecuted in their own land, I was being forced into a life in exile. It saddened me to think that such suffering could still exist in a supposedly modern western European country in 1997. After getting out of bed that morning, I packed my sports bag and asked my mother to give me a lift to the station.

"Where are you going, Robert?" she enquired.

"Portugal!" I stated.

"Don't you mean Paisley?"

"No, Portugal!" was a final reply.

This request had come as a complete surprise to her - I had intended it this way. Heading towards the railway station, despair was written into her face because she could tell that something was wrong. Although this journey was to be one-way, I knew that in all honesty, one day I would have to defy logic and return to confront this living hell. Nobody really knew about my departure until I had arrived in Portugal with the exception of the supervisor at the workshop in Cumnock, who had been taking an increasing interest in these activities. I had, however, been careful not to reveal exactly when I was going.

In spite of hearing all sorts of rumours about flying, there were no nerves, even though this was my first time on an aeroplane. My only concern was to get away undetected. Anxious about going through Customs at Manchester Airport, I was relieved when finally sitting on a seat in the plane. The engines fired up and I silently closed my eyes to contemplate the freedom and luxury that the south coast of Portugal held as I continued the pattern of my life on the run from these persecutors.

On my arrival at Faros airport, I didn't have to wait around for my luggage, as it had been checked in as hand luggage. Although I was trying my best to remain inconspicuous, such rapid progress through the airport attracted the attention of the Portuguese Customs officers. Knowing that this attention could mean trouble, I kept my pace quick and ventured outside and headed for the town with the sports bag slung over my shoulder.

After having something to eat, I decided to avoid the fiesta, which was filling the streets with people. Such excitement held no attraction for me; I preferred the thought of enjoying a cold beer in the relaxed atmosphere of a back street saloon bar. This was a pleasure; drinking alone without the nagging feeling that people were in pursuit plus reminiscing about past experiences. Later on, I met a Canadian girl on the street and, as we were both English speakers in a foreign land, we quickly became friendly. She insisted that I kept her company in the café the next day. Since I had no fixed plans I arranged to meet her there for morning breakfast. Before leaving, she pointed out which café, but unfortunately, circumstances conspired against it.

The problem was that I didn't have a bed for the night, and so made finding one a priority. After a search of the area, it became clear that all the guesthouses in town were already full. But to someone who was accustomed by then to sleeping rough, the beach was as good as any plush hotel; so I curled up in the sleeping bag on the sand as I tried to make myself comfortable. However, conditions were not ideal because there was a cold breeze blowing in from the sea combined with insects landing on the only exposed area of my skin, which was my face. Both of which kept me awake. Unable to identify whether these insects were flies or mosquitoes, such distractions were bother enough, but the sound of people in the distance also kept me awake. Then a couple approached where I was lying, where to my surprise, they turned out to be two men, not a man and a woman. They approached hand in hand, one singing in English to the other, "Lend me your body tonight." Being a broadminded person, their homosexual activity didn't particularly shock or bother me: what they did in private was their own business, not mine. I just wished that they had chosen another location. Not wanting to witness their night of passion, I decided to leave Faros.

Hitchhiking out of town in the middle of the night was the next mistake. It took forever for a Good Samaritan to appear. However, his kind gesture was short-lived. Along the road, he suddenly stopped and left me standing at a complex junction on the dual carriageway. I sat on the steel crash barrier, admiring the paint deposited on it by cars using this road. It seemed as though none of them had ever had any intention of turning this corner, preferring instead to use this barrier as a rail to get round. In the half-light before dawn, I sat perched on this spaghetti junction, wondering if it were possible to find a more dangerous place to be in Portugal, also contemplating how my situation had become so crazy. Was it a real baptism of fire, or did other tourists go through this initiation ritual? I was always one for adventure, but this tarmac and steel, the gay couple and being bitten to distraction by mosquitoes had me bewildered sitting there asking myself, 'What am I doing here?'
Fortunately, another driver came to my rescue and I was relieved to be back on the road again. With hindsight, I shuddered at the thought that I had escaped being crushed on that barrier or being lifted by the police, which would have provided some record of my whereabouts.

After this inhospitable start, Portugal became a breeze as I travelled about the country on foot, hitchhiking and travelling by bus and train. The sense of freedom was overwhelming after all that had been endured; a bit like being drunk without having been drinking any alcohol, and I soon became quite emotional. With my harrowing plight over, this wanderer was in his element, having spent a lifetime travelling. I always had a need to see what was over the next mountain, and with my rambling nature, this fitted well in this adventure. Three quarters of the length of the country flowed by as effortlessly as a migrating bird on the wind, finally coming to rest up in the mountains at Braga. In the early evening I needed to find somewhere to eat before closing time. The restaurant where I settled for a meal was run by a husband and wife partnership. The proprietor insisted that I wait until his wife appeared before ordering. Apprehensive about why I had to wait before ordering, I made certain of where the front door stood for the sake of personal security, then subconsciously plotted the most direct route out, weighing up the obstacles, both physical and human, to getting there. Old habits return with a vengeance in moments like these: it's that mixture of paranoia, awareness and curiosity creating the demon inside that will never relent. Fifteen minutes later, a knowing smile appeared and gone was any vigilance and mistrust. The woman explained she was the English teacher at the local school and the only interest she had in me was nothing more sinister than the fact that this was a native English speaker. It's funny how it all pans out in time. Here I was ready to make another dramatic escape thanks to an inability to fathom out a motive for being singled out in this obscurity.

Our acquaintance made a stuttering start as the woman struggled at first to cope with my distinctive Scottish accent. She soon became more familiar with it and afterwards was kind enough to drive me to the youth hostel. It was a real novelty to have a bed for the night instead of sleeping where I fell. While the bed was never appreciated, the other amenities were, like having hot water to get washed and shaved, and a breakfast. Up until now, this had been sporadic, like waking up beside an orchard to have apples for breakfast.

SUPERGRASS

Whatever inhibitions I'd harboured beforehand disappeared with this experience in the café. It was impossible to be tracked all this distance and all the various modes of transport could never be duplicated. Now able to relax, the only complaint I held was sunburn. With a fair complexion, the prolonged exposure to the strong Portuguese sun had become a problem.

The European Motorcycle Racing Championships were being held at the racing circuit outside Braga, and I decided this would provide me with a day's entertainment. Having freshened up at the youth hostel I was in good spirits when arriving early at the circuit to watch the warm-up session and then the first race of the day. The prospect of enjoying a pleasant day out was suddenly cut short at the start of this race. I noticed the presence of a suspicious looking photographer in the sparse crowd. What made him prominent was the fact that the temperature had soared to more than 100 degrees, causing many of the locals to start complaining about the heat, and yet this character remained totally overdressed for the conditions and looked so out of place. He was wrapped up like a scarecrow, wearing a large hat, an overcoat that came down to his knees and thick trousers. He stood about twenty metres away; even though the race was ongoing, I could easily hear the click of his camera shutter. What disturbed me most of all when I glanced round at him was that instead of taking pictures of the racing action or the local girls, his camera was trained directly on me. Upon eye contact, he immediately turned the camera in the direction of the pack of motorcycles on the track and started clicking away vigorously, although there were three solid barriers between him and the supposed subject. He couldn't have seen more than the very top of the riders' crash helmets from where he was standing. No normal person would waste film on such pictures. My suspicions were further confirmed by checking out the few other spectators in the vicinity where I found nothing relevant to warrant this intrusion of privacy. I could think of only two possible organisations this character was working for. Either he was a cameraman working for the local CID, or he was working for Interpol. It could only be one of these two that would be interested in maintaining surveillance on a foreigner over such a distance and over such a length of time. If this was only the local detective, only Interpol under the instructions of the British authorities could be responsible for assigning him to my case. Having been forced to flee from Scotland as a victim of human rights violations, they continued to abuse their position and authority to cover-up their own wrongdoing.

By what other means could anyone be found in this wilderness? I have already mentioned the supervisor, David Wilson, from the workshop. The answer lies in an interesting conversation with him before I left on this excursion to the Continent, when I told him that there was a possibility I might go to Portugal. On hearing this, he became very inquisitive.

"Whereabouts?" he enquired.

"Braga!" I replied.

"Oh, whereabouts is that?" he continued.

I remember thinking at the time that his interest was more than normal. After all, Braga would be the dark side of the moon to anyone else. However, I told him it was in northern Portugal. All those thousands of miles between Ayrshire and Braga disintegrated when I realised the confirmation of this man's treachery. He was the only living soul to be told of the final destination. Once there, the undercover surveillance resumed.

Paranoia had kept my head above water for this length of time. This certainly was not the first example of his treachery, because it was rumoured that this same supervisor had informed on members of the SNLA terrorist group, who came into the workshop. I remembered back to how he had sounded out his quarry beforehand, asking if I knew anyone by the surname 'Murdoch'. The only person in the area I knew to share this surname was a former business partner of my father's, who had sold up his share in the business several years previously and gone his separate way. In subsequent conversations, he revealed that this name did coincide with that of a terrorist, who was someone he had a great deal of respect for. What he failed to disclose was his assistance given in the conviction of SNLA members or the threat of retribution such a terrorist posed. Cautiously at first, David Wilson checked out any association there could be with myself and this man, then afterwards I detected a change in his behaviour through the questions asked. A second major incident that gave grave concern about the involvement of Wilson in my persecution was a set up assassination attempt on my life. When I went to the workshop I always passed through the town of Stewarton. On leaving the town there is an option of two different routes that you can choose from at a 'Y' junction. So on the day they had decided to knock me off my motorcycle, a car making an obtrusive presence was parked just after the town centre with the driver giving an over obvious display of surveillance. The car in question, which was waiting for myself to appear, suspiciously pulled onto the road in front of my motorcycle then drove erratically up to the 'Y' junction where it peeled off to the left at great speed. Naturally, instincts told me not to follow this car. This was exactly what was required with myself now going faster than usual, which ideally was a second requirement. Now, unintentionally I had fallen into their trap as I took my second common route. As I rounded a blind corner at high speed a fire service support truck had unique positioning, as it blocked two thirds of the road. Quick reactions, due to a body full of adrenalin from the behaviour of the dubious car, helped me swerve to avoid the danger. If I had been knocked off the bike the finishing touch is then administered with a sledgehammer; a crushed skull looks the same if it is caused by the impact of the road or done by human hands. Men were on hand, outside the fire truck, to provide the finishing touches with one holding the shaft of what distinctively looked like a sledgehammer! So on what should have been my fatal day was confirmed when I arrived at the workshop to find the questionable supervisor with an acute interest in my well-being, and also inquiring if I had suffered any recent incidents! I declined to tell him about the latest incursion.

The motorcycle races continued and a larger crowd had gathered around, which enabled me to make my movements more difficult to follow. Now that I believed that the cameraman was working for Interpol in some way, I felt keenly aware that my security was under threat. When you remember the story of the three Provisional IRA suspects being murdered by the SAS on orders from MI5 in Gibraltar, there is no disputing the severity of what can happen. Maybe I shouldn't have such a cavalier attitude regarding personal safety. At times like these, however, it is difficult to take the deranged people accountable for this incident seriously. Unable to aspirate to the danger, I lay down and went to sleep under the shade of a tree, even though my status had now been elevated from being an innocent refugee from Scotland to an international fugitive in the click of a camera shutter. The intelligence reports could only look bad: indeed, this one in particular must have read like a comic strip.

"Handler has eyeball contact with the suspect and proceeds to take photographs. The suspect unexpectedly has the handler under eyeball contact. Aware he has been rumbled by the suspect, the handler turns his attention to taking photographs of the motorcycle race. Tension mounts as the suspect rolls out a sleeping bag on the ground, lies back and falls asleep. This may be a cunning ploy to confuse the confused. Assistance urgently required."

In spite of treating this threat in such a derisory manner, the realisation remained that this danger had nevertheless to be addressed. I did not believe that I would be apprehended at the circuit because of the volume of spectators present, but would have to proceed with caution once the races had finished. The master plan, therefore, was simple; I would mingle and get lost in the crowd. From their viewpoint, the exits would be the best locations for them to find their quarry. However, knowing this, I delayed my departure from the circuit by talking to one of the English riders. Once again the big wheel had started to turn and life on the run took another awkward twist, which prompted the decision to take off in another direction. So I left Braga after bidding farewell to the English teacher, and headed down out of the mountains to the city of Porto.

Desperation slowly crept into my circumstances as I expected to have to leave for another country, but there were a few days to kill before the international train ran. Seeking liquid refreshment one night, I came across a club at the university and made an effort to conceal the fact that I had walked in barefooted. Both my feet were in a poor state of repair. Blisters from walking the streets had turned into open sores so I hid them under the table to save embarrassment, only replacing the shoes in order to walk to the bar to order another drink. However, the students later confessed that they had spotted this unusual predicament the moment I had entered. It was a relief that I no longer had to suffer the pain of replacing my shoes and could now spend the rest of the evening with them off. It was obvious to them that this stranger had a story to tell and once the film finished on the wide screen television, they started to ask questions. Surrounded by curious faces, I made no attempt to speak Portuguese, so we had a conversation in broken English. I tried my best to give them a clear explanation, but there was always a doubt that they would ever get the gist of it. In more general terms, when asked where I had been sleeping, I said on the streets. One student tried to explain how hard and violent this could be in words that immediately sang.

"Portugal, it is no garden," he said.

"It's the Garden of Eden to me, amigo," came the reply. These days of sleeping rough in the gutters of Portugal had been good. To begin with, there was no requirement to be looking over one's shoulder here, although this had changed, of course, with the incident at the motorcycle circuit. In gratitude, I would rather gladly take my chances with the drunks, muggers, junkies and street gangs of Porto than be back in Scotland at that moment. But, the wind of change was blowing that way, and so, an effort was made to return home undetected.

2. GOING HOME

As they had done before I had left home, all the same dilemmas faced then were surfacing again. What are your options if you cannot outrun them? My natural instinct said the answer was to turn round and fight them. After all, the attempt to flee thousands of miles from the death squads and the persecution of the evil regime in the West of Scotland was not working out. The pursuers could only marvel at my decision to start on a homeward direction. The struggle resumed in a tormented mind, constantly demanding an explanation of why I was about to walk into the lion's den once again. Perhaps the best defence was to continue to be unpredictable, and the last manoeuvre they would expect anyone in this position to make was a return to Scotland. It is this ability to surprise everyone around me, even myself, which plays in my favour. That said, however, you will never comprehend the adverse conditions and sheer volume of numbers that a return home was to place me in opposition to.

On the international train out of Porto, again, another suspicious and inquisitive character appeared. Only, my nature had become shy and introverted at this point. Here it was a Frenchman with his arm in a sling who stood prominent among the vast numbers of passengers. I was always wary of him. At a glance, I could see no muscle wastage in the affected limb. Having broken a leg some years ago, I knew from experience that the physical condition of the limb deteriorates quickly when it is made redundant. What this man had was not convincing. It was clearly a trick designed to portray a defenceless individual, and make the person appear more approachable. But, they would have to try harder because this deceit was never going to fool this particular rebel. Anyway, why would you meet an injured foreigner two countries from home? Being on guard before ever being in contact with him it felt so predictable that he should then single out the only Scottish tourist from the hordes of other travellers, and strangely enough, he spoke in English.
"This cannot be happening," I muttered to myself. I hadn't uttered a single word on the train and there was nothing about my person to

indicate to anyone that this was an English speaker. How could he possibly know to communicate in this language? Again, I recalled the situation at the race circuit, and felt sure that this fellow was another Interpol officer tracking their fugitive, as he deliberately selected me as his travelling companion.

Upon approach, he asked, "Where are you from?"

"Scozia," I grudgingly replied.

His second question was, "Where are you going?"

"Paree," was my reply; Paris was the final destination of the train. Sarcasm welled up inside as I thought, 'Why don't you make it any more obvious who you are with two such blatant questions?'

People I had known in the past who were wanted by Interpol for criminal activities like drug smuggling had always referred to these people as being something of a joke. Whether or not this was an accurate appraisal, or whether they liked the 'big man' image this portrayed, up to now there was no telling which. On appraisal of the current situation, I certainly found them far easier to recognise and dupe than any undercover officer from home. The train was bound for Paris, but this traveller wasn't. Unknown to him, my final destination was Bilbao in northern Spain, and when the train completed its journey in France, they were going to receive a shock that the suspect had vanished.

With me shunning the advances of the Frenchman, he left, but the experience also left a bad taste in the mouth. Vindictiveness was setting in. This incident heralded a change in personality. There was now a cold hard edge to my demeanour coupled with a raw determination to retaliate against this unceasing oppression. Having suffered all the hardship that had been inflicted, someone was about to pay the price, and this character with his arm in a sling was one dirty trick too many. The chances of this man leaving the train without a genuine broken arm were slim.

While gazing out the window at the passing scenery as the train thundered across Portugal, I reflected on who the adversaries were. The list was both impressive and frightening. Thoughts like these will tire even the most alert of minds, and with the night approaching, I lay down across the seats to sleep. Although deeply unhappy, I was also very tired but thankfully alone in the compartment therefore felt able to sleep as the carriage shuddered and rattled its way into Spain. The stop to change trains was in the middle of the night at some obscure station in Spain. At this point the guard came into the compartment to wake up this passenger, which startled me. I lunged at this stranger in the night with a knife that was hidden up my jacket sleeve while I slept. The blade came within about an inch of penetrating his tunic when I realised that it was only the guard, and flicked my hand the other way in order to disguise the weapon. Keenly aware that Interpol was on the train, and having watched most of the 'James Bond' movies, there was a warped perception of the incompetent outfit they really were. The guard had a vacant expression on his face that told how he had happily punched tickets on this very train for the last twenty years. In one sudden movement, all that simplicity was replaced by a look of absolute horror. International football supporters pose a visible threat, unlike quiet, sad individuals sleeping placidly in the night. For this being of simple pleasures, that myth was destroyed forever and this loss of innocence filled me with revulsion. The incident created a negative impression of myself, and forced me to question the distance I had travelled and the depth to which I'd sunk. Sure, if this wretched soul was going to blow his top, it was going to be catastrophic, but to puncture the lung of an innocent person who was just doing his job would be a sore injustice. I promised myself that if that is what was required in the future, there would be no mistakes. Was it right that an innocent person should be pursued to the ends of the earth by a regime no better than the Nazis? I used that question to justify the mistake. This had been an out of character action brought on by the constant hounding, maltreatment, hunger, pain and fatigue. With hindsight, the Interpol officer would no doubt receive the wrath of his superiors when trying to explain how the assailant could possibly disappear off the train right under his very nose. Without physical harm he'd suffer his just desserts.

Relieved to be able to change trains, I thought how the guard probably was as well, because he would never have thought that his job could be so dangerous. At an isolated station in the early hours, I waited for the connecting train to go north, feeling not unduly concerned about being intercepted by the local police. In years past,

I had seen Europe in an unconventional manner as a long distance lorry driver with various experiences including Customs and police, and knew how to deal with situations.

The final stretch of the train journey ended in the port city of Bilbao. I was to spend a few days there, waiting for the ship home. I hoped that by not using my return air ticket, I could enter the UK undetected via the ferry. After carefully working out how much money was left, I decided that purchasing the ticket would be my number one priority and that whatever change remained could be spent on food. Until then, living off the land, raiding what I could find in gardens, now it became a necessity. This would give me a purpose to pass the night away.

After finding out where the ferry terminal was, I obtained directions to where in the city I could acquire a ticket and went to purchase it the day before sailing. It was here that I became aware for the third time of Interpol involvement. I walked into the ticket office like any other tourist on his way home and gave the relevant information to the young Spanish woman behind the counter. The atmosphere was pleasant and friendly until the numbers on my passport were keyed into the computer. Then the mood started to change. The woman stared at the screen with great intensity, and I knew that only the details she had processed could have caused her change of behaviour. Unable to see what had come up on the screen, I waited helpless at the opposite side of the counter and watched with nervous anticipation what transpired. The woman summoned an older colleague and they spoke seriously for several minutes with various references being made to the computer screen. Only being able to speak pidgin Spanish, I could only guess what the topic of this conversation was. However, I felt sure that my details were the source of the problem. To my relief, the passport was returned with a ticket and so I gave my thanks gratefully, but the woman's attitude towards me remained unpleasant. Having grown accustomed to being victimised by the authorities, I was not shocked or horrified by this confirmation of Interpol's continuing interference. The newly found vengeful attitude with the devious thoughts it inspired immediately made me think of playing up on the notoriety. Fortunately, I realized that it was not this pair who had inconvenienced this particular client, and after the incident of mistaken identity on the train, I did not need any more innocent casualties on my record of intimidation.

With the tension high, I was aware of every move on that final morning, and found the somewhat industrial looking ferry terminal a pleasant sight. While Spain was an appealing place to visit, full of beautiful people, this particular wayward son was glad to be leaving. Feeling persecuted even in exile, nothing was ever straightforward, and my departure would not be complete without its final incident. After checking in at the port, the time passed extremely slowly while waiting to go aboard the ship - that is, before being approached by a tough looking Customs officer carrying a gun in a holster and placed under arrest. Unlike the young clerk in the ticket office, he was in the business of dealing with international fugitives, and any thoughts of making mischief with him were rapidly put aside. When he demanded my passport, there was no option but to submit to his request. It was the accepted practice to be singled out from the various other passengers.

On the ship home, exhaustion and hunger became my greatest enemies. Therefore, most of the time was spent either sleeping in the luxury of a bed or, because I had no money left, raking the ship for the most basic of foodstuffs like sachets of sugar. The ferry eventually docked on the south coast of England and I forced my way to the front of the queue, so as to be first off. I figured this would give the best opportunity to hitch a lift home to Scotland. This line of reasoning was rapidly foiled as soon as we reached the first checkpoint. There were a dozen Customs officers waiting there; I recognised one of them! He had pulled his peaked cap down to try and obscure his face and was wearing one of their large jackets, but I had seen him before listening into telephone wires locally under the guise of a British Telecom engineer. So now here he was, masquerading as a Customs officer in the south of England. He could only be a member of Special Branch to achieve this feat. Upon being convinced about him, that I nearly inadvertently said hello to him. Anyway, after failing to catch me leaving the continental train on its arrival in Paris, it was clear that they were not leaving anything to chance this time. They had personal confirmation of my departure from Bilbao from a Spanish Customs officer and brought an undercover agent down from Scotland to identify me on arrival in Britain. Incidentally, as the ship neared its berth, I surveyed the sea and the distance to the shore and contemplated jumping overboard and swimming ashore. But, it was the fact that it was daylight with the likelihood of being seen, rather than the danger or getting wet, which probably dissuaded me from carrying out this feat. Considering seriously contemplating this gives you an indication of my frame of mind and the extreme lengths to which I would go to ensure my survival.

The obstacle of the checkpoint was not going to be cleared easily. One of the Customs officers asked for my passport; while checking it, he nodded to his colleague. The second officer must have been telepathic to receive all the information he needed from a mere head movement from his counterpart.
"Come this way, Mr Rae!" he asked.
It was clear that the only way he could have known my name without having heard it or read it from the passport was because they had been anticipating my arrival. The humiliation continued as they searched my sports bag in an effort to find out where I had been and with whom I had been staying. Although others were also detained, they didn't have the same thorough search. I was given a body search and, in keeping with tradition, was detained for the greatest length of time. What a welcome home! I stood there resenting every minute of it and wished to turn around and board the ship again to leave the UK forever. If there would ever be a next time, it would be by the wet route to complete the vanishing act again.

I hitched my way up the road north until I reached a motorway café in the north of England and there met a bus driver by chance who was destined for Glasgow. Asked if he'd take a bung for a lift home, he agreed, and so I handed over the only genuine ten pound note left in my possession as payment for the journey. The only empty seat on the coach was beside a young, pretty French Canadian. As I talked to her on the journey, her innocence and naiveté soon became apparent. This girl was probably about eighteen years old and had left the family home for her first experience of life's great adventure. At twenty eight, although still young enough to be able to relate to her, I felt more like a battle hardened war veteran sitting there beside her, prematurely aged by the constant bloody conflict in some occupied land. Having lived on the edge for an eternity and having seen it all, the contrast between this renegade and her was startling. Nobody as naïve as her should be alone on the road, so out of a sense of kindness and to pass the monotony of the journey, I decided to educate her about the desperate and violent world to which I had become accustomed. Producing my only remaining ten pound note I asked her to inspect it carefully, because it was a forgery. I had borrowed it plus the one used to pay the driver on the boat home. The young woman looked shocked by this revelation, and so I explained that the only way I could get a seat on this bus without a ticket was to bribe the driver. When the bus finally stopped at the bus station in Glasgow, I wrote down my phone number where she must have seen the considerable scar on the back of my hand. The poor girl must surely have been questioning her judgement about arriving in Glasgow after being left under no illusion that my homecoming was terrifying.

On an appropriately wet and dismal Saturday, 21st of June, my travels were over as I arrived back home. They didn't waste their time demonstrating their inhumanity. It was only on the following Monday that the same policewoman, that had appeared on the *Crimewatch* appeal for the Jacqueline Gallacher murder, again emerged on television. She claimed that officers had interviewed three thousand people in connection with the case and also said that they had been to (Continental) Europe in the course of their investigation. It was clear that this was being directed at me and confirmed that this was not a proper murder investigation but a sick pantomime being played out to cause human misery and suffering. These news stories create speculation, but no consideration is ever given to the victims' families who are emotionally tormented by the cruel use of their loved one's death.

While I was abroad, the police arrived at my brother's workplace after receiving what they said was a tip-off and subsequently ruled out any connection between the vans there and Jacqueline Gallacher's murder. Of course they would do that. They had been well and truly caught out, not just with the milk that had been sabotaged but also by another reign of terror that was as vindictive as this sorry debacle. Sadly, this was not a murder to be left alone due to all the implications and damning overtones. Lurking around the corner was another reason to bring this sorry episode to a close. Jill Dando was about to play a crucial role in this gruesome saga, but at what price?

I was certainly not someone who could be described as naïve; however, I always believed they could only frame an innocent individual for murder once. Unfortunately, this reasoning was wrong. Having lived comfortably in the dangerous and unhygienic surroundings Portugal provided, I soon had only one dream - to return there. Having been hounded night and day for longer than I cared to remember, the only happiness I had found was among strangers in the obscurity of a far off land.

One lady, Jill Dando, was a rare solace in the barbaric hostilities to be experienced in the next edition of this never-ending conflict. She rose up as a heroine to oppose those people with murderous and paedophilic inclinations, but they followed their own agenda and pretended to be protecting the public. If only there were more people like her, the fundamental wrongs being perpetuated could never continue.

JILL DANDO.

The main suspects in the Glasgow prostitute murder cases were projected to be petty criminals, pimps and drug dealers, the majority of whom were mere speculation derived from reports in the local newspapers with these stories mostly police orientated. This is questionable if there is a requirement to create false rumours. The persistent rumour circulating on the street was that of Special Branch and occasionally MI5 being involved; a view that those in the corridors of power always shied away from. As with the more outrageous tales that emanated of death squads hunting down a victim in the manner of a pack of wolves, such vivid theories are sometimes best ignored. This particular story originated after a prostitute murder where the victim had multiple stab wounds with the autopsy report saying more than one assailant was responsible.

After being mutilated the final cause of death was once again strangulation. The telling point was that such outlandish theories held a grain of truth. In this overall context, why was constant mention being made of MI5?

I had never believed the problem to be simply a localised one: the deeds had turned the West of Scotland into a killing field where the apparatus to conduct this slaughter lay elsewhere. This theory was soon to be supported by the next incident, which stretched the participation to the South of England. This event and the inclusion of a second police force help to assist this view and asks if it all came under MI5 co-ordination.

It remained imperative for them to try and conceal their foiled attempt to frame me, as events were beginning to expose them as being the guilty party for the untold trail of mass murder. So on the 8th July 1997, there was a second *Crimewatch* appeal on the double murder of Lin and Megan Russell and the miraculous survival of the family's other daughter Josie. This was one of the most horrific and barbaric crimes committed in England in recent memory, where a woman and her two young daughters were bludgeoned to death with a blunt instrument in the most brutal and frenzied manner. Against all logic, the elder child pulled through this ordeal to recover from the terrible head injuries inflicted and caught the hearts and minds of the British public with her undeniable courage. The incident itself shocked a nation with its callous brutality, sending shivers up and down the spines of the population. A full year later after the incident, plus an unsuccessful *Crimewatch* appeal, the crime remained unsolved with the culprit most likely still at large in the community.

Jill Dando was in the BBC studio with all her warmth, charm and outstanding beauty that night to present the reconstruction for the second appeal, but nothing could detract from the grotesque nature of what had happened. She took a personal interest and commitment into this unenviable task that went beyond the call of duty, balancing the two with flawless precision while maintaining a professional objective stance. Exerting that extra effort to have the culprit apprehended at the second attempt by presenting the programme was to prove more dastardly than expected.

The first appeal had shown a single man driving a brown *Ford Escort*. This new reconstruction also began with a brown *Escort* with a male driver. But, as the film progressed, the car changed colour into a red *Escort*. This feat may have been acceptable in a low budget, poor quality picture or a bad comedy, but given the gravity of the crime and the violence that had been inflicted, how was it possible to manipulate the facts to such an extent? Watching the first appeal, the main suspect was described as being of stocky build, with broad shoulders and cropped fair hair. In this second appeal, not only had the colour of the suspect's car changed: the description of the suspect himself had also changed no end. Gone were the distinctive broad shoulders, the short cropped hair had grown considerably in length, and he had become younger smaller and thinner. Only the colour of the hair remained consistent. This ever-changing information was said to have come from Josie Russell, who had regained bits of her memory after the severe brain damage inflicted on her. The second source of new information was from a new witness who had come forward in May, ten months after the horrific attack, and described the assailant as being someone who had approached them a few days before the incident in a large car.

This all had an air of déjà vu about it if you remember the details of how I was first framed for murder. The discovery of a new witness after ten months was the same time scale as the new witness in the Jacqueline Gallacher murder inquiry. The car that changed colour as it drove down the road was, if that were possible, more ridiculous than a black *BMW* car changing into a small red van with white lettering. Both the original descriptions of suspects changed miraculously from being completely incompatible with my features into an uncanny likeness. They no longer needed to go to the extreme length of getting a photograph of someone to frame as they had done prior to the second *Crimewatch* appeal in the Jacqueline Gallacher murder inquiry. When the closing shot of the second Russell appeal was shown, it was a near perfect image of myself to the extent that it had photographic similarity. The final confirmation of deliberate targeting came with the buckled stance the photo-fit man presented in front of the now red *Escort* in the last frame. A shattered ankle suffered in 1990 caused discomfort and difficulties in standing for years afterwards and also made it impossible to maintain an upright posture. The red *Ford Escort* was the last car I owned, and although it was scrapped a year prior to this crime, the insurance was continued just to keep the policy going, where I was in possession of a valid insurance certificate for such a car at the relevant time. Special Branch did their homework, or more accurately, broke into the house, and so, the certificate was there to be examined by them. Combined with some local knowledge, this allowed them to wrongly assume that my ownership of the particular vehicle had been continued and overlapped the relevant period. To deliberately distort and falsify evidence in this manner is a serious crime, especially when the punishment for those wrongly convicted by such evidence amounts to half their lifetime. Fortunately, I was spared this ordeal because hard evidence confirmed that I had been in Scotland on that fateful day, and due to Jill Dando's intervention, this evidence was never questioned. These attempts to rig the facts did not go unnoticed and, therefore, one question assumes more prominence than a pyramid in the desert. If they are prepared to frame an innocent person for such a heinous crime, why are they not looking for the real culprit?

The assault on the Russell's took place in the middle of the week in broad daylight, with brute force used to slay the victims. Vicious and unprofessional, without a disguise or the cover of darkness, did the assailant rely on alternative cover to remain undetected? If so, what form did this take?

When the programme began, I was unflustered and sitting at ease watching television until the suspect car changed colour. When the description of the car fitted with the knowledge of the last car I had owned, my interest intensified. To outfox a life sentence once had required nerve and thoughtful consideration.
"Surely this cannot be a second attempt!" I questioned on viewing this incredible reconstruction.
When their new witness claimed that a stranger had approached them prior to the attack, driving a large car, I realised my sister drove a large *Peugeot*, which was often in her brother's possession. A nervous sweat broke out and anxiety rose inside as every detail corresponded with me being framed for murder again. When the

final still frame showed a face that was the mirror image of myself, my interest was absolute combined with total shock and horror. I didn't have a monopoly in this disbelief. Jill Dando immediately recognised the car had changed colour and proceeded to ask the police officer in the studio about this outlandish event once the reconstruction had finished. People may have been dazzled by her good looks, affectionate nature and charming personality, but Jill Dando was one exceptional lady whose talents went further than the image radiating from the television screen. She was intelligent, humorous, articulate and blessed with heart and backbone. She was truly a lady of outstanding substance.

The policeman in the studio, DCI Dave Stevens, answered her query and insisted that the *Ford Escort* was red and that anyone who had seen it as brown had been suffering from post-traumatic stress. To remember one brown car being driven by one male driver: where is the stress in that? Jill Dando remained unconvinced and looked in disbelief at the officer who produced this absurd answer. Clearly, she was not going to be deceived by him. After the appeal, it was claimed that there were five thousand calls in connection with this incident. The first reconstruction ten months earlier had produced only two hundred and fifty calls to the studio. Simple arithmetic shows that the number of calls increased twenty times over when, with the lapse of time, you would expect this number to diminish. Once again, Jill Dando viewed the officer with scepticism. The exaggerated figure certainly appeared to be off the scale. The police officer sat there looking silly in a situation that was all of his own making, neither prompted nor encouraged by Jill Dando, who had only to suffer his foolish antics.

In all honesty, it was irrelevant that Jill Dando had disrupted proceedings because as a confidante so eloquently put it, "If they fuck you with this, you are fucked no matter what happens."
That really did sum it all up. The fact that it was impossible for me to have carried out this despicable attack became irrelevant, and likewise, it was of no consequence that hard evidence existed to place me at the other end of the country at the time of the assault. With a photo-fit resembling a photograph of myself, the red *Ford Escort* and the large car involved, you could not simply dismiss such

information as being a figment of an overactive imagination; too many people recognised the likeness. Therefore, this was enough to start rumours locally that a paedophile was living in the area, this being the same community where children are shot at. I could see that having done my utmost, like any other decent law-abiding person, not to accept this kind of behaviour, it was all so inevitable that it should come full circle.

The desperation I had had to avoid being framed for the murder of a prostitute melted into insignificance and all the associated stigmas became mere spit in the wind: as far as I was concerned, anything other than being connected to a child murder became my priority. Sleeping rough among the litter and rat's excrement on the streets of Portugal became a taste of paradise. Now my only wish was to return there.

With a physical condition already at a low ebb, exhausted and ragged as I was from having returned home from continental Europe, the race was now run. The mental pounding I was enduring was of gigantic proportions, but I retained the ability to laugh off the most serious assaults because I had only ever viewed the enemy as dangerous idiots. Finally they succeeded in landing the knockout punch. Life from that day forward was an uphill struggle as I was unable to cope with leading such a haggard existence. For a fortnight afterwards, the sickness was running down my front every night with the worry of having the stigma of being a child killer. This effectively turned me from being a young man into a geriatric, where I found it impossible to walk from one side of the room to the other without resting halfway to avoid collapsing. I spent two full weeks sitting at the back of the shed with the lights out in an effort to shut out the outside world, only attempting to eat meals, which were inevitably rejected afterwards in the form of sickness. Basic tasks became complicated, communication was all at sea, and here was a wretched soul, tormented and destroyed. Unable to find the strength to commit suicide, I would have welcomed a visit from the death squads to alleviate this suffering.

With questions being raised against this murder appeal, the cover-up operation came immediately. Next day's papers did not have the photo-fit that had been shown at the end of the programme. Instead it had reverted back to the one of the original cropped haired suspect. The suspect that had been shown wearing a denim jacket over a red T-shirt the previous night was now wearing only a red T-shirt. I did own a denim jacket but it was something I never wore as it remained redundant on a chair in my bedroom. Again, this is an indication as to the extent of the research Special Branch had carried out. On a side note, personal curiosity had always centred on one call to the studio, which was said to have had the hairs on the back of the neck of the receiver standing up. There was never any knowledge of whom this call was about or why it had had such an effect. Anyway, with the rumours that were circulating at the time, the police were asked whether there was a paedophile living in the area. Of course, with their record locally, they declined the opportunity to quash these rumours, and later on I was approached for no apparent reason by a seven-year-old kid.

"You make me sick!" he said.

The answer was on the tip of my tongue, "Your parents make me sick, because if it wasn't for me, you would probably be molested or shot by now!"

But, even although this verbal attack had stuck in my throat, I couldn't utter the intended reply, where only an inclination that the parents had been behind it lingered. It is small incidents like this that hurt the most, and gave confirmation as to how convincing this ludicrous reconstruction had been to the ignorant masses. The more informed people in society, like Jill Dando, were not deceived. One day, she was to be murdered in an apparently motiveless killing. Was there any connection?

Other than the guardian angel, Jill Dando, my second saving grace was my past history. Out of a town of roughly six thousand inhabitants, you could count on the fingers of one hand the number of people who had opposed the violence and terror inflicted upon them by one notorious family. When after, they finally stood trial for their reign of terror after the attempted murder of five local people, where it had acted as a catalyst to bring the trouble to a head. Even though the shooting remained unpunished, a large majority of the forty witnesses who had testified against the accused suffered violent retribution. When you are a youngster living out in the countryside, you can never choose the company you keep, but run around with those you find nearest. Unfortunately, this notorious family lived in my vicinity, and so with a childhood like this, I knew better than anyone never to be intimidated by their nonsense, but to stand up to it whenever the circumstances arose.

Many local people were too terrified or pathetic as to even see their children safe, whereas here was someone who, without fear or favour, only sought to do what was required regardless of the danger. A neighbourhood still trembling from the previous year's violence could never have the gumption to be up in arms against the rumours of me being labelled as a paedophile. The situation was further alleviated when Michael Stone was arrested for the Russell murders. Jill Dando's intervention was there to be analysed and questioned, which could explain the increasing doubt about the validity of this arrest. That also could explain why it was the source of such scurrilous rumours. The unbearable pressure began to abate. However, I have to admit, I remained devastated.

The panic button was pressed and the results were obvious to millions of television viewers. This display of lunacy was unbecoming of any professional body, but the inspiration behind it remained a mystery to the majority of the population. How was anyone to know that seemingly unconnected events in Strathclyde produced this faltering performance?

IN A DIFFERENT LIGHT

Time spent abroad provided a much needed respite from proceedings where it raised the opportunity to assess another development in a new spectrum. With only Interpol to contend with there - and contrary to public perception, the threat they posed was superficial - the absence of realistic pressure combined with ample spare time allowed me to consider the complex anomaly thoroughly. Sometimes, when a dilemma is stuck in your face you become too close to the problem to realise the obvious. A circumstance like that is compounded by the daily occurrence of being under constant attack; only when you are far removed from the environment are you presented with the space for hard thought to consider the next conspiracy. Exactly what did this entail and, in all this misery, who, if anyone, were to be the next casualties?

At the beginning of 1997, having already given a statement on the big local shooting to the police at the end of the previous year, they wanted me to come to the station for a second interview. I remembered that the first time had been against my better judgement, and with little interest being shown at the initial interview, what was the real reason for the new approach? To be kind, their method of communication was best described as being obscure. Without direct contact, they were saying to third parties that I was wanted for questioning when they held my name and address, telephone number and knew the location of the house. There was no need for such a roundabout approach in a genuine inquiry. Naturally wary of the motives I ignored the intentions of this oblique contact. With suspicions justifiably high, they were to prove to have some foundation.

Once they believed my non-appearance was to continue, this prompted a phone call from Detective Reid requesting an interview on the Saturday morning at the station, with every effort being made to give an informal impression. Unconvinced by their suspicious behaviour, but unable to find a reason to reject the call, I arrived at the agreed time. The questioning rarely concentrated on the firearms offence, but instead deviated onto trying to extract as much personal information as they could, without showing any concern about the actual crime. Directly after this meeting, an interesting photo-fit, name and with dreadful headlines such as '*Sex Attacker*' and '*Sex Fiend*' appeared in the Glasgow based newspapers, with stories of a manhunt in progress for someone attacking women in the West End of Glasgow. The policeman in charge of the investigation was being called Bob Rae combined with a photo-fit picture printed bearing a similarity to myself.

In February 1997, I was shocked when viewing an article on this to exclaim, "That one looks like me," pointing at the photo-fit, "and this one is named after me!" pointing to the police officer's photograph.

This left an uneasy feeling that such a significant development could take place. It was not until I was safely on the Continent that I was able to grasp the essence of the situation. With the time, patience and aptitude to consider the details of another conspiracy, presented with the solitude and loneliness of being in exile, I started thinking how did it all correspond? The photo-fit issued was then followed by a report that the suspect had changed the colour of his hair. Therefore, the image produced was obsolete before it was ever printed?! So, exactly what purpose did it serve? The policeman, D.C. Bob Rae, shared the same name with me, but why make such an issue over who was leading the investigation? The obsolete photo-fit possessed the following features: round face, dark eyes and longish fair hair. Why was there a similarity to myself when the description of the assailant obviously differed from the published photo-fit? Women were being subjected to sexual attacks and the headlines reflected this. Could any connection be gleaned from this? The timing of the visit to Kilbirnie police station for the second interview was immediately before any newspaper story displayed this likeness and name in regards towards the perpetrator of the attacks and sexual assaults on women. What was the significance of this? Why bother to have the second interview? The off-the-record approach had been defused by my refusal to co-operate, which instigated their telephone call in which the answers to their questions could have been received over the phone. With nothing to sign, were they after my facial expression to complement the answers? If I were not considered to be a suspect, surely my facial expressions would be irrelevant. The timing, method of communication, the substance of the news reports all held a connection to the next conspiracy. Like my position of being thousands of miles away so was the reasoning behind all of this.

With a mind resembling a pinball machine, as the initial slow thoughts gathered pace, I knew that the more I thought about it the greater would be my chances of arriving at an answer. A twist on perception struck hard: if, as I suspected, the information about the attempted murder of five people was in itself of no concern to them, then it was clear that the purpose of the interview had been merely an exercise in gathering intelligence about me. In regards to what this questioning *should* have been about; them alleged to have been involved in this local crime were said to have been caught on CCTV at the local garage when they didn't pay for the petrol they put in the stolen car they were driving. I could not see any reason against an easy conviction, if this was a genuine inquiry. Here was a key witness being persecuted outrageously, a major crime remaining unsolved and there was no other logic to dispute this fact. In the same vein, facial expression during the interview process doesn't hold any value: however, facial identity does. What had remained the greatest enigma for so long was finally solved in two words: facial identity. With an elusive personality, they needed to know what the person they were about to target looked like to enable them to doctor the photo-fit to fit my likeness. The simplest and most obvious conclusions are always the last destination you arrive at. For four months, this dilemma had teased and tormented me and now the answer was tantalisingly close. This alternative perception produced a frightening conclusion.

The photo-fit shared my basic features. The name given was also mine, and the crimes featured were the attacks on several women. Although I had no history of assaulting women, the key ingredients of these newspaper articles would linger in the consciences of people long after they had read them and alter their original perception of me in their minds. After this episode, if I were connected with harming any woman, it would be inevitable that the public would then presume me guilty until proven innocent. Here was someone about to be framed for a prostitute murder, where this exercise would be used to manipulate the thoughts of the future jury. The apparent deceitfulness, combined with the clever thinking required to execute such a ploy, was quite breathtaking. The underlying message implanted into the readers of the relevant newspapers had been done without the consent of the recipients, who had been blissfully unaware of what was going on. Months later, the name of the policeman would be transposed onto the enduring facial image and the enjambment of the headlines. The name was never over-emphasised, hence the use of a less formal, Bob Rae, when you would expect the officer to be addressed more formally by Robert Rae. The comparison with the photo-fit was also shabby yet emphasised the basic features. The time scale was also appropriate. Where the newspaper articles appeared in February and March of

1997, the second *Crimewatch* appeal on Jacqueline Gallacher's murder was in May, which should also have seen a subsequent arrest and trial six months later. The period was expedient for the transformation of the name in a person's memory; with a shorter time scale, people could easily retain more positive and accurate thoughts, thereby jeopardising the whole plot. Always in opposition to those who are capable of transgressing any law here was the serious crime of rigging a future jury, especially when it was done at the expense of the safety of women in the West End of Glasgow. Now that I was being implicated in such a catalogue of evil, the niggling thoughts that countless women were being raped, attacked, battered, molested, or even murdered to achieve their objectives were prominent. The murders of prostitutes were always rumoured to be only a small segment of the ongoing terror campaign. Now, conclusive proof was fast emerging to support this theory with the unveiling of their next wicked deed.

Realising this sitting in the Portuguese dust, scribbling thoughts down with a finger in the same manner as a young child would do on the beach, I pondered the newly found revelation of another conspiracy being incorporated inside the larger one. Locals here were not concerned about another crazy foreigner; for madness went with the territory as a satisfying smile replaced my pensive mood. It was refreshing to indoctrinate the new conclusion into a scrambled mind and provided a welcome boost in morale. I rose to my feet and shrugged off the dotage that had consumed my troubled mind for so long. I looked far down the valleys of lush vineyards that lay so beautifully in the sunshine. The barriers of language, cash flow and Interpol were all minor in comparison as I finally chipped the plaster off the lavatory wall, metaphorically speaking, to reveal other horrors. The sadistic cruelty being inflicted upon the women of Strathclyde beggared belief. It was so incomprehensible that it could be nothing other than true. The protagonists responsible for the conspiracy to brutalise such a large swathe of the population would have to be confronted one day. Someone was about to return. Only the foolhardy would make that journey knowing that their obituary could soon be found in the paper. The inner strength I required came from the self-belief that had been rekindled by the startling revelation that had been induced from careful thought. Only when I was at home could confirmation be made of the next conspiracy. A genuine tiredness of running from adversaries also helped to provide a second wind.

Once I was home, I only required confirmation of two details to make certain of these thoughts. I had to recheck what had been printed in the newspapers and to establish the actual description of the man attacking the women to see if his features corresponded with the photo-fit or not. This could give conclusive proof to the theory of conspiracy, but would not dispel it if there were a likeness to him. The former of these two objectives could be found in the reference library; the latter was somewhat more difficult to achieve, but far from impossible.

Immediately on return, although half-starved and drowsy from exhaustion I quickly went to the Mitchell Library in Glasgow to reaffirm my beliefs. The script of this action adventure was to continue when, shortly after arrival, I walked headlong into a honey trap. As I was carrying out research of the appropriate newspaper stories on microfilm, the solitude was interrupted by the arrival of three strangers, two men and a young woman. You live and learn by what you experience, but although I had confronted various similar incidents of this nature before, it had never occurred to me how close and personal the handlers could become. Normally the object of the exercise is to ensnare the target by not becoming the focus of attention, but they left her feeling awkward and alienated from a distance. To divert my attention away from the screen and hopefully make me aware of the presence of the young woman and, thereby, make the entrapment successful, one of the handlers sat down on my left at a neighbouring microfilm viewer. Behaving more like a spoilt child, he proceeded to make a nuisance of himself by ripping the microfilm in and out of the projector with such severity that it verged on vandalism. While he did this, I just smiled. I also smiled as he then goaded his female colleague into making a pass at their intended target. The subtleties of an undercover operation and the need to blend into the background were lost on this pair. After all, they were dealing with someone who was considered to be dangerous. The young lady had the daunting prospect of befriending someone who could possibly be a crazed animal wholly reliant upon the protection provided by these minders. As if out of embarrassment this pair were offloaded into undercover duties with the sole objective of allowing every other colleague to deny any association with them. With their stupidity, they remained oblivious to the obvious with plenty of details to support this.

They never registered the fact that the broad smile that broke out over the face of their intended target was a means of containing the laughter inside. Undeterred, they continued gesturing to the honey trap, who remained at a distance, to come over and make an acquaintance. Their signals seemed more suited to flagging down a passing taxi than to a covert manoeuvre. My head was beginning to shake with laughter and disbelief at their antics, and others in the library were beginning to notice their presence. If this continued, someone would have to act out of kindness and ask them if they were Special Branch. However, the trio finally upped sticks and left. Was this the double-cross? Capable of evading the most professional operators in desperation, all that remained were these two dummies. They were so extremely clumsy that no balanced person could ever believe the security forces employed them.

To her credit, the honey trap showed reluctance to participate in this failed operation. She probably felt it was like being asked to indulge in incest. All the unfortunate woman could muster in response was a half smile that flickered like a neon sign in the rain. Never close enough to be able to establish contact, she moved hesitantly on their blatant instruction, clearly viewing this matchmaking exercise with contempt. She had reason to. It didn't matter that the two handlers had the combined intelligence of a plate of scrambled eggs; my appearance resembled that of a sewer rat, with dirt ingrained into the skin and hair matted with grease. This vulgar presentation told its own story of a desperate, relentless persecuted man, whose urgent priority of finding supporting evidence of a conspiracy took precedence over hunger, rest and hygiene. The basic laws of human attraction were devoid of these circumstances, but again the most obvious reasons for the plot to remain unaccomplished escaped these minders. Had she been given an assignment to infiltrate a terrorist group, her safety and life would automatically have been sacrificed by those empowered with her protection. Their first action that afternoon was to betray the cover required with conspicuous movements and then to continue unabated when the operation should have been instantly terminated. It was a sordid affair for anyone to find themselves in, to be asked to degrade themselves in this manner and destroy their pride and confidence. Thankfully, I was aware of the event and left afterwards feeling sympathetic, with no malice towards her, in the predicament the two inept accomplices had created.

The act of fleeing Scotland and then returning well versed in the art of dodging such pitfalls as these inspired confidence and also let me know that my guard had not slipped. However, the warning dealt by such an early approach could only be expanded upon. It was with the second Russell appeal in the offing, which left me virtually paralysed and unable to complete my investigations. The newspaper cuttings I had found indicated that devious practices were being used, but the attacker's actual description remained elusive.

What progress had been achieved on this front was soon surpassed firstly by events on the 7th August 1997, when the pervert who had been attacking women was convicted, then sentenced five weeks later to a minimum of ten years imprisonment. So on the 8th August, the newspapers had that much sought after photograph of Grant McCaskill on display for me to compare with what I believed to be a doctored photo-fit to assist in my wrongful (future) conviction and finally confirm the theory that there was a conspiracy against me. I examined his complexion to see how it related to the bastardised photo-fit. The longish fair hair he should have had was in fact short and brown. The round face in the projected image wasn't McCaskill's: he was slim faced. Lastly, those hard dark eyes were also absent. Not a single feature corresponded with the falsified photo-fit; my case was beginning to prove itself. There was also a degree of relief to see him convicted after being simulated in likeness and name to such a series of depraved crimes. With accusations of being connected to a child murder, there was no reputation left to be tarnished thanks to the conspirators involved. This vindication felt like a breath of fresh air to this ailing person amidst all these incomprehensible troubles.

The second event was on the memorable date of the 11th September 1997, when this sexual deviant was sentenced. It was a momentous day in the history of Scotland for three reasons, two of which were apparent and the third for the most unlikely coincidence supporting this theory. That day was the 700th anniversary of the Scottish patriot William Wallace's victory at the Battle of Stirling Bridge, which occurred only thirty miles north east of Glasgow City centre. Today, the victory is both distorted and magnified by Mel Gibson in his blockbusting film 'Braveheart'. Present day history was also being written as Scotland voted for and secured the reconvening of her parliament after three hundred years absence under the terms of devolution. In all this sense of occasion amidst historical event both past and present, was anyone going to notice the third scandalous happening that day? A proportion of the female population certainly did as vehement disquiet arose concerning the circumstances of Grant McCaskill's reign of terror. The date of his sentencing was too convenient to be ignored. It guaranteed that this news story didn't take centre stage. However, this reduction of precedence could not detract from the situation. You are only left to wonder if any manipulation took place to secure this collision of dates, and if so, who possesses the power to institute such a diversion.

Whatever had occurred, as the need to conceal their skulduggery became apparent, the conclusion was inescapable. A story emerged that McCaskill was caught back in December 1996 on a victim's window ledge. He was already known as a sex offender at the time, and the police recovered his fingerprints linking him to his crimes, although they later claimed that these were smudged?! Afterwards, he was then shockingly released to assault even more women. Instead of languishing in prison awaiting trial, he was given a second opportunity to torture the female population, until one of his victims betrayed his identity and the complexity of the conspiracy. A former girlfriend informed on this pervert, where her intervention left the police with no alternative but to finally detain him. The media news report was accompanied with the spokeswoman from Strathclyde Rape Crisis airing the sentiments of many as she verbally chastised the police for their handling of this case. In all awareness of what was actually going on, I listened to this speaker criticising the police and questioned her future safety. The other lady who had raised her head above the parapet in this way had been Jill Dando. Only Jill Dando was a celebrity of international renown; a nation's sweetheart and an irreplaceable idol to so many, which afforded her with a superior defensive protection in its own right. In hindsight, having considered the safety of these two women that day, it is haunting to think that one of them is now deceased. At the time I presumed the spokeswoman to be in the greatest danger, being Scottish, female and forthright in her criticism, but Jill Dando went on to further antagonize them responsible.

With McCaskill paraded on television, this produced an opportunity to judge his appearance, plus a single photograph of the offender was published in many newspapers. I was suspicious of this picture, believing it was a trick photograph being used in a futile attempt to make him appear remotely like the falsified photo-fit in order to disguise the police corruption. Whoever was responsible must have stuck the camera very close to his face when taking the picture. This practice has the photographic effect of making the face appear rounder than it actually is. What revealed this illusion were his ears, which had become paper thin in this deceitful photograph. The malpractice was consistent, as both the culprit and Strathclyde Police received the wrath of many angry women for their respective wrongdoing. This was irrespective of the elaborate ploy with its clandestine motives and evil intent ever being disclosed.

I had never been capable of dissecting all the insanity of the conspiracies, the scheming and plotting with timing to confuse the most logical of minds. Only now through assumption did a pattern emerge. With Grant McCaskill apprehended and released in December 1996, shortly before the police came looking for me for that second interview, it was as corrupt as I had suspected. As well as the need to extract as much personal information about myself, they needed that crucial facial identity to be able to compose the falsified photo-fit. It was only after this interview that the inquiry into the sex attacker in the West End of Glasgow became a news item with the shared name, facial resemblance, in combination with incriminating headlines. This revelation was insignificant in comparison to the next incident that provided the answer to an anomaly that had dogged my troubled mind for so long: why jeopardise the safety and wellbeing of countless numbers of women with an intricate plot but attempt to murder me before its completion? Some of the assault victims would be emotionally scarred for life, and their suffering would have been pointless if they had achieved their objective, because I would have been dead before the conclusion that I was being framed for murder materialised. Once again, the obscure timing of events fell into place now that I benefitted from a greater understanding of the situation. Grant McCaskill's second and ultimate arrest was not the result of thorough police work, but merely because of the actions of a former girlfriend; otherwise the attacks would have continued. Such a blessing for the women of Glasgow was a curse to this soldier of fortune because the timing corresponded with the assassination attempt with a timescale which could never be explained until now. The motive for it was also apparent with numerous victims being attacked unnecessarily and the ensuing furore surfacing with the source of their attentions unscathed. There were no half measures here; the cover-up involved murdering their source (myself), thereby disposing of another incriminating accuser. All this occurs in what is supposed to be a democratic civilised country, where military personnel are used to exterminate unarmed and unsuspecting members of the public. When considering the deaths of others, it is questionable just how many met that same fate. After inflicting needless murder and suffering on so many innocent civilians, for once they were to meet their match the night they came to assassinate a quiet, introverted person, who surprised them with his ability to mock and undermine his persecutors. This failure reinstated the original plot along with the glaring omission that would emerge one day to betray the conspirators involved. The next fault with the resumed master-plan was the exposure of the doctored milk, and finally the twisted abuse of the murder of Jacqueline Gallacher and the apparent suicide of the first main suspect to terrorise members of the public had reached a conclusion. A detour off to the Continent came full circle to be home in time to watch the wheels fall off their bogey with Jill Dando ridiculing the second attempt at framing myself followed by the exposure of this other debacle involving untold misery afflicting many female victims. What they coveted most still eluded them: a conviction to further fool and mislead a gullible public. Instead their victimisation of one individual rebounded back on them with the exposure of their treacherous deeds laid bare for future analysis and aptly demonstrated the level of inhumanity being inflicted upon the people of Strathclyde.

That important day commemorating William Wallace's finest hour combined with the successful vote for the new Scottish Parliament could have come close to achieving an honourable treble if only the rule of law was upheld. Scottish police forces are self-regulating, where one has an obligation to investigate the supposed wrongdoing of another. Had this principle been adhered to the terror would be finally at an end, and that would truly have been a momentous day for so many people. Nobody could claim ignorance of what was going on because this scandal was brought to the attention of the majority of the Scottish population, but all that was forthcoming from Strathclyde Police during the news report was an ominous silence without the decency of a reply. This lack of response contributed to the affront to human rights, law and order, accountability to the public and democracy, all of which contrasted with the various instances of media manipulation in order to perpetuate the widespread suffering and terror. A warning salvo was fired at the protagonists involved. However, they would continue to play God with other people's lives and livelihoods, above criticism and aloof to natural justice.

The crimes of Grant McCaskill ranged from being a Peeping Tom to the very serious crimes of breaking into homes to attack victims, threatening to murder and rape women. At the time, it was played down by the fact that he never raped any of these victims. Unfortunately, there was no truth in this claim because 18 months after he was sentenced, he was convicted of such a crime, which had been well hidden under the carpet at the time. Rape can be one of the most traumatic of crimes for the victim, and this particular case was an extremely distressing and brutal ordeal for the young woman attacked. This case was an excellent example, giving credence to the overwhelming impression that facts were habitually being concealed and the course of justice was being perverted.

After the battering my physical and mental condition had already taken, while watching from the sidelines here, it was enlightening to be vindicated about the details of this conspiracy; only this theory was repulsed by another wave of victims. My capacity to respond was missing because I was so low in self-esteem and demoralised by their vile actions. Although Michael Stone was arrested for the double murder in England, there was no telling whether he was actually guilty or not, or if his imprisonment was the result of a panic measure designed to counteract the events in the *Crimewatch* studio. The possibility for an early release for him was always prominent in my mind to reinstate the suspicion that I was a child killer.

To conclude another sorry chapter, all the mistrust, suspicions and suspected terrorism unfortunately had far worse foundation than expected. My every movement to date had been appropriate in avoiding the excesses of the ongoing cruelty, and finally the conspirators involved began to surface. What appeared as insanity did have a fairly plausible logic to it with the answers presented, and although my mental condition was poor, I still remained capable of seeing the deranged mentality of those who were involved, engrossed in their murderous agenda. The thought of the police having a policy of impartiality rang out like a grievous insult with the ever-increasing number of victims. Was Jill Dando to become included in these statistics? She certainly resented a child murder being investigated in any other way than the right and proper manner it should have been. Her stance was admirable. However, the atrocities behind the manipulation could prove dangerous, and there was no process available to warn her by. A question mark was raised over her future safety, where an eerie ability to predict the future was inherited from knowing the full context of the situation, which proved correct with the Grant McCaskill fiasco. The details in the ridiculous reconstruction of the Russell family where the car changes colour, or the suspect whose distinctive broad shoulders suddenly vanished, or the number of telephone calls about the appeal multiplying by a factor of twenty, could never be covered up. Nor could the fact that Grant McCaskill was molesting women at a time when he should rightly have been remanded in custody. You grow old fast contemplating what happened and why it happened because the slaughter was to continue unabated. Only further exposure could (hopefully) bring it to a halt because the rule of law was only being abused as another weapon of terror against the public. At this point, my Jobseekers Allowance was ceased under dubious circumstances and a minor motoring offence was received due to the complicity of their evil deeds. This would shortly involve a court appearance. The crushing blow was this second Russell murder reconstruction, where something inside had died. Gone was my jovial attitude that said, "Call that an assassination attempt, that'll be another honey trap then. Hospitalise me! These idiots are more likely to do themselves an injury."

I came home to fight or die, and I for one was growing tired of dying. No; a stand against the oppressors was paramount for the future safety and liberty of myself and every other citizen in the West of Scotland. Both Jill Dando and I would contribute to the high-risk task of revealing the truth. In my own defence, there was no other viable alternative than to run that risk because I was a condemned man anyway. Better to die on your feet than to live forever on your knees: one of those silly romantic sayings that Jill Dando   fulfilled   so   tragically!

3. FIGHT THE BIG WAR

On the eleventh hour of the eleventh day of the eleventh month in the year 1997, the fight back began. That was the time of my trial on charges of minor motoring violations directly caused by the campaign of terror being waged against me by the security forces. The intervening months between my return home from Portugal and this court case were passed slowly, biding my time for this long awaited confrontation to come to fruition.

The decision taken to use this occasion in a provocative and imaginative manner was not made to retaliate against the ongoing terror campaign, but merely to make that vital stand and provide some much needed leeway in the constant strife being inflicted. This indispensable course of action took a leaf out of their book where both the law and the media were to be used advantageously to oppose the oppressors. This was a reversal of what had been happening, where such abuses were used to perpetuate the misery. Now the same principle could be applied to expose the evil conspirators. This stance was expedient for a change in fortunes, where the hunted could become the hunter. The mentality of the insuperable was resurgent, where instead of paying homage to the vile-minded protagonists the only wish was to antagonise them.

Those thousands of miles travelled in desperation instilled in me the determination ruthlessness and cunning to accomplish this deed. It was a cold calculated gamble of epic proportions that was going to epitomise another crazy day in a crazy life. In all awareness of the grief and suffering experienced by the bereaved, I knew better than anyone that what was about to be conducted could compound their sorrow. With this sentiment prominent, my intentions were that if it was properly handled, it could provide them with the greatest remedy for all their emotional torment - the truth. People left bewildered and distressed by the loss of a loved one should not have their anxiety prolonged by those people empowered with investigating the death abusing this trust by flaunting the victim in a subordinate way. It had always been a one-way street until now where some bad publicity could act as a deterrent to those butchering and damning the population and actually save many lives. So what was being contemplated in order to ensure immediate and future prosperity?

I was standing trial for an incident that was the result of police and Special Branch victimisation, and legally, there is a legitimate defence in such a situation. The defence testimony, which told of me leaving the doctored milk samples with the police and fleeing the house in terror in the belief that I was about to be murdered was exactly as it occurred. It also was revealed that this had formed an intricate part of being framed for a prostitute murder in which the actual suspects ended up dead. This could all be construed as an over-reaction. However, once again, another death assisted in corroborating the essence of the defence. Three days before the court case, Charles McGregor was found dead. He once stood trial for the murder of his wife, the second of the prostitutes to be murdered in this sequence. As I have originally alleged, the police investigators did not classify the death as a murder case and the newspapers reported that there were no suspicious circumstances surrounding the death. Why is it that all these coincidences and conjecture form a logical pattern? The defence case presented also centred on the Grant McCaskill attacks on women, yet two months previously the police could make no response in connection with this scandal being revealed. In addition to this was their failure to reply with their findings on the milk samples, which I had left with them for analysis, along with no convictions for five serial murders. There was plenty of circumstantial evidence to support the basis of this elaborate defence. In conjunction with the media being informed in advance, I hoped that by recalling this story under oath, it would be published in the newspapers and bring this killing spree to an end and give me some respite from the relentless persecution.

This method of revealing the truth and presenting it to the public was the only viable option left open to me. When I had approached the Press several months previously as a lone member of the public, they had been reluctant to assist by printing my story, even though I had presented first hand evidence of a bottle of the poisoned milk to be independently assessed. These tabloid newspapers did share a degree of guilt by blindly printing stories that effectively furthered the mass murder, when their instinct, as journalists, should be to question the logic of what is being fed to them. Now was the only opportunity to rectify the disproportionate amount of propaganda by exposing the perpetrators, where legally speaking, anything printed about the court proceedings has no repercussions on the newspaper.

COULD IT BE ACHIEVED?

On that morning, I borrowed my sister-in-law's car to drive to the District Court in Greenock. On the way there, I took a diversion. Armed with a list of telephone numbers and a pile of loose change, I stopped at a public telephone box in the tourist town of Largs. The purpose of this was to call the various newspapers to inform them that a story was breaking concerning Glasgow's murdered prostitutes in the Greenock District Court that day. Asking for reporters to cover the story, the timing of the call was appropriate to allow them to leave Glasgow and travel the 26 miles to arrive in Greenock before proceedings began. Then I drove to Greenock from Largs to meet up with whoever had gathered at the court. The building is very small and situated up a lane, which on that morning was strewn with construction debris. Hidden from view and unaccustomed to serious crime, the surprise, which I was about to spring, would place it on the map of heresy. One freelance reporter and two lads from the Glasgow-based *Evening Times* turned up to cover proceedings. In the time before the plea was made and before subsequently standing trial, I reiterated the story to these members of the Press. Some people never realise the significance of an article featuring a photo-fit where the likeness was of poor quality, the policeman sharing the same name and the news items of women being attacked as being a method of rigging a jury. Only the freelance reporter, who was older, more experienced and possibly more knowledgeable, had started to grasp the significance of this information in relation to the plot. The other two remained oblivious to the hidden agenda behind the news articles. Some people automatically switch on, others only do so after a period of time and the less intelligent or susceptible never see the reasoning. It was difficult to explain... Apart from this, the story had ample facts and figures, evidence and coincidences, common sense and reasoning, that finally, the majority of the tale would register with this trio.

The judge had the accused appear first off. When he asked again what plea was being submitted, I steadfastly replied, "Not guilty." From his viewpoint, surely this was the wrong plea, with no obvious defence and with the two witnesses against the accused both being police officers. Unknown to the judge, I had checked with a capable local lawyer on the previous Friday who confirmed that if you have been victimised by the police to the extent that you have committed a crime, you have a legitimate defence. In this case, it was a motoring offence. You will certainly never find a more extreme case of victimisation than the one about to be presented.

Then the call came for the case to begin. With the three men from the Press in position in the court room, and with myself conducting my own defence, the moment had arrived. I cross-examined the two police witnesses like a snarling wild animal. All the injustices I had suffered contributed to the fury of my questioning. It was an unsettling performance as the composure of one of them visibly slipped in the onslaught. How was he to know of the background to this anger, being little more than a pawn in this game of Russian roulette? Then I surprised the judge and took the stand to present a defence. This probably shocked him because it seemed to everyone that I did not have any defence, with the judge suspicious of the constant phrase of, "Not guilty."
The crux of the defence argument was the poisoned milk, which I had submitted to the police during the campaign of victimisation and the fact that I had been forced to flee from home on an illegal motorcycle. What had at first sight appeared to be the most trivial of motoring offences forced the court to be adjourned in the middle of this deliverance to allow the council to go into recess to discuss proceedings. Out of courtesy, the judge asked if I wished to make any final comments before he retired to his backroom chambers. Was there ever! The entertainment value in that court room was high, as I produced a Press cutting from Sunday's newspaper and waved it wildly about and shouted, "There's the story of Charles McGregor, who stood trial for the murder of his wife. She was a

working prostitute and he was found dead only three days ago. I was to be dealt the same fate!"

Although the three accompanying journalists had been bombarded with stories, newspaper cuttings and insight, this final piece remained hidden in my jacket to be produced as a surprise even to those struggling to comprehend a mountain of facts and escapades that had already been made available. There was more to this retort than the legal professionals could imagine. On the Saturday night that Charles McGregor died I had came across one of the local members of Special Branch, from the Russell family, who was looking in a terrible state. Judging by his manner, if anybody had just taken part in a murder this young man had. The Sunday papers were checked with the intention of finding who Special Branch had murdered the night before. Shocking as it sounds, this death was one coincidence I wanted to find. If cross-examined on the subject this information was going to be revealed, but in reality they only wanted the subject closed.

The trial resumed with the judge insisting that the defence could only be given in mitigation, saying that he could not accept evidence from another crime. I protested, but had to accept his judgement as a continuation of airing the exploits that had created this hearing. Although diminished, the purpose of exposing these grievances remained. I was always going to be found guilty because of his decision and so concluded proceedings. Asked if there were any final comments to make, I replied, "I put that poisoned milk into the police five months ago. Sergeant Webster was dealing with it. When it is their first duty to put the safety of the public first; why have they never got back to me about it?"

The judge summed up this extraordinary recitation to mention leniency shown during the case, then handed out a fifty pound fine, which I agreed to pay on the spot. My licence was to be endorsed with three penalty points, which was irrelevant. I believed that my next destination would be a return to Spain, so they could keep it as a souvenir of a gallant failure. I sat there thinking of how the issue had been circumnavigated, so drained from my exertions and so totally despondent that I never even noticed the court officer with his hand held out awaiting payment of the small fine. The gloom mounted as I considered what had happened. All the anticipated members of the Press to cover the story had been reduced to three who were unlikely to provide any exposure for various reasons. The two less capable reporters had been unable to digest the complexity of the matter, and thereby remained unconvinced about the truth of it. It was, therefore, safe to assume that it would be unlikely that they would print any of the material. The freelance journalist did have at least a limited understanding of the story, but the fact that he was not affiliated to any particular newspaper and, given the incriminating nature of the story, it was doubtful that he would be able to sell his piece onto a national newspaper. On taking the stand, I had been boiling over with frustration. For someone who is normally a slow and dour speaker, I was, for once, chattering away so fast that it was requested that I should slow down and start over again. With this, could it ever be recorded accurately, as desired? Did the law change in the last four days between reaffirming the perimeter of the defence and this court hearing? Or was it simply down to a difference in interpretation? Whatever, this evidence should have been delivered in defence, not mitigation, giving the clearest understanding possible. Consumed by these dismal thoughts, I realised that the only golden opportunity to make that vital stand had strayed from the intended purpose and so crawled out of the courtroom a dejected man.

Before leaving the building, I saw that the trio from the Press and the two police officers had congregated. The one who faltered under questioning now took his revenge and lectured me like a schoolteacher would when disciplining a disruptive pupil. Dimmed, but not broken in response to his stern words, I noticed his face plummeting for a second time at the mere mention of Special Branch. Was he out of his depth? Could he read the warning signs, or was the significance revealing its ugly head?

The deed was done, and no matter how unsatisfactory the outcome there was no going back. So I left by going down the stairs into that narrow lane. The tall buildings created shadows and along with the bright sunshine over the Clyde estuary, it was very symbolic of the light at the end of the tunnel, which still remained distant. I walked with the freelance guy towards the car. He asked me if my life really was in danger. I assured him that it was, giving him various examples of how they had tried but failed to end it. After apologising to him for the waste of time this exercise had been, we parted company with the sentiments of good luck. Now came the time for a decision about whether or not I should stay or go abroad. It had been wrong to be so public-spirited by automatically paying the fine. The reduction in funds made the price of a one-way ticket to Spain debatable. Also, the borrowed car had to be returned. These were the two concluding factors in a transient return home.

I returned home that night to be confronted by my mother.
"What were you in court for today?" she asked, "Was it something major?"
Instantly I dismissed this by saying, "No, something minor, a road traffic offence."
"Oh, then what's the (*Daily*) *Record* doing on the phone looking for you?"

Caught out by this telephone call, it was time for me to own up. She had been ill at the time of these events and so I had felt there was no option but to keep it quiet. Now an explanation was required. But how do you explain something of this magnitude to someone who was unaware of the corporate corruption that existed, whereas this life was an education to the most worldly of people? I attempted to relate what had happened to the unsuspecting woman who started shaking increasingly as details were revealed. In all seriousness, I tried to calm her distress by saying, "But they're not that good anyway" in reference to the notorious family passing the house two nights before the major firearms incident with the possibility of this being their first intended victim. It was not that believable with those suspected of the attempted murder of five people, but it was impossible to express that the most professional killers in this country had failed to execute her son. Likewise, attempts by others of lesser ability could never be rated.

I checked the papers the next day to find no mention of the court appearance and the havoc created. On the 13th November, I left the university after trying to find work abroad and I bought a copy of the

Evening Times where they had a full page story which read as follows:

——

I'M BEING FRAMED

MAN MAKES
BIZARRE
MURDER
CLAIMS IN
COURTROOM
A man has stunned a Scottish court by claiming police are out to frame him for the murder of Glasgow prostitute Jackie Gallacher. His claims form a tangled web that pulls together murder, rape, attempted murder and international intrigue.

Robert Rae says he lives "in fear for his life."
He made a complex string of allegations to back his claim, including his alleged portrayal by police as a sex fiend behind attacks on 20 women and the killing of six ... including vice girl Jackie Gallacher. He admits driving a red Renault van in the Glasgow area ... cops have linked the driver of such a van to the unsolved Gallacher murder probe.

PHOTOFIT

The girl was found wrapped in a carpet in a lay-by near Bowling. Rae also claims the police photo-fit issued prior to the arrest and conviction of Grant McCaskill - who got life earlier this year for stalking Glasgow women after his girlfriend shopped him - bears a striking resemblance to himself.

Jackie (26) was brutally slain and her body dumped in a lay-by on the Glasgow-Dumbarton road last June. Now Rae has put himself firmly in the spotlight. Yesterday, he amazed officials at Inverclyde District Court where he was on trial for a minor motoring offence. He declared: "I am being framed for the murder of prostitute Jackie Gallacher."

Rae (29) was charged with driving his 125cc motorcycle without having a Basic Training Certificate. When magistrate Ronald McEwan asked what Rae's defence was, the unemployed cabinet-maker stormed: "I fled my house at 4.20am in fear of my life and to prevent a major scandal breaking.

"The scandal involves the attacking of about 20 women, six of whom were murdered. The police are actively framing me for the murder of Jackie Gallacher."

SHOOTING

He claims that a police photo-fit released during the West End manhunt identified him. He claims that he frequently used his brother's red Renault van - similar to one being sought in connection with the murder - to drive into Glasgow. He also claims that he is an eyewitness to a gangland shooting in Beith and this also makes him the subject of police interest.

The two traffic cops who flagged him down in Greenock - Constables Patrick Martin and David Ryan - sat stunned in court. The magistrate found Rae guilty and fined him £50. Afterwards, Rae said he was "doing a runner" - possibly back to Portugal or France, where he says he slipped through an Interpol net earlier this year. A leading detective working on the Jackie Gallagher murder team said: "I can categorically deny that Strathclyde Police frame anybody. This is a live inquiry and it would be wrong to identify people who we have, or have not, interviewed."

Accompanying the article were two photographs: one of the unfortunate victim, the second larger picture of myself holding up the Press cutting with the circumspect photo-fit under the headline (in reference to Grant McCaskill): "*City Sex Fiend Strikes Again.*"
When the two reporters asked for this photograph to be taken it was done totally unprofessionally, setting the form to be repeated throughout the court proceedings. On the small landing on the stairs, which are only the width of the steps squared, with my back hard

against the wall, this pair insisted my head should go further back. Due to the lack of available space, I reluctantly squashed my chin into my neck, creating a small double chin. Again they insisted the face should go further back, so I obliged by tilting my head back until it rested on the wall. This distorted photograph had even less of a likeness to the incriminating picture issued as a photo-fit, and thus the difficulties explaining matters afterwards were exasperated. In all this strife it was the worst timing to have drawn the shortest straw. The story was written in a confused and crude manner, aided by a lack of understanding by the authors. Very simply, it was the bullet in the back of the head that I feared; not a scandal breaking, but there was no mention of the milk or, for that matter, the policeman with the identical name. The writing was far from kind and the words, "*in fear of his life*," were never uttered, but fortunately, this amalgamation of the context did appear and acted as an insurance policy against being murdered. It was a lifesaver in disguise, raising the stakes to new proportions by daring to challenge the sacrilege being peddled by an efficient killing machine.

What was of importance was the concluding statement in the story, which read, "*I can categorically deny that Strathclyde Police frame anyone.*"
This incredible ability to discredit what had been written was retained, with every opportunity used to have a one-sided argument that always reaffirms their views and opinions. Under a veil of respectability and trust, the mass murder campaign was continued where only by destroying this bond between public and police could the termination of be achieved. Here read another example of this principle. Unable to answer the repeated accusations of implicit savagery, they resolutely denied them, thereby sacrificing the lives and safety of innocent civilians once again. The final sentence of their reply was more about threatening than it ever was about investigation, commenting on who had been interviewed. The nearest this inquiry came to interviewing me was once their grand scheme of framing an innocent person lay in tatters, when they backtracked and ruled out any connection between the van I could have been driving and the one supposedly used in the murder of Jacqueline Gallacher. Unlike the women's groups two month previously, this expedition into the unknown had extracted a reply,

albeit more in the lines of psychological warfare than in the interests of law enforcement. Just maybe that catastrophic failure wasn't entirely worthless, as I previously contemplated sitting despondently in the courtroom two days before. The story, although it had been misrepresented, had appeared and in simple terms could either be investigated or the killing would continue.

This misrepresentation, the distorted photograph and the highly controversial substance of what did appear created the next nightmare. I had been originally desperate to avoid the murky world of prostitution, murder and the associated stigmas that went with both; now with the newspaper story I had delved into another unpleasant situation. The public response was a blizzard of abuse without giving me the opportunity to explain the unfortunate predicament. As someone who had been to hell and back, I really didn't need the never-ending torment of muffled threats, depraved stigmas, name-calling and subsequent ostracism. The most vehement and damning were from those whose failings, betrayals and cowardice had resulted in what had occurred and were now trying to raise their own profiles by running down someone who had already lived up to the bravado they aspired to. This left me with the greatest mental block that persists to this very day, where if they succeeded, they could only make themselves look no better than child molesters within the context of the situation.

Without the right of reply, the supposed reason for the outlandish newspaper story was three-pronged. Some perceived this incredible defence was to avoid a £50 fine and penalty points on my licence. Such reasoning from people that small-minded didn't deserve to be dignified with a reply. Being of a reckless nature when it comes to motoring, I had racked up fines and points annually from the age of sixteen and had always accepted the punishment. Already being in possession of an impressive list of minor motoring violations that could easily fill this page; why should another insignificant offence ever justify the most spectacular of defences? Others, in reference to their own drug habits, gave this as the reason for the article. Having never been known to abuse drugs, it is unlikely that I should take such a notion immediately before appearing in court therefore jeopardising the most trivial of offences for something more serious, such as contempt of court. In court, that was the only constraint to which I gave consideration towards avoiding, when pushing the judge to the margin, when delivering the defence that was later reduced to mitigation. The third and commonly accepted opinion was that of insanity. Most convenient temporary insanity fitted the proposition best of all, a condition which, if such does exist, is instantly ruled out by the fact that this story ever appeared in print. Herein lies a paradox where the substance of what was heard had to have sufficient weight to ever receive coverage, and by its very appearance, it receives that much needed credence. Every day, courts are told fanciful tales, which never warrant media attention; the element of truth has to exist, the context one way or another has to be substantiated, and the speaker does need a certain amount of credibility. Further complementing the paradox is the fact that this epic story received a response from none other than a spokesperson representing those against whom the incriminating accusations were being made - Strathclyde Police. It could be argued that the Rape Crisis spokeswoman, whose outburst failed to receive any response, is in greater respect of being labelled insane than someone who could commandeer an issued statement. Her criticism was more than justified, as countless victims in whose defence she spoke will testify.

Reading from the Press cutting to here, those with superior cognition of the situation will have noticed an interesting quandary about the denial to rectify the misalignment in the newspaper with what had preceded it. Surely a simple explanation was all that was required to stem the growing consensus insanity produced this performance. As always, however, the dark forces of evil prevented such a basic misinterpretation being ratified by a source as equally shocking as it was effective. Your best judgement could never guess where the definition of madness originated, or why such an erroneous diagnosis in the face of insurmountable evidence could entertain any credibility. It was my own brother who perpetuated this lie. In a story where conspiracy revolved around conspiracy, paradox complicated paradox, and incident followed incident, this anomaly requires closer inspection.

At the beginning of that year, the brother in question found himself a new girlfriend called Helen Stewart. The timing of her appearance fitted well in the impending scenario. On initial contact, far from being deluded by paranoia, I was not the only one to have the immediate impression that she was as genuine as a £3 note. The social work employment with the homeless she claimed as an occupation is a favourite cover-story for those operating incognito. At times the groupie traits she displayed were inappropriate for someone of the social standing she supposedly held, especially in light of the fact that she was older than him. She took little interest in any subject but always seemed alert. When inquisitive, her attentions focussed on myself instead of her boyfriend, until the actions of this blonde changed one night. I unintentionally made a consubstantial remark in Helen's company one Sunday night that caused her to light up unexpectedly, but instead of leaving her to squirm in the self-conscious show of ostentation, my brother spoke up and defended her, which defused the situation. Needless to say, Romeo and Juliet separated only days later, which was rather predictable, as a result of the behaviour that had been exhibited previously in the house kitchen.

Later that same night, I was lying awake and heard the locked front door being opened, intruders entering the house and departing again, locking the door behind them leaving everything intact with one exception. This was the first of many house visits known to have occurred. The next morning, my brother complained that he was last to go to bed and first to get up in the morning, and that what he had left on the kitchen work surface had disappeared. I now believed that sooner or later incidents like that would register with him though knew that his unrealistic stubborn nature could never accept a reasonable explanation. He was someone who would argue that black is white rather than admit to being wrong. Unfortunately for myself the penny never dropped. A more convincing example of this was when he heard someone on the roof of the house in the middle of the night, which could have been someone bugging the house, and had myself go out and investigate. Unable to find the moonlight steeplejack, I returned empty-handed. Irrespective of what they were doing and likewise not sighting them, only the gullible could not realise that all these incidents shared a central theme. They say there are none so blind as those who don't want to see. Helen's impeccably timed appearances to offer solace and provide suspect interpretations for many unexplained riddles gave real foundation to the cynical beliefs held. She persistently returned after their falling out, offering employment, which basically entailed me sitting idly out of the vicinity for £400 per week. Left impoverished because my unemployment benefit had been ceased; why did I give lame excuses and refuse this nest egg?

In the wake of all this, the most surmountable and revealing conundrum remained unheard. With her boyfriend's brother being framed for murder, it was surprising that this woman should excel herself as one of the best authorities of Glasgow's murdered prostitutes. With claims of culprits, knowledge of who the owner of the small red van allegedly involved was, and why the police had failed to apprehend him, and other relevant snippets of information all forthcoming with timing to correspond with a cover-up. If only the police knew of Helen, then many of Glasgow's mysteries could be solved?! On the other hand, the quintessential substance of the claims being made mirrored some of the newspapers being used for propaganda purposes. A police source used to manipulate the Press when it was demanded; so, who was her source? Here were the words of a charlatan expressing a view different to the commonly accepted belief that alleged a Special Branch massacre. All of this takes us back to the syndrome of being too close to the problem to realise the obvious and not having the breathing space to accept an alternative opinion. This repeated predicament was now consuming a brother where the symptoms are left to affect myself. Written here without the complexity of the dual faceted use of a bastardised photo-fit, the first time this scenario occurred, it is difficult to understand why this brother was unable to unravel Helen's interjections or the unexplained happenings. Unlike his younger brother, he never shared the same level of intellect or ability to comprehend the concealed logic hidden in the enigmas presented by dubious sources purporting to be reliable in fact. This crazy situation was to manifest itself into the impossible circumstances that developed, which produced the afore-mentioned denial to rectify the simple misrepresentations that appeared in the newspaper article. Only slight discrepancies needed clarifying. However, if your own brother makes accusations that you have gone mad, people fore-warned by this are not going to give you an audience to explain the misconceptions associated with this most outlandish story.

Vindication of all this came at a high price with the lengths, the number of people informed, the amount of distortion required and the methods used to ridicule this story. Those who were hoodwinked were not to know that he was plied with guidance from the Devil's advocate. What really caught the essence was the final affront, when the doctor was called behind my back to further the insinuations of madness. Unaware of what was going on, this doctor appeared at the house and suggested that a psychiatrist should be consulted. Realising then what was happening, I believed there and then that this was conclusive proof to verify the story because the same person had featured earlier in the events. Doctor McCormack, in all her honesty, admitted that I had approached her previously to have the sabotaged milk analysed, and if this confirmation didn't sway the GP's judgement, nothing could. Thinking they had tripped themselves up by pushing too far, however inconceivable it sounds, she persisted with assessing the supposed ailment. The lunatics really had taken over the asylum with multiples of victims from various incidents supporting every word said. It shows the total desperation when the last line of defence is to discredit someone by engineering a campaign claiming they are insane. Others taking a passing interest in this final insult adhered to this view, fully aware of the situation realising the options left to contain these actions were limited, and with the oppressors being challenged the need to discredit the story was paramount.

In particular, two contentious points stood out for criticism, the contaminated milk and Interpol. First hearing of this poisoning of suspects during secondary school, today only firsthand experience could describe the contamination process witnessed through the clear glass. It also made sense of an oblique saying, "The milk filled the Maze."
Uncertain if this was army, British Intelligence, terrorist or media who had coined this unusual quote, only now was it possible for me to interpret such a riddle. It was in reference to the past situation in Northern Ireland where terrorist suspects were poisoned prior to

arrest and trial, thereby increasing the likelihood of conviction, and where the sentence was served in the Maze Prison. A second source of ridicule was Interpol, which did appear in print. The truth is Interpol are nothing to be revered or respected, where only the advent of the computer has increased their effectiveness. With no more than an adequate service provided, the ports and airports directive is commonly issued to trail suspects. Those who are unable to segregate fact from the fiction presented on television are never going to accept the distorted status of this policing organisation. Ignorance played the greater part in receiving abuse from these two conducive subjects opposed to any foundation to warrant the haranguing encountered.

Thankfully being a person of reliable character who is not known to have fabricated such yarns in the past, there was no problem making people believe what I am telling once able to explain the story to them on a one-to-one basis. With plenty of evidence to support the story and with no apparent reason for me to exaggerate any of the details, the handful of people I had informed, who had no preconceived ideas, knew that this could be nothing other than the truth. Unfortunately, this was a mere handful, and so with every stigma, social affliction and depraved crime being levelled against my name, you could now add insanity. The only real one was a suicidal man struggling to hold the pieces together. Finding the strength and the will to continue remained the biggest obstacle to overcome. For all this, people of an open-minded persuasion claimed that what was written there was only the tip of the iceberg. They knew of some of the more daring exploits that I had embarked upon. With the mainstream current flowing against us, others knew that the contents of the article carried an element of truth and the following questions were being asked:

"Why have there been no convictions when it is impossible to murder someone in the centre of Glasgow without being noticed?"

"Why do the suspects in these cases suddenly end up dead themselves?"

"How was it possible to change a black *BMW* into a small red van?"

"Are the police committing these murders?"

"Why did they syringe a virus into your milk?"

"Why are you being targeted by them?"

"Why are so many drug addicts found dead?"
"Why do the down-and-outs disappear?"
"Why is there no evidence from the security cameras?"
"How many have they murdered, who is behind it all and why do they get away with it?"

These countless unanswered questions did hint at more of a larger conspiracy, and at me knowing substantially more than had ever been revealed. As the months slowly ticked by, so did a steady trickle of accusers change their viewpoint with words of agreement in support of this cause. They said, "You predicted that would happen."
"You claimed that months ago and you were right."
"You always maintained that Special Branch were responsible."

This new popular opinion put the onus onto my brother. Why did he work so hard to discredit me? Maybe I should have answered this with a tale from his former girlfriend, Helen Stewart, when this stupid brother told me a story of her knowing who was responsible for Jackie Gallacher's murder. She claimed to have the culprit as one of her homeless clients, driving a small red van. He doesn't sound too homeless, does he!

ANOTHER DETAIL

Whatever nonsense was bandied about became irrelevant. The response to the newspaper story became the important factor. I returned to the workshop down in Cumnock to be greeted with a disgruntled David Wilson and an important source to his irritation. He volunteered the information of his own redundancy along with the timing of being informed of this termination either on the afternoon immediately after the court appearance or the next day. This made perfect sense as the word 'supergrass' flashed through my mind. He was rumoured to have informed on the terrorists. I tested the theory by supplying him the destination in Portugal to give to the authorities, which resulted in the resumption in surveillance by the over-dressed cameraman. Remembering these incidents, I had never revealed to him my intention to make a surprise stand in court. This was the second major contributing factor that would make it look as though he was holding out on his handlers which resulted in instant dismissal from his council employment. Finally the pieces were starting to fall into place, and the controversial stance at the trial was made more valiant than imagined. The termination of the supervisor's employment was a small victory but nothing to gloat about because I only viewed it as having been self-inflicted. I had always done my best by him, so having never done anything to inconvenience this supervisor, why did he behave in this manner? The SNLA terrorists who had come by the workshop were his friends and they were the first to be betrayed by him. It did pose questions about his scruples. The more I pressed him about the redundancy, the more vague his answers became, especially after I revealed my latest exploit in court. The timing coincided with his initial confession and his futile efforts to try and conceal the relevance gave away his status (as an informer) plus the need to cover up his treachery. His loss of income was complicated by the fact that the man had a wife and a young family to support. But this was minor in comparison to the loss of liberty or life that he could have contributed to through his treachery.

RISK TAKING, HEART BREAKING

The appalling situation once again reached crunching point; nobody could make such claims of this substance in the light of so many unsolved serious crimes and not have them investigated. What was going to happen here? Answer: an honest investigation resulting in the imprisonment of their own was never going to happen, so the likely outcome would be similar to the first airing two months previously. They would shun the whole affair. The hypocrisy could be accepted with only one exception; people were being murdered here and will continue to be murdered unless some kind of deterrent is instigated. The more the situation was pondered upon, the more the realisation affirmed itself. The stakes had now increased to an astronomical level and I was looking over the precipice. What now? It was no longer fashionable to be murdered with the newspaper article saying what it did, and it now went beyond being hospitalised. What was written was cruel, but it meant the difference between living and dying, where someone would have to live with the consequences of the stigmas of being associated with the murders of women, possible child abuse and prostitution.

In circumstances like these, there is always an immediate response, which can be little more than nonsense followed by a secondary severe reprisal. The first had come and gone with the supervisor receiving his comeuppance. When considered from this viewpoint, it looked like justice, which is such a rare commodity in the West of Scotland. The need to curtail these activities became imperative before overall justice could be secured to incriminate the whole murderous regime.

Time to further these objectives ran out with an incident most people would hold in bewilderment. For all the torrid abuse received by others, they could never comprehend that what was attempted was lion-hearted in the extreme. We are not dealing with an isolated murder here, but more of a present-day genocide, where a sole dissident can be easily suppressed. A few days later I had been away from home, whence upon return to find that sheets had been swapped on my bed. It was strange that such an event should happen. The bed sheets that had been removed were more old-fashioned plus made of cotton and matched the bed. By contrast, the replacements were linen in texture and much more modern. I was not the first person to hold this complaint but was fully aware of why such an apparently obscure incident should occur.

The repeated failure to secure any convictions for the prostitute murders combined with the deaths of the various suspects made a wary public more sceptical about the situation. There was increasing doubt over who was responsible, and suspicion was turning on the police force deployed to investigate these crimes, where the contempt for the female population was made manifest by Grant McCaskill's reign of terror. The pressure was mounting and the desperation to avoid being exposed had certainly brought the situation to boiling point. Obviously, the reprisals against me for even attempting to confront such an evil regime would be sudden and devastating. That story in the *Evening Times* gave an undeniable statement identifying six murdered women. The deliberate crusade to rubbish what had been written and to frustrate a simple explanation clarifying the distortions printed, in conjunction with the refusal to investigate my claims, presented them with the opportunity to further the slaughter. No moral judgement was made on the lifestyles of the murdered women, and it did not state that there had been six murdered prostitutes, because only five of them had shared this profession. The sixth woman was Lin Russell, who was caught up in the ongoing scandal. There is no void here, and there was no void. What did appear was accurate in detail surrounded by other misconceptions. To create a void out of what was written and to fill it by murdering a sixth Glasgow prostitute would incriminate Strathclyde Police, whose response was publicly aiding and abetting a mass murder campaign. This was extremely serious in nature, but if blood was already dripping off their hands with previous murders in this sequence being attributed to their co-operation, another used to conceal their atrocious crimes would become readily acceptable. It is this very insight that contains the logic for another kill.

The divergence in tactics now was to utilise the Press report, which connected me to the attack and murder of various women. The greatest irony here is that what they failed to do by sacrificing the safety of women in the West End of Glasgow was now achieved to perfection by trying to curtail their murderous ways. Only a foolproof conviction of myself for the next murder could enhance their position and alleviate the concerns of the public regarding the implication of the police in such dreadful sins. How else was it attainable to finally frame an innocent person in a definite manner in the wake of the constant failure to secure any convictions?

The moment I found that the bed had been interfered with provided me with an unfortunate answer, which led to a daunting conclusion. One of the most convincing pieces of evidence retrieved from a crime scene is a DNA sample and bed sheets are an ample source. The transplanting of a DNA sample removed from the house to the vicinity of the next murder victim, especially if it were a prostitute, combined with what the newspaper story stated, would certainly result in a conviction. Any forthcoming trial originating from such entrapment methods would force the defendant to resolutely maintain there never had been any association with the victim. However, the evidence would contradict such an honest claim in the thoughts and beliefs of a jury. The scenario was sufficient to overcome any discrepancies, alibis and lack of motive presented. Although the story was wearing thin, the authorities responsible could still rely upon the same respectability being abused throughout this terror campaign to convince people of the wrongful guilt of the accused.

When you sit thinking over these various things: the proposition in the context of why I was originally targeted; the belief that the intention behind the reconstruction of the Glasgow prostitute murders on *Crimewatch* was to frame innocent civilians; why Grant McCaskill's attacks on women were prolonged; and now with Jill Dando's life expectancy called into question; you become aware of the systematic process being used to further the carnage. The scary element of this theory was that if I was correct about my suspicions, another murder of a prostitute in Glasgow was imminent.

I was living in intrinsic fear, laced with frustration that, having done the utmost to oppose those responsible, only two weeks separated the controversial court appearance and the news report of the murder of a sixth woman frequenting Glasgow's red light district. How predictable it was that only days separated the sheets being swapped and this woman being murdered! Your worst nightmare becomes reality before your very eyes where you are unable to influence the outcome in any way. Less predictable were the events that followed this crime and the surprise that I remained at liberty. Nothing short of a minor miracle could appease the impending arrest and subsequent trial, but, what did?

An unusual feature exposed itself as I watched the news bulletin on November 25th 1997 about the murder of a young mother, Tracey Wilde, who was found dead in her flat on the north side of Glasgow. The television camera showed the block of flats in which she lived crawling with police, detectives and media reporters. All this was normal for a murder investigation, or so it appeared until the camera panned down the street to the junction where a British Telecom (*BT*) transit van was sitting. As soon as I sighted this vehicle, the definition of this murder took a sinister new twist. This is a favourite undercover vehicle used, and from the outset it was prominent at the murder scene. Later on, a second *BT* van was shown in other footage even nearer her flat. While the possibility of these two vans being genuine *BT* vehicles can never be dismissed, it is most likely that they would have been politely asked to vacate the area and return to duties at a later date. The alternative was that these were undercover personnel who were on hand to monitor developments, control proceedings, eavesdrop on relevant gossip and gauge public perception about this latest murder. It had become a weird science; the possibility of Special Branch committing the crime, then overseeing the investigation with a deliberate presence was a new phenomenon that further complemented all that had been previously alleged. On this same news program the head of Strathclyde Police appeared talking on another subject and looking very smug. This is not the behaviour of a professional, unless, given the record of convictions his force had in connection with these murders, his pleasure came from another dimension.

The disclosure of possible undercover vehicles being there at the scene did little to alleviate the probability of being framed for murder for a ridiculous third time. A far more substantial disclosure would be required to ruin the next plot. For instance, an accurate description of the killer would certainly assist in disrupting any future prosecution. If only you could get that lucky! Stranger events have occurred, and not only was the murderer seen leaving the victim's flat, his description was initially accurately reported in the media and a final impossibility materialised. The killer was someone I knew. The minor miracle required to remain at liberty was occurring from the depths of degradation summarised by the Press conference that was staged. The victim's mother was paraded in the most distressed state making a heart-rending plea to the public to come forward with any information that could assist the police. The familiarity of this had an unsettling tone. Where the same police force only days before had publicly aided and abetted this murder. Now they were taking advantage of the situation created by abusing the mother's distress to appeal on their behalf. The word 'sickening' never really catches the grotesque essence of the scenario. This audacity demonstrates exactly how they were able to continue when the circumstances of Grant McCaskill's attacks should have been investigated over two months previously and the resulting punishments would conclude the whole episode: not something that was in the interests of the butchers responsible. So it was only a matter of time before Tracey Wilde and many others would be murdered unless alternative means of curtailing the slaughter were implemented.

The man witnessed leaving her flat at 2am on the Monday morning, wearing a dark suit and driving away in a blue *Ford Escort* had his features accurately reported. The defining line is drawn here. If this was a genuine murder inquiry, an accurate photo-fit would quickly appear. If British Intelligence were responsible, the paramount need would be to conceal his identity. After such an accurate and instantaneous description was issued, like the culprit who attempted to drown another woman in the River Clyde, no such crime solving measure would be forthcoming. The illegitimate process became all too apparent when they were keen to produce a versatile photo-fit during Grant McCaskill's reign of terror which bore no resemblance, thereby allowing him to carry out further attacks.

With the killer seen and his description recognised by myself, but bearing no resemblance to this complexion, once again a method of obscuring the truth would be required. How could they alleviate the situation without arousing public suspicion and not issue a photo-fit? The answer appeared days later with claims that Tracey Wilde was present at the drop-in centre on West Street at 3am on Monday morning. Now they were raising the dead to further their objectives, where the time referred to on a miserable winter's night becomes removed from reality. This fallible principle, morbid in context and devoid of realism, would one day be their undoing.

Every suspicion and fear regarding these murders came to fruition with this latest killing. The shortage of eyewitness accounts, the absence of CCTV footage and the lack of positive leads believed to be suppressed by the perpetrators in other instances was finally overturned here with the requirement to disguise who was responsible. The first convergence in this vein was the reported sighting of the victim in the company of a man driving a car in West Street. This would most likely require an eyewitness followed by film shot inside the drugs rehabilitation centre later on showing the unfortunate lady, and finally those elusive CCTV pictures from the area in the centre of Glasgow used for prostitution were produced depicting the alleged victim. All of this removed the focus away from her flat and the first suspect. However, this was contradicted by the fact that it was there that her body was found strangled and, once again, where she was actually last seen alive late on the Sunday night. All three sightings and footage had to be falsified to accomplish the impossibility of her rising from the dead to criss-cross the city of Glasgow at such a late hour. How the efficiency of the investigation procedures suddenly increases with all that was revealed here in contrast to the continual failure to broadcast any legitimate video footage from previous similar murders. The only solace here was the poetic words of Jackie Gallacher's mother once again passing comment on television on the latest murder. Finishing with the words, "If you believe them," said in an unconvinced tone in reference to the police. For all the gruesome prospects encountered, those four words were confirmation that I had achieved an ambition. Members of the public were less trusting of the police and likewise were less likely to be led like lambs to the slaughter. Casualties would continue afterwards, but a period of change for the better was surmountable.

A KILLER IN BLACK

Seven months before this latest act of evil should have seen my own execution when two military men dressed in combat fatigues came calling. In the rural location at night, both were dressed all in black, this being the best camouflage for the circumstances. Tracey Wilde's killer was seen wearing a black suit, an urban camouflage for the precincts, but who was he and why was this murderer so readily identified? A military man? A policeman? A member of the Secret Services or an unrelated assassin? His connection to the despots involved concurrent to allow full co-operation between the two, where identification of one man could wreck the apparatus installed to viciously terrorise the West of Scotland. The impetus to pursue the genesis of a murder was too seductive for this very reason. Paradoxically, the need to go looking for him was not the case. For a reversal of this became reality.

Near my house is the clubhouse of the local golf club and, adjacent to which there are several passing places on the single-track road. Many months before the latest calamity, a blue *Ford Escort* sat in one of these lay-bys. The car had a large aerial on its roof, and the male driver, who was the only occupant, perfectly fitted the description of the man seen emerging from Tracey Wilde's flat. The only detail to differ was the length of his hair, which was longer than described prior to her murder. The house was bugged, and more often than not, this bogus CB radio enthusiast was sitting there listening into the family home, because he was Special Branch. Another diversification on this theme was a second aerial in a spiral twist around the magnetically mounted large aerial, and a luminous green glow transmitted from a small screen in the dashboard was apparent inside the car. The house was being kept under both visual and audio surveillance on this occasion.

With their lackey responsible for killing the unfortunate lady at his master's demands, what followed was of the most twisted and vile methods ever experienced, and which, in a rare admission, I do confess was clever. Only such evil people, best described as an insult to humanity, could produce such an extraordinarily hellish galvanisation as the one about to be experienced. All along this terror campaign was absolute; they would capitalise on the deaths that were occurring through the framing of innocent people victimised at random. Tracey Wilde's murder took their depraved principles to an even greater depth. What were the *BT* vans doing situated there at the murder scene other than to put on a show of strength to further petrify an already scared population? That is how it could be perceived. Make it obvious who is responsible in confidence that the public could do nothing about its own massacre anyway since the law had been reduced to a structure of oppression. When the law fails so has democracy, and here is another example.

The blue *Ford Escort* made a return to its position near the house with the driver sporting a short haircut, matching the description of the wanted suspect. Sitting inside the car, his expression was always blank to disguise his covert purpose. However, this was to change, again revealing who the murderers were, and thereafter capitalise on the suffering. Now he was sneering and smiling in a menacing way whenever I was in contact with him. This is the ultimate death threat: the killer situated outside your house with a recent murder unsolved and unlikely to be as a constant reminder of what they can do when unhindered by the law. The smiles and growls answered the longstanding question as to why all this was happening in one word; pleasure. It was like that nightmare apocalyptic vision of the future that every school kid seems to be inundated with. This is the beginning of such a prophecy: the ultimate blood sport of killing people for pleasure and laughing at all who oppose them. Just in case the significance of this passed you by, this is 1997 in Strathclyde, and the nightmare is a reality. Murders and victims are being racked up without justification with a barbaric cruelty unknown in any civilised country for the sole purpose of other's enjoyment. After thinking how someone could participate in such sinister actions, the most frightening conclusion was that this was probably not his first kill. That smile betrayed an unfaltering confidence, and Tracey Wilde certainly was not his first victim. The unanswered questions associated with the crimes being committed are inherently conducive with pure evil when answered, and offer no relief to the inquisitive. It was vile and inhumane beyond comprehension, extracting that last little bit of misery from the most appalling crimes.

Police involvement in the ongoing massacre was always a contentious subject, and now they would display behaviour similar to the childish actions of bullies mocking a victim in a school playground. There was a daily and regular occurrence of police cars passing the house, sometimes stopping and revving the engine and accelerating away to make sure their presence was obvious, but it was not just noticed by myself for a man who often walks this road did comment on this increased activity. They were conducting themselves like second rate terrorists, and the inescapable fact remains, this murderer stationed in his blue *Ford Escort* was also being passed by the same police officers. A potential serial killer was ignored when it was not in their interest, increasing the constant and complete affront to law and order.

All the way to Christmas, the blue *Ford Escort* would appear and position itself near the house. Another development was the appearance of a burgundy *Peugeot 305* with two men looking every inch like CID emerging from the vehicle outside the front gate. Whether they knocked on the door or not is uncertain as I lay down and fell asleep on the bed, beyond caring, and knowing it was in my best interests to be in court anyway. To be tried for this murder would have been another gamble, for at that point I would most likely be convicted. But, any further exposure could act once again as a deterrent until such times that an investigation could be conducted by international human rights bodies. With circumstances like these, exhaustion and apathy are predominant over self-preservation.

The announcement that DNA evidence was obtained from the victim's flat was rather predictable and failed to provoke any rash reaction, even with the foreboding knowledge of how incriminating this could be. The culprit was seen and recognised, the car involved was incompatible with any vehicle I could have borrowed, and three credible alibis in my favour at the time referred to all assisted in alleviating this situation. It did not, however, prevent another wave of victims being included with the introduction of another new devious tactic: simply, DNA testing hundreds of men under the pretext of being possible suspects. The unforeseen aggravation this caused in trying to explain to family, partners and wives why the police should request a DNA sample in connection with a murdered prostitute is enough to fracture any relationship. With the same police force driving past the perpetrator on a daily basis, this exercise certainly was not about investigation. So what was it about? Was it an involuntary experiment in genetics, a mechanism for raising the divorce rate, or was it the favourite option, a power-crazed regime oppressing the population once more? Financing such treachery is never a concern for, as long as the truth can be concealed, they over-tax the community to pay for their own terrorisation.

Vindication nestled with the extraordinary omission of who was not approached for a DNA sample; this being myself. The non-compliance, I believed, arose from the sighting of their killer being accurately reported, as well as the implications concerned with further targeting someone in a failed plot, and their refusal to reply to the milk situation reiterated under oath in court. All congealed to verify that the charade produced for public consumption had no apparent basis as an investigation. The events following this in the subsequent months will conclude a positive result by proving their guilt, where to accomplish this meant reversing the impossible.

[Four and a half years later the police finally extracted a DNA sample, only once every other tactic against me had failed, as they continually struggled to dispose of their number one target. Arrested in a joint operation by regular and undercover officers for walking in a public park (my arrest for an incident prior to this was for driving home alone!). Desperation is apparent as they continually produced fictitious situations in liege with a corrupt law that allowed it all to happen.]

A genuine murder inquiry concerning Tracey Wilde should have seen a reconstruction on *Crimewatch* on the January 1998 programme due to the urgency of the potential situation. With the sick pantomime being orchestrated, some deviation from the norm was required to divert public attention away from the non-appearance on television and to prevent suspicion growing. The week before the programme, still photographs were issued from the CCTV cameras in the city centre claiming to be the last known movements of the victim. This was the first appearance of what was alleged to be falsified footage. The other video evidence at the earlier time of 3am from inside the drop-in centre on West Street remained undisclosed. The two times supplied for the CCTV pictures of the red light district were 3.30am and 4am early Monday morning, which becomes ridiculously removed from reality. The original time given was 4am, and then later on a second time of 3.30am was attached to other CCTV pictures as though an effort was made to rectify the silly situation being fabricated. Having heard years beforehand what was allegedly being conducted by the authorities with basic reason supportive of what was being said, I knew better than anyone to religiously avoid this area at the period used for prostitution. It did not, however, deter me asking others about Glasgow in such areas as to the relevance of the authenticity of the said time in reference to this profession. The consistent reply was that this trade, like any other business, operates on supply and demand, and at such a late hour the appropriate quote used was,

"There is not even litter blowing about the streets at such a time, never mind punters looking for sex."

Consistently it was said the women involved finalised their activities hours before, with most clients about to start work soon afterwards on the Monday morning. The detail of the pictures produced further complemented the assumption that they were falsified. There was a single man striding down the street, which appeared quite meaningless, and others of a couple in close contact who conveniently had their faces obscured by the woman's umbrella. All that technology in an area of many local government buildings with high quality security cameras and all that could be obtained were these oblique pictures, which quite frankly could have been of anyone. No opportunity was missed to inspire fear into the community. One photograph in particular had such a device included. Already mentioned were the British Telecom vans at the crime scene, the blue *Ford Escort* near my house, and now what distinctively looked like the front wheel and quarter panel of a police *Range Rover* included in one of these CCTV pictures!

How inconceivable this sounds. The victim was found dead in her flat in Barmulloch, the position on the street she used to ply her trade was known, and there was a full description of the culprit and the car involved, complete with times. Any competent detective could single-handedly solve this crime with a minimum of effort. All that was required here was simply to trace their steps from A to B using the network of cameras installed in the city centre to build up a complete picture of the driver and the registration number of the vehicle as he went. Entering and leaving the centre of Glasgow the streets are all one-way, reducing the possibilities of route taken. Again this evokes the question of why such phantom killers can operate and go undetected and hints at internal assistance outside the capability of an ordinary member of the public. The claim that Tracey Wilde was the woman hidden under the umbrella in the issued still pictures was suspect in the extreme, and two months later, further doubt was cast on the validity of this identification with another revelation.

February 1998 also failed to see the murder featured on *Crimewatch*, but unfortunately, another woman was murdered in Glasgow's red light district during this month. Margo Lafferty was strangled, and afterwards, finally, a youth, Brian Donnolly, was convicted of her murder, but not without complications. The Press conference staged in connection to this latest murder showed reluctance on the part of the police officers present to confront the Press as they gave agitated replies that contained an air of reticence. It emerged that Margo Lafferty was well known to the police by participating in a liaison group that was set up to provide police protection for the women working in this notorious area. It was also admitted that she was a friend of Tracey Wilde. Before the conviction for this crime, Lafferty's neighbour was also found murdered in his own home. The only comment I had to make after the trial was, "No 19 year old could ever walk out of that."

This was said irrespective of his innocence or guilt in reference to me because I was older and wiser to the methods being deployed to secure a wrongful conviction. There was little surprise when the original verdict was overturned two years later only to go to retrial which ended in a second conviction, but the evidence was suspect with the killer seen on CCTV pictures not wearing Donnelly's jacket. After this I was not the only one sceptical about this sequence of murders.

[The court case against Donnelly had a convicted sex offender, who was in the vicinity of Glasgow's red light district the night Margo Lafferty was murdered, as a witness-come-suspect, in the court case that convicted him. This is a clever tactic, one I had seen before. The family name 'McPherson' was always given in connection with the murder of Jacqueline Gallacher. This surname is synonymous with them that run the brothels in Edinburgh. People could be easily fooled into thinking they have found something by connecting, McPherson to brothels - brothels to prostitution - then on to the murder of J. Gallacher.]

Finally, on the 24th March 1998, the reconstruction of Tracey Wilde's murder was shown on BBC *Crimewatch*. I asked others for their opinion on the film produced and they described it as being weird. I had not seen the programme and therefore could not influence their judgement. It warmed my heart to hear that the public response had turned to suspicion so that they no longer trustingly accepted what was being relayed to them, although it remained repulsive as to how this doubt had been achieved. Film footage from inside the drop-in centre on West Street showed Tracey Wilde with a time seconds before 3am at the bottom. However, modern technology can easily remove and superimpose a false time onto the film. Footage of her standing there herself held little value as a crime solving development. The greatest value it possessed was to convince people that she was still alive after the incident at her flat, which took place over an hour earlier. For my theory to be proved correct, both this and the still pictures issued had to be falsified. It is no great revelation that intelligence agencies around the world are known for deceptions. The reason the reconstruction was so unconvincing was because of that infamous umbrella deliberately obscuring the face of the person below it. There was a story that the item referred to did not belong to the victim but was claimed to have been borrowed just beforehand from another working girl in this area. It was uncanny in the extreme that the women involved in this brutal industry, that carry the minimum of accessories, should have a convenient spare umbrella that could be borrowed, especially with the ludicrous time of day given. On that miserable cold wet night, the participants in the vice trade had the centre of Glasgow turned into a busy place, contrary to the accepted logic!

It has been said that serial killers create patterns in their crimes. The circumstances here created such similarities of sequence. Weeks after the long awaited *Crimewatch* appeal, the police made the statement that they were looking for a student living in student accommodation. Words to this effect were applied to conclude other such murder investigations concerning prostitutes. This unimaginative display had a resonating ring to it, where such a repetition would soon be acted upon. The inability to secure convictions conflicted with the fact that every resource, including television appeals, were made available. After the reluctance to reconstruct the murder of Tracey Wilde for *Crimewatch*, a year and a half later a second appearance was made on the programme. The murders I claim I am being framed for all have second showings on the BBC appeals programme. The victims all had accompanying deaths. Jackie Gallacher had the first suspect in the black *BMW*. Lin and Megan Russell had Jill Dando. And, now Tracey Wilde had her friend Margo Lafferty plus another undisclosed death that could also be connected to her murder. Sunday night strangulations after which the victims are found with articles of clothing removed are another common feature. The threatening investigation procedures deployed, where the police would interview suspects in their own homes, causing inconvenience and embarrassment, were always featured in the media after these murders. Because of the lack of positive leads, the totally unassuming all-encompassing statements issued cast suspicion over the whole population. Statements like, "The perpetrator could even have been a woman," were prevalent. Tactics of the police deliberately delivered terror to the community. The area used by the victims, their habits and lifestyles, all had a common theme, yet they refused to admit that there was any connection between the various murders. This in itself was another similarity.

With suspicion and hearsay rife in the community, coincidence and conjecture apparent to even the most casual observers, this remained insignificant to those for whom criticism and the rule of law has little bearing. A substantial development out with the ordinary was required to make an impact that would produce a result with far reaching consequences and leave everlasting implications. Who could indulge in such a practice, mastermind the complexities of it, and execute the plot to achieve these ambitions? The answer lay with the one who had been persecuted relentlessly, dodged the bullets, Interpol and a prison cell to fearlessly oppose the bloodthirsty despots responsible. The war had begun; the stand in court for that minor motoring offence was as contentious as it was inexplicable. Now the day was dawning to launch an attack, complicating the substance contained in the aforementioned text. This could be to the greater benefit of the whole public, not just to those who were involved in prostitution, and would only be to the detriment of the killers and their allies.

We are all victims paying taxes to a regime that could make any third world despot shrink in comparison. It was just that some suffered more than others. The next alleged casualty was large in stature without any connection to the process of attrition and will shock the most broadminded of readers. Who next, where did they fit in, and why was he victimised?

The crusade embarked upon was, as ever, without any viable alternative. I was forced down an avenue that did not have a clear destination, where only fate possessed as much guidance as any real objective being followed. In my own words, "I am too far gone to help myself now," which is a statement, people were entitled to take any way they want. Deception played its part in continuing the struggle when it was crucial to deceive everyone, even those nearest to me. The basic interpretation of the phrase referred to the importance of not allowing the present predicament to rest when it was imperative to exasperate the situation to cause visible fractures that the public could recognise, leading to their protection combined with my own safety. However, at this point in time, here was someone with their sanity in question, so a misunderstanding could easily be surmised from what was said, possibly deliberate in intention. The distractions implied in order to buy time were quite clever, where one day, clarity will reign once an explanation is granted.

In the meantime, it was irrelevant how people perceived the present situation until the next episode was delivered with menace and vengeance. As the citizens of Strathclyde need to know, once you stand up to the bullies and their cohorts, only then do you cease to become a victim. This principle is compelling, regardless of stature or disposition.

4. THE RAT CATCHER

Where are the safeguards when a secret police force starts operating beyond their jurisdiction as they seem to do in a Third World state? The rule of fear, intimidation and excessive surveillance applied to an unaware community by means of stealth replaces both law and democracy itself. The resulting oppression cripples the economy, which blights the people and tarnishes society. The problem is more acute than envisaged, with the culprits not readily identified: the participants can be your next door neighbours without you even knowing. Only the occasional inconsequential comment hints at their covert existence; for example, "He joined the army when he left school, but I'm not sure what he does now," is the type of telltale line that indicates clandestine activity.

Like a kind of mafia, they rely upon a code of silence, secluded in their own indifferent community, and operate in a twilight world. These nameless and faceless individuals are automatically given immunity from prosecution for the crimes they commit, all except that of murder, for which a defining line is drawn. A police force, the intelligence community and government have no pardon from a charge of murder, and what is at stake here is an unnecessary campaign of mass murder against innocent civilians.

To further complement the concealed existence of the alleged murderers, nondescript companies are set up to employ such people without attracting attention from the public or others in the business world. Special Branch front-companies can employ not just their own, but equally importantly, unconnected members of the public. With this integration, nobody would suspect there was any connection to the intelligence community. A company outside the security business with a workforce comprising only former police officers and military personnel automatically attracts suspicion, but the addition of others alleviates such concerns. A superior alibi is provided when underhand deeds such as the falsification of timesheets occur to cover up a covert operation so that the legitimate workers will remain certain their fellow employees could not be involved.

The start of 1998 remained inexplicably quiet with the man in the blue *Ford Escort* elsewhere and the police presence non-existent, all of which had become a refreshing relief to me. The 3rd of February of this year was one of the most miserable, cold, wet days on the calendar as I sat at home watching heavy rain splatter onto the window. Obviously, there was some significance to remember the fine details of the weather that day, which was verified by viewing the local midday news on Scottish Television (*STV*). A report featured the counting of the unemployed with a prominent government minister appearing in connection with the article. As is the case with an employment-related issue, the short commentary also included film footage from inside a job centre. The reason for this particular day being so memorable was the person shown looking for a job. It was me!

The second interesting feature was the choice of job centres. It was Kilbirnie, which is situated a full twenty five miles from the broadcasting station. Countless other job centres were by-passed in the selection process. The third point was the greatest enigma: the last time I had signed on was the 10th of April 1997, and if this video footage had been taken that day, then obviously, the film had been in cold storage for ten months. With hindsight, it was indeed from that day because of a combination of events. Watching the news report, I could see myself wearing a brown suede bomber jacket with the camera view showing my right profile and back as I surveyed the vacancy boards. As I was about to start self-employment, I had ditched the principle of dressing down, which indicated a requirement to receive benefit. Hence, this was the only time I was there wearing the suede jacket. There was a camera positioned rather obtrusively on a tripod inside that office on the referred to day, pointing in the exact direction of the view shown on television on the 3rd of February 1998. This was totally conclusive and important evidence, and so I marked the calendar with the letters 'TV' for future reference.

An uneasy feeling automatically replaced my surprise at finding myself making an unsuspected guest appearance on a news report. Having already been a full-scale victim of the most horrific of dirty tricks campaigns, the significance of what was witnessed was not apparent, where only fear resided regarding why. The logistics, high-level contacts, the authority and power on display here in conjunction with an obscure job centre, and the appearance of Henry McLeish MP - who was regarded as the second in command to the Scottish Secretary - in an interview with the Glasgow-based *STV* crew all hinted that another conspiracy was underway. Only time and perseverance would reveal any deceit behind the latest anomaly.

My ability to suss out which local companies were connected to British Intelligence in previous years was given a short circuit. The terrorists down in the Cumnock workshop, although being strangers, openly spoke about being pursued and harassed by Special Branch. As a newcomer there, the brief period of overlap between going there for the first time and them being arrested and subsequently receiving prison sentences had one interesting event for the topic of conversation. I was working at one side of the bench and they were on the opposite side. The local front company for Special Branch was called 'Acre'. The name was particularly appropriate to these terrorists because of the grief inflicted on them. Having shared such experiences, years later I was readily in agreement and saw their point of view. Back then, the two locations given for this suspect company were Irvine and the main street of the small village of Dreghorn. Shortly afterwards, while I was running a local girl home to Dreghorn, we were passing the base used by *Acre* and I inquired who was in there.

"The security people," she replied.

The status of this company was confirmed by both the terrorists who were being targeted by the personnel, and also members of the local public.

By the middle of February 1998, I was still perplexed by my appearance on television a fortnight before. Rumours started to circulate about the accidental death of an industrial cleaner at *Bridge of Weir Leather Company*. The interest in his death was magnified by the disclosure of who his employers were: they were none other than the suspected Special Branch company of *Acre*! The low key media coverage of this death further fuelled suspicion. Although a local incident, the news reached me not by the usual channels of local news footage, but by word of mouth. Intuition told me that there was significantly more to his death than it just being an unfortunate accident. This dubious set of circumstances was about to be convoluted by a final riddle.

Another fortnight after hearing about this incident brought the time scale to the beginning of March and the last in a sequence of three incidents. After a two month absence, the blue *Ford Escort*, which had been positioned close to the house as a deliberate method of terror, made a return but with a revealing alteration. They say that fear sharpens the mind, and to be in constant contact with a murderer gloating in the gory aftermath of what he had done to that defenceless woman, I can assure you, is awe-inspiring fear. This is especially the case when the police presence was only there to assist in the slaughter. He was someone who I'd never known, but after that grotesque ploy I would be able to pick him out of a crowd at a minute's glance. When the blue *Escort* returned, it only took the merest glance to identify the driver as not being the original. As I was driving home on the single track road, this car came charging round on a blind corner at high speed and deliberately ran me off the road. Minor incidents like that were a regular occurrence and the hazard was totally irrelevant, but the fleeting glimpse I had of the aggressor was more than enough to realise that he was a decoy. Not moving from the grass verge, which the car had been forced onto, I observed the other driver leaving on the by-pass in the direction of Kilbirnie. This was also a diversion from the person he was trying to impersonate, because the original always departed in the Glasgow direction. This impostor was better built. He had a rounder face without the reddish colouring around the mouth, and now wore thick spectacles. The only two areas of consistency were the short brown hair and blue *Ford Escort* with the large magnetically-mounted aerial on the roof, although admittedly, the car was now in an inferior condition to the original, which could be due to the passage of time. For all the endless months of its continual appearance the previous year, there was no point in writing down the registration number due to the fact that registration plates could be seen in the reflection of the sloping rear window as they sat on the parcel shelf. I presumed that this was to enable them to change the car's identification at will. In Northern Ireland the security services used cars with phantom registrations for covert exercises. Such vehicles were known as Q-cars. The driver who was used to impersonate the original driver was also a frequent visitor to the area. Previously, he drove a small blue and white van, which was again stationed there with a large aerial on the roof. The colour scheme was similar to old *British Gas* vans with blue at the top and bottom and a white horizontal band in the middle section, and was what I always equated as being part of Special Branch.

After methodical consideration, I came to a startling conclusion about why an impersonator should replace the original driver. If he was out of the country or laid-up in hospital, the requirement to clone him did not exist. It was only if the original were dead, where a need arose for them to convince me he was still alive that they would go to the bother of making him appear alive. This was not as entirely morbid or devoid of reality as the issued CCTV still-pictures of Tracey Wilde were. Potentially, her killer was also now dead, possibly murdered.

Running down the possibilities, I came to the final conclusion that Tracey Wilde's killer had been seen committing the murder and he had been murdered at the *Leather Company* just outside Bridge of Weir. This impostor was being used to fool me so they could finally solve one murder out of a sequence of six. This meant laying the blame on someone who was now deceased and, therefore, could not possibly be there to answer any accusations, thereby attempting to dupe me into believing that it was two different individuals. This reckoning came very close to the final outcome. Only, the murder remained unsolved and was unlikely to be because of the next twist in this complex scenario.

The long awaited *Crimewatch* appeal featuring Tracey Wilde's murder was finally shown on the 24th March 1998, and only the small concluding part commenting on the success of the programme was viewed. I heard to my surprise that the suspect in the blue *Ford Escort* had phoned in to eliminate himself from the inquiry. It was now four months after the crime, so why exactly did he choose this particular time to own up to having any involvement? It is quite possible that the reason for the delay in showing Tracey Wilde's case on *Crimewatch* was; they were waiting for the memories I had of the original *Ford Escort* driver to diminish, produce their clone, then finally have it presented on television. A complete trail of unbelievable incidents that night had a new addition, one that was partially predicted. The belief that the murder mystery was to be solved was wrong; however, the motives behind the impostor appearing in the blue car now became apparent. The phone call to the BBC studio was the concluding element in a catalogue of deceit, completing the illusion that the culprit was not the man seen at the crime scene. The impersonator was supposed to fool the general public into believing this to be possible, when in fact it was definitely impossible, and that night finalised with the appropriate comment prominent in my mind, "No; I don't think so."

An undeniable flaw in all this skulduggery was detected immediately as it occurred, where the exploitation of which could only complicate the matter and expose the evil conspirators. After a long wait, fraught with danger, the moment had arrived to accomplish an amnesty for the unsuspecting victims in Strathclyde. The day of the lion hearted would once again materialise to launch an attack capitalising on the glaring omission presented here, which was not only to the detriment of both police and the intelligence community, but shockingly, to the Labour government.

I kept close scrutiny over the local news reports on the progress Strathclyde Police were making in this investigation and it was never once said that the blue *Ford Escort* driver was anyone other than the genuine article. The close monitoring of developments certainly confirmed that this suspect had been completely eliminated from the investigation, and then that well-worn phrase, "We are looking for a student living in student accommodation" was rolled out. This was the cue to put a master-plan into action because I knew that this reiterated line was used to conclude the murder investigation in the public eye, just as it had been used previously with other murder inquiries.

The starting point was to gather the correct information, analyse it, then act upon it. The first question was: who did die at the *Leather Company*? Incidentally, although it was known as the *Bridge of Weir Leather Company*, it had the trade name, *NCT*. A young father of two, Raymond Stevenson, who had been promoted within the industrial cleaning company *Acre* had died recently at the leather producing plant. Married and living in the village of Houston, he was twenty-eight years old at the time of his death. All these basic details fitted well with the description of the suspect at the victim's flat, the blue *Ford Escort* seen near the golf club house and the assumption that he was a Special Branch agent within this suspected company. His age corresponded with the wanted suspect, and the direction in which the car posing as a CB radio enthusiast left the vicinity was towards Houston, unlike the decoy. Raymond Stevenson also had a background in the British Army! And finally, promotion within his company would have made him less accountable to other employees, if he was indeed a Special Branch officer. *NCT*, or, *Bridge of Weir Leather Company* depending upon how it is known, is said to have supplied the leather to cover the seats in the Houses of Parliament. Only high level contacts within the British Establishment would secure that contract.

The second question that had to be asked was, "When was he killed?"
Shocking revelations have never been in short supply up to now, but the answer to this simple query overshadowed all that went before it. Raymond Stevenson died on the 3rd February 1998, the same day as my television appearance, and to confirm this I rechecked the calendar for the letters 'TV' because I could not believe the collision of these dates. Two months after this eventful day, this surprise was checked and rechecked because of the magnitude of the revelation of another conspiracy, one which had the potential to bring down the Labour administration in Scotland. Having continually stood on the viper's nest in the past, I realised that this revelation surpasses every other major conspiracy detailed previously. The murder of Jill Dando constantly failed to have any viable motive attached to it, but here were pointers to a powerful motive, if indeed British Intelligence were responsible for assassinating the celebrity. The coincidence of these two dates was one of the nasty quirks best left undiscovered because of the gravity of all the implications it contained.

On the miserable wet day referred to, when I sat watching the midday news broadcast and saw myself on the programme I was wary about why this peculiar event should happen. I suspected that there was some kind of hidden agenda behind it and so watched all the other news bulletins that day. The intended purpose was that it guaranteed my whereabouts and so Raymond Stevenson could be murdered without any knowledge of with me. Considering that the plot was successful and a government minister had assisted in the conspiracy to murder, it becomes irrelevant whether it was intentional or otherwise. He is either guilty of neglect, or the charge could be as serious as conspiracy to murder, where forthcoming events will bear this out. The clone who attempted to impersonate Stevenson can be easily found: I know his address. The coincidence of what happened that day can never be passed off as such once the full details are revealed. Finally, if my DNA is planted inside Tracey Wilde's flat, resignations from political life will not be required as no prison inmate is allowed to be a member of parliament.

An explanation of the background to this will produce an unfaltering recognition of criminal wrongdoing in a society where the law has been undermined and will give credence to everything previously alleged. Prior to my unemployment benefit being ceased, a request was made that I appear between signing-on dates at the Job Centre. Because this was an unscheduled appointment, I had the right to claim travelling expenses, when in doing so signed my name under that of two others, thinking sarcastically, "Is this their hit list?"
Fortunately, I kept this humorous interjection contained for they may not have shared the joke, but it did in fact become a reality. One of the two names above my signature had had his benefit stopped, and on leaving the office, he had told the staff rather abusively his thoughts on the subject. He subsequently received a six-week prison sentence. Suspicious that applications were receiving interference and preventing me from finding employment, I embarked on one tremendous effort to start in self-employment, so as to be free from any unnatural, illegally imposed constraints. A small grant is obtained to assist in this objective. On the 10th April 1997, I entered Kilbirnie Job Centre optimistic that an end to both the claiming of benefit and any suspected underhand practices was in sight. However, in light of the final affront about to be experienced, this over-confidence was a wrongful frame of mind. After the second door in this office, the open plan design that day had an unusual feature. A large camera was set up on a tripod standing to the left. I walked past this obstruction, wary about the possibility of this video equipment being live. The first indication of this was the huge smile the office clerk gave when I gave my name. Having been systematically messed about on previous occasions, she certainly was not going to give a display of affection now, and sinister motives were expected right from that initial contact. A male

counterpart, Mr Tyre, was given the task of interviewing me, and he also appeared rather pleased and smug as he informed me that my benefit was being ceased. He finished with the words, "Go home and we'll take a decision on this and let you know in due course."

Such a tremendous effort exerted by working over a hundred hours a week to break an impossible circle and the minute I succeed came this crushing blow, which deliberately scrapped all the plans set. I was totally deflated upon knowing that the superhuman exploits could not be surpassed therefore left silent and despondent. On departure I walked in such a manner so that the camera could not get any more footage of me, but to my right was the window to a small office in which I could see two men who were not part of the Social Security service. No time limit was placed on the words 'due course', and even with the assistance of a lawyer, today, as with the poisoned milk, a satisfactory answer has not been received about the reasons for this termination. Only the speculative answer of a deliberate and wrongful termination of benefit to provoke a reaction from me with a camera recording the evidence remains. I read in the local newspaper about their other client receiving a jail sentence; here the prison cell was not the threat, but the fact is it only takes five minutes in captivity to end your life with what is purporting to be a police force in Strathclyde. For all that had happened while still at liberty, who could take that risk in confinement?

I returned to the Job Centre afterwards and asked for the exact reason my benefit had been stopped and the reply was that I had failed to sign-on on the 24th April 1997. What a strange reply, when it was their refusal on the 10th that left me in limbo afterwards awaiting their decision. The lie was exposed when the assistant produced R. Rae on the computer screen corresponding with the 10th of April. Certain this was not the case, I asked to see the hand-written signature for that date. He left and duly returned with the form, which should have included the print. Bewildered, this office clerk stared at a blank line, and finally realized that he had been caught out. He referred me to his colleague who had originally terminated the claim. Being more buoyant, this Tyre tried to put the emphasis on myself, claiming that a false claim had been made but then backed down from this invalid argument and offered an appointment to sign on again. Rejecting this futile approach, I stood up and left with the brave words, "No, I'd like an appointment with a court of law."

These bold words should have come to fruition in any democratic country other than Scotland, where the law was habitually being abused to persecute innocent civilians and was failing to protect the victims. On consulting a lawyer, I asked repeatedly if he was prepared to take this case to court; only upon this agreement would his services be retained. Ability was not a consideration here because I believed the case could easily be won and the lawyer was only there for the formality; backbone was the only credential required. Correspondence began between the two reiterating that the reason for termination was the failure to sign-on on the 24th April. Once this was exposed as being fraudulent, a second reason materialised: this being a failure to participate in one of their courses. Again it was strange that the accused should actively be included on an employment-related course at the time. The final contempt summarised was a refusal to recognise any participation on the said course, claiming they had no evidence of this involvement. This last default was contradicted by the small booklet kept as a record of appliance for employment, where it was written in black and white. A satisfactory entry was written and initialled there to verify their acceptance. The lawyer knew their intentions were less than honourable as they didn't just make a fool of him for he had been led up and down the garden path and he was the first to acknowledge this. It was heart-warming to see the contempt they had shown towards this legal professional: the humiliation he experienced knew no bounds.

Now came the moment of truth, the anticipated day in court. The solicitor reneged on his word, saying this case was better suited to someone with 'specialist expertise' and so referred me to the Legal Services Agency. I arrived there and detailed the circumstances, to receive the reply, "What are you doing here? Haven't you got a lawyer? Why isn't he taking your case to court?"
I attempted to reply that I had a lawyer, but he was hiding behind the office door when I was last there. Starting to feel silly about the situation that had been imposed on me, I realized I didn't know why I was there either. To everybody's benefit except my own, it was all

fizzling out with the run-around experienced. The exercise was not totally wasted as it detailed the discrepancies to an independent body, with this solicitor's best offer being a compromise of taking the case to a tribunal. This was rejected because anyone was capable of doing this themselves (in this case, months previously) and for what purpose but to give them a second opportunity to accomplish their sinister ploy.

The 3rd February 1998 was a frightening day. Henry McLeish MP surfaced with the latest unemployment figures, but the greatest irony was that it was an indifferent count that had risen that day by at least one. How the video footage shown then was obtained certainly held more grievances than you could count accumulating into another conspiracy, where a person is victimised unjustly for whatever objective. Was I stupid enough to believe that any enterprise could get off the ground in Scotland while struggling against a deliberate oppression that was making a mockery of all these initiatives to create employment? Forever patronised afterwards, you keep hearing how the Scots lack ambition, fail in entrepreneurial spirit and are reminded what a poor country we live in. It is a view that is contradicted by their history, success abroad, and the undeniable wealth of this nation. All faith is also lost in the law when you struggle to be a law-abiding citizen and yet mere survival requires you to become a minor crime wave just to remain alive due to the impossible circumstances you find yourself in. Rapidly transforming opinion says anarchy is a better solution, giving the people the right to retaliate without fear of imprisonment, such was the sinister scenario predominant in Strathclyde. That once proud boast that Scots Law is the best in the world sounds like delusions of grandeur. There certainly were plenty of implications to when Raymond Stevenson died encapsulated in intrigue from such a high ranking source.

At the time, I was so numb and devoid of any positive feeling but somehow developed the realization that the magnitude of this was breathtaking. They may have enjoyed their slaughter of countless victims, probably mercilessly butchered, but to have murdered their own, the inhumane creatures responsible must have been stung to the bone. Blind devotion to their superiors of questionable sanity could only be strained here with the thought of how easily they themselves could be disposed of. Consideration of why he was killed presented no logical answer because silence is a primary requirement; only the inevitable feeling persisted that the West of Scotland was indeed a killing field. Left empty, with values so depleted, a general lawlessness summarises the whole episode. The fatal day that Jill Dando was shot dead only held a feeling of inevitability surrounding her death, having been predicted a full year and seven months previously. Had she lived in the West of Scotland, it is doubtful if her execution would have been so prolonged.

I was under no illusion about what really happened to this Special Branch murderer: only the biblical saying, 'Those who live by the sword shall die by the sword' was appropriate in this context. The problem is that the people involved in professional cover-ups are an art form unto themselves. This only suggests how corrupt our society actually is. It was always going to be difficult to inflict irreparable damage on the consortium of supposedly respectable public bodies and officials responsible. Undeterred at the prospect of attempting to dislodge a few noses in high places, I continued as always with reckless abandon. Listening to a story, which I unfortunately cannot recall, of the corruption involved in no less a fundamental institution than banking, gave the inspiration to launch an intricate assault on the protagonists responsible here...

Information from these events was collated and then distilled into a simple statement which was explicitly indicative of what had happened yet carefully constructed to offer no recourse to the accused. Far from being literature, the straight-forwardness of the writing held its own entrapment. As I was writing the message down, I pressed hard to leave an imprint on the paper below, then turned this second sheet upside down and drew in the small statement without any clue to whose handwriting it was. The completed master copy went to a photocopier to produce samples, which were never handled so as to give no forensic evidence that might reveal the author. Only the envelopes could produce any minute clues. This simple message, written to look like the faltering words of a child, held its share of incriminating substance. It read as follows:

"TRACEY WILDE WAS MURDERED BY THE MAN IN BLACK SUIT SEEN LEAVING HER HOME AT 2AM. STRATHCLYDE POLICE MADE NO EFFORT TO TRACE THIS MAN BUT PRODUCE FALSE EVIDENCE TO HAVE HER ALIVE AFTER THIS AWAY FROM HER FLAT. THIS MAN WAS SPECIAL BRANCH OFFICER. RAYMOND STEVENSON FROM HOUSTON HE WORKED FOR ACRE A SPECIAL BRANCH FRONT COMPANY. AFTER CRIMEWATCH 24th MAR 98 THE MAN IN BLACK SUIT PHONED IN TO ELIMINATE HIMSELF. NOT ONLY HAD THE KILLER ELIMINATED HIMSELF BUT A DEAD MAN HAD MADE THE CALL. RAYMOND STEVENSON WAS MURDERED AT BRIDGE OF WEIR LEATHER ON 3rd FEB 98 BY HIS OWN PEOPLE."

At around 10.30pm on the Tuesday night of the 14th April 1998, three letters addressed to the news desks of three newspapers were posted at the post box outside the sub-post office in Nelson Street, Tradeston in Glasgow. The addresses of these three newspapers were within a one-mile radius of this location. With a sense of mischief, an element of danger and a disregard for the implications of whose reputations this exercise could destroy, I only wished for a response with names attached in the defence of this ploy. Feeling like I had just poured a gallon of burning oil down a drainpipe into a rat's nest, I sat back and watched to see what vermin this scheme was about to flush out. After this Tuesday night excursion, with the collection and delivery of the post presumably the next day, followed by the alerting of the security services and quick consultation, a response was expected finally on the Thursday evening or Friday morning.

What could be vindication happened on the Thursday afternoon of the 16th April, when a row blew up between Henry McLeish MP and the head of Grampian Police, Dr Ian Oliver, supposedly concerning leaked information from a report in connection with murdered schoolboy, Scott Simpson. Awareness here rocketed, knowing they could not disclose any police or Special Branch involvement in the two murders referred to in that photocopied message. If the Intelligence community believed that one of their own had rebelled then produced this message and the source could not be found, a row would be staged in parallel wherewith used to warn the culprit to cease their activities. The question of whether this was the case or that a genuine leak of information had happened concerning the tragically murdered child requires some background to assess the situation properly.

Dr Ian Oliver was acknowledged as being one of the most articulate and clever figures within the British police service, where his appointment as Chief Constable of the Grampian force was gratefully received. His high profile, changes of operational procedures and ambition, however, did not always endear him to the people of the North East of Scotland, who are more accustomed to a slower pace of progress. The Chief Constable's career came to a premature end with tabloid revelations of a relationship with a married woman half his age. After which, it was agreed he would remain in position until the 1st June, and then take extended leave before retirement three months later. With his career about to be terminated, it would be dogged before concluding with controversy from another source: the bungled investigation of a child's murder by a known paedophile.

Steven Leisk abducted then murdered schoolboy Scott Simpson. The attention of the investigation had been focused upon the victim's family at the time of the initial disappearance and it failed to recognize the involvement of a stranger. This undue targeting of those nearest to the victim is common practice, but unfortunately, it proved to be wrong in this case, which marred the whole investigation. It was further disclosed that they had failed to find the child's body in an area that they claimed to have searched already, and that Leisk, a known sex offender, had been living near the park from where the boy had disappeared. Finally, it emerged that Grampian Police had failed to identify him as a suspect in the early stages of the investigation. Because they had not been as thorough and competent in their inquiries as public perception would allow, these revelations were complicated by the vastness of area within Aberdeen required to be searched plus the confusion over Steven Leisk's registered address. Leisk was eventually arrested and convicted of the crime, but the public was antagonised by the Chief Constable's staunch defence of his officers involved. To appease the disquiet, a social work report was compiled on the subject, but its publication created another furore. It was issued at a time when Dr Ian Oliver was in Taiwan on police business. On return, a Press conference was staged and his response was less than tactful when he accused Henry McLeish of disreputable behaviour. The two prominent individuals squabbling over this first report and the timing of its appearance was distasteful for all concerned, with a dead child being the crux of the friction. It was agreed that Graham Power, the Deputy Chief Constable of Lothian and Borders police force, should commission a second report to look into Grampian Police's handling of the case. A month after this was agreed, Dr Ian Oliver was caught up in controversy once again as the afore-mentioned relationship with a married woman became public knowledge, resulting in his early retirement from the force. Then on the 14th April 1998, I read in the Press that the awaited report was now available and contained thirty-six recommendations and conclusions, including a front page exposé in a tabloid newspaper. That same night I posted those three incriminating photocopies that included the deaths of Raymond Stevenson and Tracey Wilde.

Two days later, the infamous row blew up most definitely concerning a leak of information to the Press. The imperative question to be answered; was this a circuitous method deployed by the security forces to act as a deterrent against any further leak of information believing it was done by one of their own?
A detailed analysis of what actually occurred from the middle of April onwards wholeheartedly supports this view.

REASON 1: THE TIMING

After posting the photocopies, I predicted that if a response were to materialise, the earliest estimated time would be on the Thursday evening. However, this account did not take into consideration any urgency on the matter. With the benefit of hindsight, of course, there would be urgency to prevent information of this distinction from getting out into the public domain. The first public airing on local radio of the circumspect row concerning Scott Simpson was in the middle of Thursday afternoon, only a few hours earlier than expected - impeccable timing. The assumption that this was a staged row was supported by the following statements: *"How irresponsible this is of the person doing this! How damaging this type of thing is to the police!"* and, *"...The most damning report on the police since the war."*

Criticism is healthy, especially when considering the prolonged agony one family had to endure with the loss of their young son. Any shortcomings in procedures highlighted then amended can only be of value in the future. So why should the afore-mentioned irresponsible person leaking information be so damaging to the police? By contrast, it is certain that the above statements all corresponded to the released photocopy. Astonishing as it may sound, a preview was printed in the newspapers on the Tuesday morning, over two days previously. So for what reason did this bitter dispute erupt that afternoon if in fact it did concern the Scott Simpson report, which was, in any case, starting to become public?

REASON 2: THE BEHAVIOUR OF HENRY MCLEISH M.P.

The first report materialised in January 1998, six months after the murder of Scott Simpson. The two main areas of concern were the legal and social work practices. The killer and known paedophile, Steven Leisk, had been previously convicted at Kirkwall Sheriff Court, after which it was argued that due to the type of crime, past record of this convict and the likelihood of him re-offending, this case should have been referred to the High Court. Had this happened, a harsher sentence would have been handed down and Leisk would not have been at liberty at the time he killed this child. The second source of contention was Leisk's supervision order, which had a further two months to run before completion when he committed this murder. Again, it was deemed that this crime would not have happened but for this critical blunder on the part of the social work department. Grampian Police were not the focus of attention here with these two complaints overshadowing any discrepancies in the police operation related to this matter. Dr Ian Oliver consistently made a firm defence of the actions of his colleagues: a situation which deflected attention away from the officers directly involved but produced an arrogant portrayal of the Chief Constable. With public opinion against him, a reputation suffering and the fact that he was abroad when the report was released, Henry McLeish capitalised on these circumstances to claim that he was 'astonished and angry' that the Chief Constable was not present at the time of the report's publication. Public support for the minister was galvanised at the expense of Dr Ian Oliver, although the main criticism in the report was not directed at the police. Therefore, the conduct of Henry McLeish smacked of opportunism. The return of Dr Oliver from Taiwan was particularly reminiscent of the scene inside Kilbirnie Job Centre; deliberate provocation to produce a predictable outburst recorded by a television camera. Unfortunately, he did not maintain a dignified silence and rounded on this government minister. In doing so, he further alienated his position in the community, whereas a bit of restraint could have exposed the tactics of McLeish. Having been in a similar situation, I remained one of a minority who felt the bickering was avoidable, and that it was repugnant and disrespectful to the memory of a dead child that political gain could be achieved from this scenario. An honourable minister could have averted the situation by making a polite request either to delay or advance the publication of this report to a time when the Chief Constable was in a position to reply. Or if this was not possible, to delay comment until Dr Oliver was back in the country. In any case, a Chief Constable always leaves a deputy in charge when he is not present. Did this squabble ever have any real foundation?

Three weeks later, when Henry McLeish re-emerged on television, I was mistrusting of this minister and viewed his appearance on 3rd February with scepticism. The horrific revelation that a prominent government minister had fronted the television broadcast and that I was shown on the news bulletin inside a job centre all on the same day that Raymond Stevenson died was dismissed as a coincidence at the time. This was not from any belief that he was an innocent party who had been coerced or cajoled into participating, but more from the terrifying consequences and unbelievable magnitude of what was occurring. Potentially, here was a government minister suspected of participating in conspiracy to murder!

Finally, in the middle of April, the same activist surfaced again in connection with what could be a cover-up operation, although admittedly, the ongoing row was between himself and Dr Ian Oliver.

However, the conduct of this minister became deplorable, suggesting alternative motives. With the behaviour of Henry McLeish under scrutiny after his suspected indirect participation in the murder of Raymond Stevenson, only immaculate principles could now discredit the opinion that the incriminating photocopied statement had created a staged disagreement with this hidden agenda. His actions would only fortify the assumption that I was the instigator behind the acrimonious dismissal of Dr Ian Oliver, and not any leaked information on the murder investigation as purported. Appalling conduct was evident with the *Daily Record* proclaiming on Friday 17th April: 'I Will Shame You!' printed in massive letters on the front page with the target being the Chief Constable.

McLeish failed to answer accusations that he was behind this and, more seriously, that he had reneged on a verbal agreement that the meeting prior to this was in confidence, where a concerted effort was made to defy this trust. Dr Ian Oliver was not slow to highlight this shameful conduct; however, being the victim of such underhand methods, he remained perplexed as to why matters should be developing as they were. As the argument raged it became apparent to those not blighted by emotional feelings, that Dr Oliver had the upper hand over the Home Affairs Minister, who would soon conspicuously disassociate himself from the confrontation leaving others without the baggage of a blemished reputation to continue the heated exchange.

REASON 3: THE THREE-DAY DELAY

On that Thursday afternoon with the radio announcement that information had been leaked to the Press words like 'official documents', 'confidential information', and 'leaked information' were used, where the most eye-catching of which was: '...the most damning report on the police since the war.' It was a strangely revealing state of affairs that the competitive Press should be in possession of this information of outstanding public interest yet have nothing to print on the subject?! With newspapers vying for sales, whatever happened to the front-page news stories to correspond with the description given on both radio and television? Having wondered for a long time what leaked official documents actually contain, it would be catastrophic if the photocopied message was indicative of what is secretly held. Then, to conclude what was assumed, an announcement was broadcast that the leaked information on the Scott Simpson report would appear in the Sunday papers. This extraordinary admission meant a three-day delay, and for myself, vindication of my own involvement, where only the slightest doubt lingered prior to this. Plenty of time existed to exaggerate and over-emphasise the original damning passages extracted from the report in order to conform it to the criteria of how condemning it was supposed to be.

REASON 4: THE COMPLICATION
INCLUDED IN THE SCENARIO

I was unable to find out what, if anything, was said to be with the Press, but after hearing that the report would appear in the Sunday newspapers this provided me with an opportunity to put a final twist into the impending scenario. All along, the cover-ups were professional to an exemplary standard, and this one was about to be thrown into the dustbin of history unless a complication could be included to raise eyebrows throughout the country. Not about to let murderers and conspirators off the hook in this State-sponsored terror campaign, it was time to act again. Three more of these photocopied messages were sent out. Two were despatched to the women's groups; the final one was destined for the constituency address of the Labour MP, Irene Adams. This was the clever part, where the one sent to the member of the government could be denied in a cover-up, but the others were unlikely to participate in anything of this sort because of the details the statement held. This secondary tactic was equally as deceptive. The photocopied statement would arrive by design on the Monday morning at the Labour MP's address and reveal whom the culprit really was, where I predicted that an immediate response would come in the late afternoon or evening. No intelligence or police-related source would indulge in such a practice with the obvious security arrangement the MP would have in place (plus, with a possible internal witch-hunt ongoing searching for the intelligence related leak), thereby deliberately revealing my own involvement. All along, my personal search was to find the conspirators involved in the mass murder ongoing in Strathclyde, and with this ploy I was about to fully expose government involvement.

The moment of truth arrived on the Monday night of April 20th. This was the appearance of the Scottish Secretary of State, Donald Dewar, in accordance with the prediction that my latest attack would receive a response at that exact time as he made this television debut in connection to the Dr Ian Oliver situation. It was a once in a lifetime moment where the waters parted: he was either for or against the people, who were being subjected to the most appalling crimes. Forever the optimist, I was sure there was only one reply he could make here: admit that the whole argument was staged right from its initial conception four days previously. He would then apologise to Dr Oliver for the undue distress caused, denounce Henry McLeish and have him ostracised with the contempt he deserved, and finally launch a thorough investigation into the never-ending murders in Strathclyde, focusing the attention on Special Branch/Strathclyde Police involvement. Even at this late hour, this terrible saga was salvageable and genuine political gain for Donald Dewar and his party could be readily achieved. The security forces do not pay this man's wages. As with everything else, the taxpayer was funding them to become a victim of self-sponsored terror.

The momentary hesitation between the broadcast focusing on the Scottish Secretary and him uttering a word felt protracted with the anticipation of seeing where his allegiances lay. The suspense and optimism I held was immediately shattered as Dewar spoke angrily, and concluded by telling Dr Oliver to, "pack his bags and go now."
This man did not need a platform to air his views; he held the power, position and authority to end the campaign of suffering, but with this interjection, he made the ultimate betrayal of the Scottish nation. It was the uncharacteristic fury with which he spoke that belied any illusion of a diplomatic dispute with the Chief Constable. Oliver would now definitely have to be removed to cover up the genuine motive behind all this animosity. The unparalleled revulsion this provoked was beyond comprehension as I left the sitting room rather than unceremoniously switching off the television with my boot directed at Donald Dewar's face.

"Keep the red flag flying." I muttered this favourite phrase of the Labour Party now that I knew what that represented: the blood of the Scottish people.

How appropriate that the rhyme from which this phrase comes from should mention traitors and cowards. The contrast between someone who would have sooner died in the gutters of Portugal than submit to the despots responsible and the one who holds the ultimate responsibility betraying every principle and moral duty to continue the terror created an array of feelings, with frustration and rage predominant. I could see visions of the sickness on the front of the shirt, blood on both feet, the photo-fit resembling a photograph of myself, a killer gloating on his latest calamity, and the distressed mothers appearing on television mourning their loss. I could feel the insanity of attempting to counter-attack the military personnel deployed to eliminate another defenceless victim, the stigmas of being a child killer and a serial killer, the jibes, insults and humiliation. I could feel the loss of every value and principle I embraced, the alienation, torment and frustration, the point of physical collapse and the spontaneous suffering being inflicted on others in Strathclyde. This Labour government had waited a long time to be back in power. Is this how they repay the commitment we made to them? The two most distinguished members of the Scottish Labour Party had become embroiled in the defence of mass murderers, where the participation didn't align itself with the supposed purpose then, and it is unlikely to be manipulated into a satisfactory cover-up today. Aware that I had sealed the fate of Dr Ian Oliver with that final complication, where the ensuing persecution would verify this, I remained unsympathetic towards him with the public humiliation he experienced. He and others appeared to forget that this manipulated furore had stemmed from the murder of a child and not from personal grievances.

REASON 5: THE HIT AND RUN TACTICS DEPLOYED

Justice requires both sides of an argument to be heard so that an honest, balanced assessment can be made rather than a biased view from only one of the participants. After the photocopied statement was sent, it was fitting that McLeish should emerge as a man perceived as having more reason than most to try and deter any further exposures. Allegations of a secondary leak attributed to the minister's office surfaced immediately after the rumpus began with deplorable tactics to discredit Dr Oliver. An injustice that contrived to support the idea that the origin of this hostility was not that produced for public consumption. At this point, the Chief Constable could have closed his briefcase and tendered his resignation instead of retaliating by expressing revulsion at Henry McLeish's behaviour; after which the minister became suspicious in his absence. The repeated description of the Scott Simpson report was sufficient to have Dr Oliver removed from his post by its own merits, if the continued claimed substance was accurate. Surprisingly, this was never accomplished. I was then aware that my complication would produce a response later in the day on the designated Monday. And, at the introduction of Donald Dewar, I realised that the tactics to evict the Chief Constable would turn decisively nasty after mocking them by way of revealing who the perpetrator really was. Confirmation of this was swift and accurate, again supporting the prognosis of the photocopy as being word perfect as the government conspired to halt any further leaks. Realizing they had been duped, the need to remove Dr Oliver became paramount to cover up the apparent omissions in this conjunctive predicament.

With the Scottish Secretary roaring, "Pack his bags and go now," but unable to stomach any more of his outlandish behaviour, I departed without witnessing the next convincing action to ascertain what was being alleged. Donald Dewar was challenged to appear in a live debate with his opponent on the *Newsnight* programme. According to the Press he was reported to 'react furiously' in his refusal to participate. Being the aggressor who was savaging Dr Oliver, surely he would welcome this opportunity if the disagreement was genuine without any hidden agenda. So what was the reason for the determined refusal? What had the Scottish Secretary to hide?

Fully aware of the complication included, the next convergence in this theme was Graham Power, the author of the supposedly devastating report that was failing to live up to its billing. Mr Power conveniently disappeared off the scene with the light-hearted statement that he had gone fishing. The humour here was ill-conceived. A scandal of epic proportions was underway, an alleged cover-up equally as sinister, and all that was forthcoming was a comment so moronic that deceit is automatically suspected. Once again, Dr Ian Oliver was victimised by the report and then refused the opportunity to answer the accusations by the absence of Graham Power.

The list goes on and on. Duncan Crawford resigned from the Police Board, which automatically increased the pressure on the Chief Constable to do likewise. This event certainly appeared to be stage-managed, after reading that his position was likely to be re-instated once Dr Oliver had retired. The character assassination of Dr Ian Oliver was so masterful that, even today, people remember this greedy, arrogant and vindictive man, who cast a poor reflection on the Police Board who appointed him. It is strange how selective the memory can be. After the resignation was finally announced, the Chairman of the Police Board, Pat Chalmers, had to issue an apology for any remarks attributed to him that suggested that Dr Oliver was holding out for a larger financial settlement. During the wrangling prior to his retirement, such a contribution assisted in demonising the Chief Constable and created the everlasting impression of a selfish, evil individual, who was manipulating proceedings to his own advantage. With the benefit of this extraordinary reflection, the propriety and judgement of Pat Chalmers appears inexplicably flawed. It was just another contradiction where those of questionable morals remain in position while the victim is dismissed against natural justice in an unrelenting campaign designed to discredit him.

An abundance of examples suggesting dubious tactics to remove this prominent individual consistently did not align themselves to the situation. On the 24th April 1998, it was announced that he would depart with a month's notice and his retirement would begin on the 24th May. It is strange how his previously announced retirement dates of the 1st June, with extended leave until retirement on the 1st September only had a matter of days in separation. Why exactly was such an effort made from different quarters to remove him fractionally early from what was a long career? Did the answer lie with Pat Chalmers as a comparison, to keep the parties guilty of wrongdoing in office at the expense of democracy?

REASON 6: DR IAN OLIVER

A staunch defence of his officers involved in the Scott Simpson murder investigation placed him at odds with the general public. This was exacerbated when Henry McLeish verbally attacked the Chief Constable in January. The blunt and forthright reply he gave, although justified, left Dr Oliver out on a limb unable to restore his credibility and therefore vulnerable to future reprisals. When this subject again came under the spotlight in mid-April, support for the Chief Constable had already deteriorated because of the disclosure of his extramarital affair, and Henry McLeish attempted a second assault with gratuitous conduct. The anomaly here was how the sterling job of ridiculing the Chief Constable in the tabloid Press allowed this next injustice to go unpunished because the public had a distorted view of who the villain of the piece was. Consistently, the devious practices of his adversaries were underlined, whereas he miraculously maintained an honourable stance until the threat of legal action was considered; not to remove the Chief Constable, but him retaliating against orchestrated aggression. This had a particular relevance to myself upon being so cynical about the law. Could someone of his stature actually bring his grievances to court? Where would it lead if this happened? The photocopied message I sent at the beginning of this dispute required an answer because it was believed that the whole episode was fabricated to conceal its existence. Further vindication lay with the fact that complaints held by Dr Oliver were not being aired in a Court of Law. This would present the opportunity to expose the incriminating photocopy as the primary source of these hostilities in an ever-increasing ill-defined dispute that failed to comply with what was purported. The saga went quiet at this stage. Then, two days later, his retirement was announced after a consultation behind closed doors. The Chief Constable emerged from these talks, adamant that his conscience was clear, and two of his most vehement rivals, Donald Dewar and Pat Chalmers, both acknowledged his achievements in their farewell speeches. This could not be the same bitter pair who had verbally assaulted the man just days earlier?! What was the reason for this apparent case of double standards? Even after his dismissal, Dr Oliver continued to point out the hypocrisy and asked the question about why Donald Dewar and Pat Chalmers remained in office. But this, like many other unexplained riddles in this protracted row, only left what really happened to speculation.

REASON 7: A DEAD CHILD

The argument that such a crime could never be manipulated in any way becomes invalid when past events are considered. Here was someone who is being framed for murder that could be a key witness in the attempted murder of two children! Further, the second reconstruction of the Russell murders down in Kent was as outlandish as a spaghetti western. Women and children were always the first victims in the gruesome recitation, with the natural inclination of those responsible veering towards a child murder as the first option to cover-up their participation in a campaign of mass murder.

The ultimate contradiction is that any reasonable-minded person says that the murder of Scott Simpson, even with the apparent shortcomings included in the investigation, could never be abused in the manner being alleged here. This error of judgement, in fact, directly allows such a thing to happen. People in general have their emotions distorted with the revulsion a child murder provokes. Only by capitalising on this revulsion did the events detailed above take place. Without this impaired temperament, the whole stomach-churning situation would not be possible. Anyone who disbelieves this principle should recap the encounters concerning Dr Ian Oliver; they will find out that he held his head high throughout this affair. It was an affair in which his ill-treatment included betrayal, falsified allegations, opportunist verbal attacks, sensationalised headlines, which amounted to a systematic campaign of character assassination so as to increase pressure on him and so on. Incidentally, the incidents mentioned above were only a broad spectrum of what was occurring; others could be used to replace these examples of treacherous deeds. It was all verging on the ridiculous when finally one of Scotland's most respected journalists, Magnus Linklater, as an open-minded individual without any inside information, questioned the Chief Constable's dismissal, saying, against public opinion, it should be revoked. A complete frenzy of hysteria blighted sound judgement with every accurate comment made by Oliver ridiculed in the process.

A final quirk, in alignment to rubbishing his words, because this could include the word 'conspiracy', was a public comment made by him and shared by David Beattie that the original outburst by Henry McLeish back in January was personal. David Beattie, being Oliver's second in command, was left in charge while his superior was in Taiwan, and he could only offer this view to explain the conduct of the government minister. This significant disclosure, which was made public once he had been dismissed, verified what I had always believed: that this repugnant public squabble was avoidable, and was created by the opportunism of Henry McLeish to raise his popularity. With countless examples of evading similar set-ups, which could have resulted in a prison cell, hospital or grave, I saw right through the initial entrapment as it occurred. Maybe someday the minority of opinion back then will turn into a majority. If McLeish had deliberately targeted Dr Oliver with unknown backers, this would make the Chief Constable a choice victim in any forthcoming conspiracy...

REASON 8: AN AYRSHIRE CONNECTION

When producing that photocopy, it was imperative that the wording was perfect. The second decisive factor was to leave no forensic evidence to connect myself to its manufacture, so as to create a complete illusion. Was I successful? The answer that I was came from an obscure source.

The local postman had not changed for years, apart from the occasional spells of a replacement who was also a familiar member of the community. The appearance of a stranger delivering the letters in 1997 was no real cause for concern. Only the interference to the mail this man delivered held reason for suspicion; letters were being opened then resealed, as evident from the ripples noticed in the paper envelopes on receipt. In the middle of April 1998 with the genuine local postman resumed to duties, the mail was not being tampered with. When I had sent that first batch of photocopies mentioning the murders of Raymond Stevenson and Tracey Wilde, the bogus postman reappeared. The obvious purpose of this was to intercept and confiscate the photocopy because they believed that their own personnel were responsible, and he was deployed as a safeguard to prevent this message reaching myself. With the Dr Ian Oliver dispute raging in the media on a daily basis, and seeing him in the mornings with the mailbag, I was fully aware of whom the instigator was in both predicaments. The whole ill-fitting episode was definitely my doing. The second batch of three photocopies was sent with the expected response on the Monday evening, which included the outrageous outburst from Donald Dewar. I knew this would allow them to deduce who the culprit was. I again felt vindicated as the normal postman returned to his duties before the end of the week.

He undercover agent went by the name Kevin Smith. The first name would be genuine but 'Smith,' being such a common name could have been taken for this purpose, therefore less likely to be traced afterwards.

The revealing timing of this covert agent acting as the postman substantiated the panic, the importance and the need to conceal the basic information expressed in that short message, which was written in a format that suggested that the author was illiterate. Fools were not in short supply here: only separating them from propriety required two strokes of genius.

THE AFTERMATH

A real hatchet job removed the Chief Constable from office, disgraced and extensively regarded as an object of public humiliation, and painfully aware of my participation. There was no remorse: only gratitude that a stubborn refusal to go had left so many unexplained ruptures in procedures. It was so complete that the Secretary of State for Scotland stood accused of unlawful conduct, which, as always, remained unanswered. The ridicule experienced by Dr Oliver was cruel, and on sending that second batch of photocopies the abuse he suffered increased immediately. However, I knew that this was paramount in order to expose them and their cohorts. On his dismissal, he faded into the background after a few public outbursts with a comfortable financial package to live on. In contrast, I was so penniless that I was half-starved at times, but could relate to him being outcast, but without this hardship. The rules, laws, public etiquette and natural justice were all breached: the double standards included were shown up when his successor was caught up in a similar situation but he was not removed from his post. In simple terms, Dr Ian Oliver had become another victim, albeit a high-profile one, of an unrelenting scandal in Strathclyde that knew no respect for people or reputations.

The accuracy of the contents of the photocopy played a crucial role in determining what occurred. With a public outcry simmering below the surface, people were alleging that Special Branch murdered this person or that person without giving them the dignity of recording the cause of death as such. There were seven prostitute murders and the allegations were that Special Branch was responsible for every one; the problem was always going to be substantiating these allegations. It didn't matter how ridiculous the reason given by Strathclyde Police became, how unbelievable the circumstances became; without hard evidence to support what was being claimed, it could always be denied. Now a killer had a face and a name. There was police and Special Branch involvement to change the murdered man's cause of death to death by industrial accident, as written in the photocopy. Dr Ian Oliver was subjected to appalling treatment to disguise its existence. The government minister, Henry McLeish, could not be dismissed as a rogue element because others within the Labour Party had acted in conjunction to secure the unlawful dismissal of the Chief Constable. The personal crusade to complicate and determine the accuracy of what was being surmised held an incentive to embark on this ploy, because I feared that my DNA was planted into a murder victim's flat. Once democracy and justice are reinstated in Strathclyde, which important individuals will find themselves in prison?

What had happened here was a real breakthrough. The murder of prostitutes was averaging one a year with the clinical strangulation indicating specialist expertise. Now this death rate was curtailed; a small victory for human rights without the intervention of Donald

Dewar attempting to conceal the truth having any bearing on the outcome.

My confidence rose. Corresponding details supportive of another cover-up became evident with the first convergence only days later. I was reading in a Sunday newspaper that the last three prostitute murders could be connected. No doubt this was being said solely to discredit Raymond Stevenson as the killer of Tracey Wilde, because he died before the last murder was committed, but with it, the possibility of framing any innocent person diminished substantially. I was grateful for small mercies, and welcomed the fact that this could close another chapter of terror, where anyone targeted is unlikely to fit into all three sets of circumstances when being totally innocent. The beleaguered status of those responsible became apparent with the next day's papers contradicting this by saying, yet again, that there was no connection. Here was one opinion to appease the concerns of some and denials to appease the concerns of others. I was always in a no-win situation, so it was gratifying to see those people with blood on their hands sweating it out in impossible circumstances. Unfortunately, they reneged on their word and went on to secure the conviction of a youth, which was later to be ruled unsafe, to be convicted again when his appeal failed. When the situation started to look insecure the head of Strathclyde Special Branch, Jim Orr, was drafted in to lead the investigation of Glasgow prostitute murders, then ideally placed to cover up any involvement.

The death of Raymond Stevenson was kept unusually quiet when it occurred. This was overturned by the inquest, which was given full exposure by both television and the Press at the end of 1998. The timescale was now over a year since the murder of Tracey Wilde. Memories of any witnesses, that fatal night at her flat, had diminished by the time his photograph was being extensively broadcast. On seeing this picture for the first time, I exclaimed, "That's not him!"
Later on, I was reassured that it was indeed Stevenson: only the picture that was used bore little resemblance to him. This was borne out by the fact that having asked others what age they thought the person in the photograph was, I never received an answer outside the 30-35 age bracket. He was twenty-eight when he died, so this

deceptive image had reversed the ageing process. Moreover, this was said to have been an old photograph of him, which would have him much younger than twenty-eight when it was taken. Determined to spot any illusion with the farce involving Grant McCaskill, where the same picture was used throughout, here, the principle was again compelling. A frightening aspect was to emerge during the court proceedings when I read who his workmate was at the time of the incident that killed Raymond Stevenson. A British Telecom engineer with an identical name to this work-mate entered the house to fix the telephone. The problem was these workers were Special Branch agents masquerading as *BT* engineers. The man in question, Peter Ritchie, was of an abnormally large size and easily distinguishable. The imagination goes into overdrive at how up close and personal this could be when you think how effortlessly this giant could overpower a smaller foe. That day I asked to see his ID tag several times with good reason. Before any involvement detailed previously concerning myself materialized, reports were made public from a prostitute murder that a giant of a man was witnessed being in the vicinity. At the time this was alleged to be Special Branch agent Peter Ritchie. Now here was in all likelihood the same man inside my house. As innocent people picked on were being found dead all over the West of Scotland, big Peter Ritchie was free and unconcerned living in Saltcoats.

On reconsidering the sole photograph of Raymond Stevenson that was published showing him sporting a bushy moustache so that he would not be recognisable; I knew for certain that others were unlikely to. But, wasn't that the purpose? Having spent years on the receiving end, I was the first to notice any deliberately included fabrications, and found this latest edition was well incorporated into a chain of deception. I had delayed the decision to post the incriminating photocopy until the bogus investigation was exhausted. My reluctance continued even after I had heard the repeated statement that the culprit could be a student living in student accommodation. The reason for this was to prevent Strathclyde Police reneging on their word that the suspect in the blue *Ford Escort* had been eliminated from the inquiry because I was fully aware that they would do this. The second reconstruction, which took place a year and a half after the first, provided me with full vindication after hearing that this person was again a wanted suspect. I was not at all surprised that Raymond Stevenson did not previously rise from his grave to telephone the BBC studios, so this left only the gaping faults in the movements of Tracey Wilde requiring closer scrutiny.

As with the backstabbing and the sinister ploys to remove Dr Ian Oliver from office, recounting what happened here only creates disbelief that the whole episode could go unchecked where it leaves more questions than answers. The predictable sick pantomime continued to cripple a community, except that now the curtain was beginning to fall on the evil protagonists.

THE CONCLUSION

Metaphorically speaking, to see Judas betrayed, the hangman hung, and the top gun shot down in flames all in the space of five months is an awe inspiring accomplishment to anyone else. But here, there was no sense of achievement, only bewilderment. The scruples of those who were ultimately responsible put into question; why does anyone work for those people, keeping them in position only to be betrayed for their loyalty? Why assist in the misery to become the next victim? Can they not see that the decisions being taken are of questionable sanity? Knowing that I'd saved countless lives, the three servants-turned-victims was an acceptable trade-off without which no conclusion could be realized, where only Dr Ian Oliver should not have been included. The path that had been embarked upon was always going to be bloody and messy in acceptance of what was required to curtail the activities of these butchers plying their trade on the streets of Glasgow. Long and arduous the distance travelled, the route taken physically, mentally and spiritually, to be at a destination or conclusion, no one could ever evaluate, being haunted and tormented by ghouls hell bent on another kill.

From start to finish, there was no point in any of this, killing people for pleasure: committing genocide, undermining law and democracy.

When that photocopy was sent out, only wishing to identify who would defend the indefensible, it was Scottish Labour Party members who became implemented in succession. How they could ever equate this with the supposed socialist values they held is a mystery unto itself. Scotland has a minor socialist party whose leader is another target of the Secret Service, where the Labour Party Home Secretary has to sign the warrants against him. The situation had come to an impasse. Unable to provide a satisfactory cover-up, a secondary attempt would only help to verify everything I have detailed where the present status was ill conceived in the extreme. All those attempted wrongful convictions, which in the process perverted the course of justice, only to have the two most powerful politicians in Scotland framed in the ongoing conspiracy. This result surpassed all expectations. Nobody could foretell what fools would publicly go on record to defend mass murderers. This was as shocking as it was ugly.

Donald Dewar had placed the reputation of the Scottish Labour Party at stake, his own political career and his future liberty, where a powerful motive to murder Jill Dando had now materialised. This situation was surpassed by events when two and a half years after the extraordinary intervention by the Scottish Secretary in the acrimonious dispute, he died as a result of ill health, which had no doubt been contributed to by this diabolical scenario. Jill Dando was murdered a year and a half before the death of Donald Dewar. It was his duty to either resign or to oppose the oppression. Instead, he furthered the objectives of the murderers responsible, and had to live thereafter with his conscience and the consequences. The decision was his own and the legacy tarnished a long political career and the credibility of his party. The peculiar actions of his Number 2 were implicit of a deeper rot ingrained in the officials presiding over the West of Scotland. During research of the subject while milling through letters from the public published in the newspapers I detected a response supportive of Dr Ian Oliver, either for his admirable stance or the compromised position the Scottish Secretary attained. It was incredible to find that one of the contributors was none other than Henry McLeish MP. Equally incredible was the topic of the letter because he had denied he was engaged in any vendetta against the Grampian Police Chief Constable. How condescending it was to read this version in the absence of answers concerning the minister's behaviour relating to the most serious of matters. He contradicted the claim that the dispute was personal, now a culminate response to one accusation was heard only if it prevented any backtracking at a later date. At face value, how the other unanswered accusations could be explained away in the light of this not being a clash of personalities requires the most imaginative of reasoning. Dr Ian Oliver was not a lone voice in finding the conduct of Henry McLeish reprehensible. The conclusion to this predicament resulted in the victim being removed from office while his assailant remained in power, then he offers the most limited of replies to the many grievous accusations faced. As always, the word 'justice' could never be applied to the situation, now that the integrity of a consortium of high standing individuals in direct opposition to the Chief Constable were in question.

Faced with a situation where the truth might leak out at any moment and incriminate top officials in Scotland, did British Intelligence have Jill Dando murdered to prevent further exposure? The sacrifice Donald Dewar and his cohorts made with their involvement here could only be held in gratitude with the conspirators. Of course it all could be denied, but the number of believers was rapidly disintegrating, as you can only make a fool of someone so many times with this concept at saturation point in the West of Scotland. The saga concerning Dr Oliver had ample visible flaws. The connection was not an obvious one as the general public didn't know about that photocopy. But, who is to say what could transpire in the future? The other avenue with tangible connections to the massacre in Strathclyde was the Russell murders, where this did have a final incident with Jill Dando three months before her death. A final affront was played out in the BBC studios exposing the corruption and opposing the aggressors. Two incidents that appeared oblique in comparison to the events in Strathclyde could not afford to have any more faults in the process highlighted, where one brave lady was in a position to do so and valiantly refused to be manipulated. So with it, the substantial motive required to murder Jill Dando now had segments included one after another only if British Intelligence were her executioners.

The law being practised with legal professionals full of their own importance appeared to lack equality required to administer justice. Why couldn't the only case that I attempted to bring to trial with its certain injustices not come to fruition? Why were the never-ending errors and crimes committed by the State allowed to continue? Amazingly, there was no prevention against being framed for murder time after time. There was no surprise from this quarter when grievous accusations were made of political (Labour Party) bias in the Scottish legal system when the law is supposed to be impartial. To whose benefit could this be? The requirement to interfere has to have a present or future advantage, when yes, there are a few candidates outlined previously in the former passages to fill this need. Again, this hints at a dictatorship edging into society.

All these principles of oppression allowed Adolf Hitler to reign, where here in the West of Scotland, a new apocalypse had already begun. Only by eradicating them at source can democracy be enhanced. A warning has been served!

5. NOT FOR GLORY

With a biography that reads like an adventure book full of axe battles and renegade stories, this perception could not be further from the truth. Normally being of a quiet nature, the only real difference was that here was someone who would retaliate against any acts of aggression, whereas had others done so, they might still be alive today. The story, therefore, was one of persecution of innocent people, who were being subjected to the most appalling crimes, and most of it was by and large without their knowledge. No aspect written previously was unique, right down to being destitute and stranded down in continental Europe as another Scot recalled his own experiences. He told how he had fled Scotland where with desperation creeping in, survival meant that vegetables were stolen out of foreigners' gardens. This was told in an ashamed manner. A smile broke out over my face as I freely admitted that I had been in the same predicament. The victimisation of individual people is an atrocity that can go unpunished for as long as the truth is concealed. It is a most extraordinary situation that no action is taken when the evil is publicly exposed. Various incidents had come to light, but like a bad record, it just continued. The sole event that sets this story apart from the experienced hardship being inflicted on others was when two military personnel were deployed in the cold-blooded murder of another innocent civilian. The debate here raged either way, where one instalment followed the direction that, if this were true, the assassins employed would be SAS. When outnumbered by two to one and unarmed the chances of surviving such an attack is not feasible. Complicating this assumption was the basic fact that others who had been targeted were now dead yet a survivor tells the tale that his would-be executioners were two military men dressed all in black. Was there any viable alternative to answer this anomaly?

A relative appeared home from abroad, and at this initial meeting on his return, asked, "How have you still got your kneecaps?"
It was strange that this should be the first question to be addressed.

"They never got me: it's as simple as that," I replied, and it is this reply that may well tell its own story of evading the impossible.

Equally perplexing was the other side of the argument. It was undeniable whom they had targeted during the Grant McCaskill fiasco, with the photo-fit being a vague resemblance to myself, combined with the policeman with the identical name. Those who were in the know adhered to the view that, with all that transpired, this would not be complete without repeated attempts on my life. Why the claim that one major unsuccessful attempt was not followed by others? The missing ingredient here bewildered most observers, but what was it?

A commonly held opinion was that the death squads were yet to complete unfinished business here, where, sooner or later, death was imminent. With the passage of time, a stressed-out person became more relaxed: not the actions of a condemned man about to meet his fate. In accordance was the newspaper story, which although it read as if there was some involvement in prostitution or the associated crimes, it did reiterate the fact that I was the one to be murdered next. In reality, I had lived long after its publication. A paradox could only lie at the heart of this God forsaken situation: one with the potential to baffle any expert in sociology. It was intriguing and mystifying and often others asked; "What have you done now?"
It certainly held a copious answer.

ANOTHER SUNDAY NIGHT

When the British Establishment gives you a visit where the purpose of this call is to assassinate you, it is like shooting rabbits in a field to them: you really are that defenceless. What are your options? Do you go to the police for example, when this very slaughter would not be possible without the co-operation of elements within the police force in Strathclyde? This is not a viable option, unless you are totally naïve. If you retaliate, it will be you who is imprisoned, because once again, the culprits responsible are not going to assist those who are exposing or opposing their mass murder campaign. The only realistic answer is to run. However that is predictable, and when you become predictable that only guarantees what they came to accomplish. How far could you ever run from the likes of this before your murder was dealt? This said, for once they were about to find out that this was no rabbit that they had come to kill. Against a background of allegations that others were being murdered and passed off as victims of drugs overdoses, accidents, suicide or drowning, this execution was always going to be a little more colourful. It was going to be a gangland shooting. It was a case of the end fitting the means, where the chosen method of eliminating another civilian is deliberately fitted into one's circumstances, thereby reducing the suspicion lingering in the aftermath. This was a questionable decision because the only other incident of this nature held implications concerning Strathclyde Police: desperate people engrossed in their murderous ways where another kill takes precedence over logic. With no history of drug abuse to the extent that I would refuse medicines that were prescribed by doctors and dentists, an overdose would not be an appropriate cause of death, which left the other two favourite options; an accident or a suicide. Here was someone capable of evading the incidents deployed in entrapment, so they never got close enough to complete one of these 'accidents' or 'suicides'. The remaining alternative was an execution complete with pointers to the criminal fraternity as suspects. In humour afterwards, I would comment, "A gangland shooting, that's got plenty of street cred, but I could live without it."

In all seriousness, it is strange how the little details bother you more than the severity of it all due to their failings and incompetence. What was irritating in this manner was why the cart had become before the horse, because this murder, if it had been accomplished, had happened before I had been framed for the murder of Jacqueline Gallacher. It made sense, if there is any sense in all this insanity, to attempt the wrongful framing, and then if this failed, carry out the execution. What was originally alleged was that the suspects who escaped a life sentence for the prostitute murders were then murdered themselves. At the time, it appeared as though over eagerness on the part of the death squads created the unusual timing. Only in the succeeding months after the trial of Grant McCaskill could any logical procedure be applied to the sequence of events once his former girlfriend betrayed him. To be caught out for a second time left no recourse open to the police but to finally instigate his detention. This was later followed by the major scandal being exposed. Never about to answer any accusations with a police force implicated in such dreadful terror, my death at this point should only be beneficial as a method of covering up the evil. The other accusations concerned with the unnecessary attacks on countless women were simply ignored: the women of Strathclyde being such second class citizens in all this misery. The timing, initially appearing to be in disagreement with the circumstances, did fit perfectly, and the Sunday night being used for another murder also fitted.

So when you are up against an assassination attempt, to believe that there are only two outcomes, both of which looked rather bleak; either imminent death or going on the run to delay the execution. Neither option can be recommended. As ever that third elusive option, whatever it was, could only be the preferred choice. I held a nature that retained an unpredictable streak; regardless of the peril encountered, it was the only resource remaining to rely upon. An exceptional answer to a unique problem was required just to remain alive.

Having read the warning signs correctly for once, the weekend passed away feeling anxious that another assault was about to be confronted. I was not in the habit of it, but early on Sunday evening, I lay down on top of the bed fully dressed, and pondered what the next attack could include, having continually experienced various incidents. The bed was situated tight against the wall below three windows. In spite of the night being overcast, the view remained excellent at around 8.30pm as I gazed bemusedly out of the window nearest the end of the house, looking northward across tranquil countryside. Any distraction could interrupt this peaceful solitude, and, like a cliché from a cheap novel, it did. A small white van passing the neighbours' farm was abrupt as it startled both the tranquillity and my personal repose. At a distance of a quarter of a mile, the vehicle distinctly resembled a *Ford Courier* that was carrying more speed than was acceptable in the circumstances. Now that it had gained my full attention, I followed the movements on the single-track road as it sped down the hill. It stopped unexpectedly on a small plateau, and then suddenly raced away again. The incident was so quick that had I not observed its every movement bordered with dry stone walls, therefore would not have noticed two men jump out at this intermittent manoeuvre. It was a one in a million chance that, against routine, the only window in the house to view this event was commandeered at the correct time. Of all the misfortune experienced, this happening could not have been more fortuitous.

The unprecedented driving to deposit two military men in the vicinity is not an accepted practice about to be exacerbated by the speed and precision to which they operated. Only close monitoring of the van allowed the situation to be recorded, where these two soldiers scaled the farm gate then sprinted over the field towards a ruined cottage, which lies out of view secluded in a small wood. I am not easily impressed, but in a rare admission, could see that this pair were top-flight professionals as I jumped up to the window in astonishment. The path taken was ideal to avoid detection from the various neighbours concluding in the preplanning and single-mindedness of the mission. The fact that two predators are fast approaching was not worrying in itself: however, the efficiency and description of what was being surveyed was a fearsome prospect.

Both men were of a powerful, athletic build and ran at extraordinary pace over the rough ground. This put them outside the realms of being just ordinary soldiers. They were dressed identically in black combat fatigues, boots and carried backpacks. They certainly were not criminal hit-men who, as a rule, operate in solitary guise, or terrorists, who operate in makeshift military costume. The packs secured to their backs afforded them full and easy movement of all their limbs. We have all seen the bedraggled tourist running for a bus or train with a rucksack on their back, where the faster they try to run, the more out of synch their load becomes and increases the handicap with every step. This in contrast was professionally secured kit, purpose-made for unrestricted dexterity. The final frightening aspect was protruding up from behind the left shoulder: a pipe. At this distance, it could be a gun barrel: it is difficult to come to any other conclusion. As someone who had seen most things with broad experience, I had never encountered anything like this before. As soon as I had sighted them, the possibilities of who this pair were, can be short-listed to being SAS, SBS, Royal Marines, Parachute Regiment or mercenaries, such was the ruthless rigour displayed, although all along I suspected this to be SAS.

As they vanished from view in the leeward side of the hill, so did all hope of survival as I lay back down on the bed thinking, 'It's over'. The gangland hit they were about to imitate could be avoided, but not this. An unnatural calm engulfed the next would-be victim of the mass murder being carried out in Strathclyde. Miraculous as it sounds, there was no panic at the impending situation, only acceptance. It was surreal contemplating your own death without any regrets because I had only ever known the deliberate restrictions and animosity in the crippled status of the West of Scotland. Another wasted life was about to be extinguished with others too blinkered to see the truth. Further realisation said that it was pointless to write down my last will and testament because it would only be confiscated in the subsequent cover-up. I thought about how I had become non-existent in the system after my benefit was recently stopped, and asked myself if this was a new target group to be murdered. Here was I, someone who had never been a member of any political party, or offered any threat to democracy; didn't have a criminal career and had no affiliations with any terrorist groups yet could be murdered for no apparent reason. The only classification that remained was what they term a subversive. Only in Strathclyde could someone who desperately tried to leave the ranks of the unemployed by making a concerted effort to start self-employment be prevented and then murdered for it. A subversive I must have been to believe this possible at the time.

Well educated, not from school where once you could read and write you learned very little afterwards, but from a host of other sources, the more unconventional circumstances, the better the education. Upon knowing, as an example with similarities to the developments outside the window, that it wasn't the toughest guy who becomes the criminal godfather but the one who could both think and fight it out. A combination of daring exploits, going against the grain to achieve a superior result and an uncompromising attitude commands the respect required in the hardest of environments. With a litany of stories concerning organised crime to draw from, I formed an opinion on tonight's confrontation. If I sit here, an instant kill will be achieved; if I run, they will capture then kill me. But, what if the tables were turned? It still meant dying, where that had been accepted the moment this pair sprang from the white van, but it did not mean I would die alone. I could see no way of getting out of this predicament alive, no matter what transpired. So, inspired by my latest crazy master plan, I rose and retrieved a large hedge knife then placed it under the bed to be used later in defence. Feeling unbelievably placid about the impending situation, I lay down on the bed again, fully aware that the assailants would need to recuperate from their exertions before the final assault on the house. In slow reflection, the more this was considered, the greater became the belief that I had found their Achilles heel. The two butchers about to complete the simplest of kills would not expect to be hindered in any way, especially not by a defenceless victim. The element of surprise which they rely upon had been turned in my favour, plus knowing the territory well as a second advantage.

As with the stories that have become part of the folklore of the West of Scotland, beginning with the night a sixteen year old midget went out to battle with what he believed to be five grown men not realising it was a practical joke done by friends, or the night I had to run barefoot through a sea of broken glass on the large kitchen floor to fight off six intruders, once again the moment of truth had arrived. Two of the best killers in the world were about to be surprised by a total nobody. As the SAS hold that reputation - and this pair were in all likelihood SAS members - it defied logic, but being pressured into situations like this brings out a demon fuelled on adrenaline that is more menacing than any adversary could ever imagine. Unbeknown to them, this pair were about to experience some quality opposition. Capitalising on the only real advantage I held meant creeping up on this pair from behind in order to take one of them out. Whatever happened here was always going to be of legendary proportions, redefining raw courage and contributing a new chapter of stories to the local gossip flying around the area.

A popular misconception is the effectiveness of the shotgun, having been given the predetermined capabilities that to guarantee killing someone with such a weapon it had to be at point blank range. At a distance of more than three metres, the advice was not to bother pulling the trigger. There are many variables with the calibre and capacity of both gun and cartridge, that if you choose to murder a foe, this is generally not the preferred weapon. The last time I held a shotgun, I had refused to pull the trigger, as all it is is a loud noise and a sharp recoil. To know how heavy and cumbersome this piece of hardware really is, and in the present circumstances, it could prove more of a handicap when counter-attacking professional soldiers. Although I didn't own one, most farms in a rural community possess some kind of firearm that could easily be borrowed, but with this appraisal, I decided against this option. In order to get so close enough to engage in hand-to-hand combat, a silent method of killing would be required, and then the second assailant would have to be confronted by any means possible. If there was a time when one needed that textbook method of strangulation deployed on the streets of Glasgow, this was the hour, but unfortunately I lacked this technique.

Plenty of steep rough ground separated their present position from the house, which was no safeguard against what they had come to administer, though it bought some time. Realizing this, the only method of protection remaining open to me was to launch an attack to shock the aggressors before they could find out who had indulged in such a practice. It was a decision of bravado that could surpass the accepted view of just walking to your death. It was time to act. I drove my sister's car down to the town from where I would complete the journey into the countryside on foot. Switching off the car ignition I realised that I had left the hedge knife under the bed. It was too dangerous to return home to retrieve it. I was scarcely able to believe my own stupidity, so decided to continue with my mission armed only with a *Swiss army* knife. Desperately disadvantaged with the quality of opposition, I was now more vulnerable and prayed that I would be able to find a substantial second weapon in the intervening period before the final conflict. The gruesome prospects were multiplying by the minute as I only really hoped to kill one and then be finished off by the other, leaving two corpses behind from an evening of utter brutality. With two bodies, more questions than answers would originate from what really happened that night and leave a mystery from beyond the grave. This was my objective, rather than just being slain by them. People never contemplate that kill or be killed predicament, but this was different, only murdering as a last act of defiance, spitting in the face of the tormentors and extracting that last little bit of excruciating misery of being a rebel in a final bloody scene. With the hedge knife, a small distance separated myself from the victim. Now the pocket knife didn't afford me this luxury. No description ever catches the essence of this that the only consolation in death could be another dead stranger. It is raw un-distilled madness, induced from calm cold calculating thought laced with the grotesque brutality of haunting consequences. We all die, but some die a little harder than others.

After parking the car, I quickly looked around for any suitable object that could be utilised as a weapon. Nothing suitable presented itself, so with no time to spare under the cover of the dim light I made the move in their direction. Running over fields until the approach to the old road leading up to the deserted cottage, then reduced my pace to a moderate walk. I was not concerned with concealing my identity as a hedge provided the immediate cover upon nearing the empty house. This property, although it was unoccupied had both roof and timbers intact, and therefore I assumed it would be the ideal base-camp for the perpetrators. Surrounded by outbuildings, shrubs, overgrown gardens, trees and a small wood in the near vicinity, there was plenty of cover from which to launch an assault, with the thick undergrowth chosen as cover closing in on the building. I used the grass to muffle the steps as steady progress brought me to the position of confrontation. The crouched posture required little more than a further stoop to disappear below the branches of the shrubs, with the long grass coming up to provide perfect concealment at the end of the house separated only by the width of the road. No alternative weapon could be acquired on arrival: only the small knife remained drawn throughout held in a firm clench. Every breath felt magnified with the tense situation, with lungs like bellows sucking and exhaling air. The noises from the wildlife were exaggerated with a newly found clarity as both adrenaline and heartbeat pumped. The only sound that I was desperate to hear was a creaking noise emitted from the cottage. I was aware that the floorboards were intact, and this could verify the position of the prey. An old house like this with the windows smashed should act like an amplifier if anyone was inside. What had happened to these adversaries?

In the absence of any human sounds I relaxed with the thought, 'It's over', for a second time that night, not this life, but that of my family, for I believed the hired killers had continued to complete their mission and it was anyone's guess who they would murder. I spent twenty minutes hiding like a fox in its lair before regaining some composure. As confidence rose and the intensity of the situation receded, I emerged from the foliage. Still cautious, I checked to see if anything was disturbed with the knife-hand down at my side, now that the threat had reduced. Then, relieved that one of the soldiers had not come out of the ruined cottage to have his throat slit I became quite complacent about the peril. Standing tall, I slowly moved out into the courtyard with small gentle steps, wary of what could appear out of the building in front of me. Now I was fully exposed in the most vulnerable possible position, but nothing stirred.

Suddenly, a 'thud, thud, thud' sound came from the small wood situated above the cottage, which sounded similar to the sound of timber being chopped. All along the property was under suspicion where I hadn't considered the trees in the distance, and jumped in shock at this interruption. When I glanced over my left shoulder, the repetitive noise stopped immediately and I stared in horror in the direction of the source. The impulsive movement was sufficient to betray who was really standing alone in open ground. Unable to see either of the two opponents, I knew my actions had handed the advantage to the killers. I had blown the only favourable aspect - the element of surprise to catch them off balance – where now this offered no protection. My best guess at this point was that I was now being lined up in the crosshairs on their telescopic sights. If my bottle crashed the next thing felt would be a bullet ripping through my upper body. My tongue felt as though it had been transplanted with my heart, but I retained what nerve could be mustered then turned and looked down.

Moments like these can be described from a reckless past, when having crashed a bicycle or a motorcycle and you are flying through mid air just before the impact, your mind switches over to an obscure thought to detract from the imminent danger and produce a surreal sense of calmness. This same principle became apparent as a smile broke out over my face as I thought; 'Is this really like it is in the Hollywood movies? Does a certain amount of blood and tissue follow the bullet out as it exits your body?'

Looking directly at the knife in my hand, I had to physically contain the laughter contorting my insides and came to the conclusion; 'It's only you and me, pal'.

It all became apparent how futile the whole encounter really was. Now I had to throw this knife over a distance of forty metres at a target that wasn't even visible and make a kill. Then I realised that this was, without question, the craziest moment of my entire life. Admittedly, there were more candidates for that title than most people ever have. Gallant actions are no substitute for professional judgement, to now know that defeat and death were the only two prospects lingering.

Minutes had passed and this solitary figure remained stationary, unable to believe that the end had not happened. Now a retreat had to be considered. But how do you get out of this situation when you know that their killing range ran into hundreds of metres? The answer was half accomplished when I stared at the pocket knife. Gangland hit-men will shoot being almost certain of the target, but because I believed this pair to be serving in the British Army, I knew that they needed positive identification before the execution would be carried out. Any member of the public could have wandered into this environment. They were not about to kill and then find out that they had got the wrong person leaving a trail of dead bodies behind them. However, this was Strathclyde where every atrocity is acceptable. Provided I never allowed curiosity to permit another glance in their direction, why not just walk out of here unconcerned? Even if I had been identified, such a nonchalant attitude would create doubt in their minds, granting me precious seconds. With my head bowed down I turned and strolled casually away until the substantial stone-built building adjacent to the house acted as a shield, then bolted like I had never run before. I careered down the track, through hedges, fences and any other obstacle in my path, looking for the area of most moonlight as this provided least resistance for me to cannonball through. Out over the silage fields, I knew not to continue in a straight line and sprinted with an intermittent side-step and weave, so as to make myself a difficult target. The greatest hurdles were the drainage ditches, which were difficult to pick out in the half light, where I sometimes misjudged the edge when jumping and would sink back in. Never certain of the position of the others, I kept the haste of this departure sufficient to evade their attentions as I returned to the car. Reflecting on how I was caught like the proverbial rabbit in the car headlights; this motor vehicle was sanctuary for a wanted quarry. With little more than exhaustion, some minor scratches breaking the skin and an excess of mud spreading as far up the legs to cover one knee I realised what a fortunate escape I had had. Then I made a promise to myself that there would be no more mistakes, no more cat-and-mouse stuff, no more death-defying stunts and no more confrontations: it was time to run. This was unscheduled as a third final problem surfaced to complement a night of hazards. To be on the run, both money and provisions would be required and this would mean a return home while unaware of the whereabouts of the soldiers.

I returned home very briefly and stopped the car outside. I didn't choose clothing but just tipped the contents of one drawer into a sports bag, collected a sleeping bag, money and food as I swept through the house before leaving. Brushing past one of my brothers, I said I was off to work in England and promptly left the house. It would be safer for everybody concerned if this target were out of the vicinity. The car had been filled with a full tank at the local 24-hour petrol station in order to complete the journey.

This vehicle belonged to my sister and having previously tested the theory, there was reason to believe that a homing device was fitted. Another motor I had been using had the smell of soldering inside it one morning. Inquisitive about this, I had removed the radio to find objects on the wiring that were not there when inspected a few days previously. Their presence was to prevent interference from the radio obstructing whatever device had been hidden elsewhere. Tonight's car had already been involved in a revealing incident. One day while leaving Glasgow on the motorway, I switched on the radio at what was believed to be the pick-up point and then witnessed the large police *Rover* racing back in the opposite direction with its blue lights flashing shortly afterwards. Now approaching the suspected stretch of motorway at 2am heading towards Glasgow, if there was any transmission from the car, there was every reason to let them know their murder was foiled. So raced along at the wrong side of 100mph, the radio blaring with Bob Seger singing appropriately enough, 'Hollywood Nights' to give them the best possible signal in any detector, and roared into the night. The rebel inside showed his hand once again at this obscure time of day, swiftly passing through Glasgow and to my bewilderment, watched a police *Rover* racing on the other side of the M8 back to where I reckoned the pick-up point to be. I laughed at what was possibly the same car being fooled for a second time with its pace and blue flashing lights.

After all the excitement the journey down into England was tedious, and with the heat building up in the car, so did the smell from the putrid mud on my legs. The drainage ditches that supplied the offending muck were filled with a rotten mixture of stagnant water, slime and soft mud, and this produced a unique stink. This gave cause for continuous stops at service stations on the route in an effort to clean the grime off. It was ironic that the predicament produced by the contortions required to get a foot into the sinks in the public toilets was a bigger challenge than the SAS had been. At the period of time, only lorry drivers were active as they received a fright when they entered the toilets to find someone scrambling in embarrassment to conceal their purpose. Once the physical mud had been removed, and the jeans had been changed for a clean pair, this terrible stink prevailed. That night I slept on the back seat of the car, to be awoken the next morning when a car approached my secluded spot. It was the police estate vehicle that was used to patrol the motorway. At a distance, I shouted an explanation and they drove off. It was a strange decision that they didn't investigate these circumstances further having lain there with a back door open with my bare feet protruding out.

After an absence of two days I returned back home. There at the end of the road, a *Dunkin Donuts* pick-up truck was stationed like a sentry. The driver was sprawled over the bonnet, sunning himself wearing small round sunglasses in the glorious spring sunshine. This company is alleged to be associated with American Intelligence, which was supported by the fact that, on passing, his leisurely posture changed drastically as he jumped to attention and immediately betrayed himself and his surveillance purposes. It was an indifferent homecoming after having left at the threat the military had posed, only to see at first hand an international dimension included. However, there was every reason to believe the suspect to be local.

The borrowed car was returned to the owner, and then months later, I told my sister the full story. Her reply was, "I wondered why the car had done an extra two thousand miles."
It was quite a distance considering it was only here for a new set of spark plugs!

PERPLEXING AND CONFUSING.

The claim that I had gone head-to-head with the SAS sounded like a figment of the imagination. However, such a proposal was not always accompanied with the conclusive element to make it believable. Very simply, it was to die; not to win or even to evade, but just to go out in a blaze of glory. The mentality that allowed such a prospect to come to fruition had been tested in the past and it undoubtedly remained the sole reason for my present existence. Afterwards, telling of the night two military men in black came for another kill. This was a superior outcome to the grizzly expectation that was attempted. Reminiscing about this with the canteen culture that exists in the armed forces, I believed there was little doubt that the two who were responsible received endless humiliation at the hands of their colleagues for failing to kill a pathetic civvie, with all the contempt that amasses. This was not a terrorist or a rival army member, but a small quiet unarmed individual of limited means.

What was not perceived at the time as being a victory obviously was if only for the sole statement of fact: they never tried that again for another seven years. The mind games must have torn them apart trying to decipher how I knew they were approaching and how to counteract the aggression, and why the mission remained unaccomplished.

Very little happens without the culprits being known, which is why the Glasgow prostitute murders were so unbelievable. Had a member of the public been involved his name or details would be widely circulated by now, regardless of standing trial or not. With the passing years, the two men dressed in black have never been named in connection with this Sunday night excursion; a converse departure from the stream of information about other assailants while your own would-be executioner remained anonymous. This ill-conceived state of affairs increases speculation about SAS involvement. Later on, I was known to wear an army issue tee shirt from a former SAS member as a badge of respect for my actions that night!

At the time of this attack, what I described as thuds similar to wood being chopped could in fact have been three gunshots, such was the consistency of the sound. Years later, having being given a similar description for gunshots did I question if practice rounds were fired to check their weapons and release the tension the soldiers were living under. The difference between the sound of a shotgun blast - that I am accustomed to living in the countryside - and high technology rifles used by the SAS could account for the muffled noises, in conjunction with the distance separating us, with them being inside a wood at the time to further dampen the sound. Both this wood and ruined house had been used previous to this military operation by local members of Special Branch in other operations against me, indicating as always British government involvement. I have never been under any illusion as to the full and bloody participation of the British authorities as they reduced what was once the most technologically advanced area of the world to what is approaching Third World status, complete like such places, with death squads operating.

A friend used to comment on the *Dunkin Donuts* shop that once sat on the corner of Union Street and Argyll Street Glasgow, to which he claimed was, "The dodgiest place in Glasgow."
He made claims that the customers in the early hours of the morning were predominately drug dealers and pimps. In the end I owned up saying this is exactly what a company associated with the intelligence community wants - these kinds of people are of more

value to them than the average law abiding person. Strathclyde Police have had a *Dunkin Donuts* vehicle in their possession for a number of years.

The conclusion of perfect alignment in the overall pattern of events will silence any detractors who assume this confrontation never happened. The timing of it did fit in, but when the next assaults are considered, the chasm at the heart of the scenario becomes bridged. This set-up murder to fit the bill of being a so-called gangland hit was before the appearance of the *Land Rover Discovery* outside the house with the covert cameraman. The failure of these soldiers resulted in the original flawed attempted conviction for the murder of Jacqueline Gallacher to be reinstated. The original allegation of who they frame for these murders if a conviction is not achieved will become the next victim was not apparent here. The next major incident was the double murder of Lin and Megan Russell, which was destroyed by Jill Dando. If they had a loose end that could not be disposed of by killing, they would have to continue attempting to frame for murder until success was achieved exactly as it occurred. Then, at the court appearance for the minor motoring offence, it was another targeted person who was found dead three days beforehand. Why was the source allowed to proceed using this platform to beguile his tormentors? The newspaper story appeared to be somewhat twisted, although it reiterated concern for my future safety. One commentator said afterwards, "Putting that in the newspaper wouldn't save your life. If they wanted you dead, they would still murder you."
"Could they?" I replied ambiguously, with a wry smile.

Was this opinion correct? What were the other undisclosed factors that belied my present survival? Every possible assumption could be debated then dismissed with the only one remaining being that the SAS did indeed try and fail in the cold-blooded murder of myself. Those who are not prepared to accept this view have mounting contradictions to vacillate their perceptions of the situation. Implicit in this is where in Houston graveyard lays the remains of their own man, which is not the accepted form. Today too many people are telling similar stories of death squads operating in Strathclyde, of innocent men being framed for prostitute murders, of those picked as suspects being allegedly murdered then the murders covered up, and here was I still at liberty also promoting the same views.

Two months later, having fled to Portugal and witnessed the photographer taking photographs of me, is it any wonder that I could not take the threat of Interpol involvement seriously, that I fell asleep under a tree when under surveillance. Anyone else should be departing with haste. The incident on the train, where I unintentionally tried to stab the guard after mistaking him for an international police officer, was an act of desperation because I knew that capture could result in death. It was not the accepted practice that a total stranger should be injured for no apparent reason, however I knew the peril being imposed was at a unique dimension.

A change in attitude, an unpredictable element to complicate the expected behaviour, the ability to comprehend other alternatives, and a ruthless streak were all qualities that could be utilised to circumnavigate the most impossible of imposed situations. Others never held this ability, and they are dead today. In sad reflection, I knew I had no right to be alive given the quality of the opposition. The most difficult of settings to digest is that this all occurs in a supposedly civilised country: it is against belief and logic and it is against the Geneva Convention!

{At the end of this book, under *Miscellaneous Details*, further SAS involvement is detailed.}

ANOTHER DAY

This could rattle on for ever explaining set-ups, gizmos, nasty tricks, methods of sabotage, exploits and daring adventures, which sound all action, all singing and dancing when the fact is this hides the reality. Only by condensing what has happened is a distorted picture conjured up concealing how it really was, with the majority of the time spent under house arrest with the cottage itself bugged. I was to find light-bulbs had been exchanged inside the house for them from the *Ring* company. This brand is known for producing bugging devices disguised as ordinary items. Interesting stories could fill these pages like when passing a car on the dual carriageway with the driver pretending to light a cigarette with the built-in lighter, where in actual fact he was speaking out the side of his mouth into the lighter. The fact that the cigarette in his mouth never actually lit betrayed the fact that the lighter was actually a microphone. Instead of continuing in this manner, here is one day in my life...

Through the night, I lay awake in bed listening to intruders outside being industriously busy sabotaging a van. The vehicle receiving this evil and unwanted attention belonged to a friend, which in the morning I will have the dangerous occupation of driving. This is a regular occurrence where the same self-tapping screws, as one example, are used to puncture a tyre, so unconcerned I fall asleep and examine the damage inflicted in the morning.

I get out of bed in the knowledge that the new day already has had certain obstacles imposed and go down the stairs past the telephone. If you lift the receiver, you can hear the voice of the wife of one of the neighbouring farmers on a crossed line. We live over a mile away, but usually two large *BT* vans can be seen in the vicinity of this farm stationed beside a telegraph pole with rubber covered connections. They are positioned there for several months. It is not at all a convincing disguise since the telephone network in outlying areas is very basic, therefore, it should be possible to solve any genuine fault in a matter of hours. I have watched their activities when passing their position slowly on the single-track road. The supposed engineer is there with a headset on, directly listening into the line from this junction. At the start of 1997, the British Telecom engineer came into the house to fix the phone. This was a little odd as far as I was concerned because it was in perfect working order. It is clear therefore, that his actual purpose was to plant a listening device inside the phone. It was only after this installation was applied that the vans started to appear continuously, where their purpose was to listen directly into the house. A second attempt to repair the phone occurred on the 28th April 1997; on this occasion there was genuine damage that required attention. The engineer entered the house and was led to the telephone in the living room, and then I retired to the kitchen and left him alone to carry out the repair. Although the door was closed, the sounds of him at work could be heard interrupted by the squeak of the cupboard doors being opened and closed. It made sense that this was some kind of deviation, because he was not a genuine engineer, searching for whatever evidence that could be found in the vicinity of the telephone, supporting everything that was suspected. His guise was blown wide apart fifteen minutes later when he re-emerged looking somewhat embarrassed and shameful, admitting that he could not fix the telephone. Doesn't that just put everything into a nutshell? Those who are good for nothing are in the position to cripple an economy where failure inspires failure. Decent working citizens against their better judgement pay for these people, and there is no mechanism to regulate their activities. This is as predictable an insult as it is sick. Maybe if this idiot had spent more time examining the telephone instead of the contents of the cupboards, the illusion could be maintained. Then he appeared saying that a new phone was required and he promptly fetches one from the van. He made a great play out of opening the polythene bag in my presence, demonstrating that it was sealed to convey the idea that it was a standard phone, and in the process, emphasised the fact that this phone had a secrecy button. Once it was installed, he had to pass through the kitchen to leave. Before leaving, I inquisitively ask, "What was wrong with it?"

The engineer replied that it was old and worn out. His steps quickened, clearly because he knew that other people's phones don't suddenly age and wear out. My glance in his direction had transformed into a stare because it was clear this answer had been a blatant lie. The feeble excuse given didn't hold water because the telephone hadn't suffered from the wear and tear for I had deliberately broken it. Any capable *BT* engineer would automatically have been able to work this conclusion out. As he was nervous and anxious to leave the house, I fired another question at him to mock his stupidity and incompetence, "Where are you going next?"

"Anywhere ... Irvine, Barrhead, just wherever they send me."

Anywhere far away from here was my guess. He grabbed the front door handle in order to affect a hurried retreat before I had a chance to ask a more searching question such as, "Was that an *Infinity* inside the old phone?"

An *Infinity* is a sophisticated listening device. He sped off with the evidence that had been deliberately confiscated during this exchange of telecom property.

To continue: after breakfast, it is time to go to work. I didn't wish to receive any mail, because with a stranger delivering the letters the tampering is obvious. The new postman, Kevin, is easily distinguishable: he is taller, heavier and balding than any local member that he has suspiciously replaced. When I see him, I know to expect deliberate interference with the mail. You can only wonder how the property warrants could be obtained to make all this possible. Either the Home Secretary or their Deputy has to sign the appropriate consent forms and what are the grounds for him/her to do this? It is not reassuring to know that someone away down in London has signed away your life to be the next victim of the slaughter in Strathclyde. Confirmation of this agenda is hard to conceal: there are so many examples to confirm it. While working at the Chinese take-away, it was no surprise to see the appearance of *BT* as they erected a small red and white tent to excavate the pavement immediately outside the building. It was an awkward choice of work site, particularly when the telephone wires actually entered the rear of the building. The most likely purpose of this work, therefore, was to bug the property: this being one of their favourite methods. They dig down and plant devices under the floorboards while the unsuspecting target in the building above remains oblivious to what is going on. The street is of brick pavement set in a herring bone pattern with double yellow lines. After their activities were complete, the whole length of the shop front had noticeably been renovated. This was evident because of their failure to replace the bricks in the order in which they were removed. With the double yellow lines in such a distressed array it resembled a piece of modern art. Recognising that the building was probably now bugged, one inquisitive body asked, "Is there a serious triad problem in this town?"

"No, there is no triad problem here: you are talking to the source of the problem," I replied.

They had made it so obvious that even casual observers could see the extent of their activities without any prior warning.

Anyway, returning to the subject of trying to go out to work in a sabotaged van, with no viable alternative because I had no source of income after the fiasco that resulted in the termination of my unemployment benefit claim. The van was reluctant to start at first because of the damage that had been inflicted, but eventually the engine rumbled into life for a transient period. It was a lottery how long this would be sustained, so I nurse the stricken vehicle into Glasgow to attempt a day's courier work when aware also that the CB radio used are on open airwaves, where any hacker could listen in if he was on the same frequency. By midday, with the life in the engine slowly expiring, the inevitable breakdown is fast approaching. The van finally reached its last gasp in Govan. Fortunately, I managed to park it up in the grounds of the Southern General Hospital and get it off the road.

The next incident would reveal if the radio transmission was being monitored. In this position I radioed in requesting assistance, so that the parcel I was carrying could be transferred to another courier. I had, of course, to give out confirmation of the breakdown and present location. On receipt of this call, a motorcycle was despatched to collect the package at the hospital gates and proceed with the delivery. While waiting for the pick-up a red *Nissan Bluebird* approached. The male driver gave a cameo performance glancing in my direction as he entered the grounds and stopped a matter of metres away. He was so busy adjusting the rear-view mirror in order to keep me under surveillance that he failed to realize his car was illegally parked on a box junction. His attentions continued until the motorcycle arrived to continue with the delivery. Unable to cadge a lift off the rider I was now left stranded. I left the van and went to hide in the nearest bus shelter. This also drew the attention of the driver in the red Japanese car and he drove out of the hospital grounds shortly afterwards. I watched this car disappear up the road and then decided it was time for me to do likewise. So I set off in the opposite direction and headed towards the city centre. On a small back street, a little white van stopped in front of me, and the driver asked if I could tell him how to get on to the A737.
"Where are you going?" I asked, assessing his credentials.
"Ardrossan," he replied.

Under any circumstances, this was too convenient that, having broken down, this man now presents himself as a lift home. It was just too much of a coincidence and so I rejected any attempt at such a promising prospect and replied: "The motorway's over there. Just follow the signs for Irvine."

Moments like these come thick and fast. Only by thinking on your feet and rejecting such advances saves your life. It's a real cloak-and-dagger world where you are constantly side-stepping the players on a frantic merry-go-round. I watched this second suspicious vehicle leave, and then, for the second time in the space of ten minutes, it was time to follow this example. Having been a victim of a set-up breakdown, complicated by surveillance and followed by the offer of assistance, I had become substantially more anxious, so I departed in my well-practised manner of crashing through hedges, down walkways and over fences.

When I managed to summon a black hackney cab, my distressed state was apparent, looking ragged and breathing heavily. My predicament was further complicated when I remembered that taxi firms are a favourite undercover company used by the Intelligence services, so I tried to keep conversation with the driver down to a minimum. Nearly every day in life I am reminded of this as a local Special Branch family, Houston, set up a taxi firm to deliver the neighbour's kids to school. Not being sure of the present driver's authenticity I remain an awkward customer in the face of continued questions combined with local banter, and asked to be taken to the BBC studios on the north side of the city. It was an ironic choice of destinations when you think about the misfortune that was inflicted on Jill Dando. Before abandoning the van in the hospital grounds I wisely gathered a sample from the throat of the fuel tap of the sugar that was used to contaminate the diesel using a strip of *Selotape*. Again, they had made no secret of their handiwork to the extent that it was easy to deduce that castor sugar was used, and it provided me with evidence of what I was claiming was going on. The visit to the BBC with this piece of evidence was not fruitful. I only received advice about which independent television companies to approach, but believed this would be quite futile due to the strength and resources of the parties responsible for the terror.

With an overall feeling of rejection and despair, I went back out on the streets of Glasgow and wandered here and there contemplating what other options were open to me. Finally, evening fell and I decided to make the journey home on public transport. As a precaution, I phoned home to say that I would be coming back on the train, and then would take the bus; such is the prevailing paranoia that phone calls to the house are being monitored. Only to be caught out by this measure of safety. I missed the bus that was prearranged by mere seconds in an intentional last minute grab. Now I had to decide whether to take the train in the full knowledge that they could have been forewarned by the call I had just made and, therefore, be able to mount an attack, or wait an inordinate length of time for the next bus. The assessment was that if I took the train, it would give them less time to set up such an ambush than it would if I waited for the following bus. However, I knew well that their personnel could easily cover both options. So I felt that the only safe options were to get a car home or by making a trick call and then run and jump on the bus as proposed. Weary after a full day trekking about in adverse conditions, I chose the quickest option of the train journey because this could provide some entertainment in that spirit of defiance. It might seem that I possess a death wish, but this ability to walk into these situations then return unscathed was becoming second nature.

Alert and aware of any untoward happenings, this journey always promised to be an exciting one. I intentionally sat in the middle of the train. The initial movement of the carriage from the station heralded the appearance of the ticket inspector. This was quite a surprise because having made this journey about a thousand times before, I knew that the normal routine for the guard was to start at one end of the train and gather tickets plus collect fares as he went to the other end. It was against all logic, therefore, that his first customer should be me sitting in the middle of the train. Because I hadn't purchased a ticket at the station, I bought a single to Lochwinnoch. The smallest of incidents were mentally noted knowing that the minute details would betray any underhand practices. I expected that this espionage thriller would begin with the most unlikely clue, whence number two and number three would sit directly in front of my deliberately chosen position. Accompanied on this journey by two large men, who entered the carriage in succession, as if they were together, only to separate on embarking. The first man sat diagonally ahead of me: the other sat diagonally in front of him through the open passage that contained the doors. They shared a dress code that verged on being a uniform, where both wore those brown coloured overcoats that spies and detectives always seem to wear. At the end of the Cold War if you ever wondered what became of the protagonists, this pair of heavies were the living embodiment judging by their costume, builds and posture. My assessment was that this could develop into a potentially dangerous situation. Otherwise, I found it hilarious to think of them roaring up to the station in a twenty year old French-made car, abandoning the vehicle in the middle of the street with the doors left ajar and running into the station. This fantasy captured the essence of the scene and relieved the tension in a real and present production fraught with peril.

The train continued on its journey without any movement coming from the assumed threat until it had left Johnstone. The guard who had sold me the ticket entered the carriage again and had my undivided attention. I had suspected he was involved in the impending assault. My guess proved to be correct when he directed a nod of his head at the duo wearing the overcoats. Both of whom clearly understood this obvious signal. Suspicion was further fuelled when once he had made this signal, the guard turned on his heel and retreated back in the direction he had come in. This was a deliberate and purposeful act, and I had no other plausible answer for these actions. Originally I had believed that he was the third man in this set-up arrangement because he was tall, and feared the trio could attack at any moment. It was only after discussing this incident later that it became apparent that the railway employee had been coerced into participating.

The line is urban up to this point, passing through Glasgow, Paisley and then Johnstone. After Johnstone, it becomes a rural setting and the number of passengers aboard that night was scarce. These were ideal conditions that did not bode well for my security after the definite signal was directed at the two suspected assailants. Relieved that neither the attack happened, nor did the ticket inspector reappear as I now felt the deceleration of the train upon approach to Lochwinnoch station. What now? The definition of what was happening chimed in at the right moment as the inspiration to avoid the conflict presented itself. The principle of conjuring up outlandish answers to evade the impossible was masterful. The next addition was equally incredible as I closed both eyes and fell asleep.

The warning signs had been read correctly right from the initial concept of that telephone call home, to where the guard knew the destination of this passenger from the destination shown on the ticket he had sold. Then he attempted to convey this information in a discreet manner to the dubious duo after the penultimate station. This was clearly an instruction for them to leave the train at the next stop, to have their target follow this pair off the train without him (me) becoming suspicious. Forewarned about the imminent danger when I noticed the over obvious body language of the guard upon delivering the message. Lochwinnoch station is an isolated, unmanned platform, secluded in rural countryside, and handles very limited numbers of passengers outside of the normal rush hour. Disembarking here would present the assailants with the most ideal conditions to inflict untold injuries undisturbed, but only if I followed them out of the train.

I continued to sleep on until I heard the doors click shut and felt the movement of the train as it departed from Lochwinnoch. Only once the train had resumed its journey did I spring back to life, to find the pair of knuckleheads posing as idle passengers had gone and this relieved body allowed himself a mischievous smile.

As I carried on to the next stop at Glengarnock it was satisfying to think how infrequently trains actually use Lochwinnoch, so I knew that this pair would be stranded in the wake of this latest ingenious evasion. As strangers stand out in a close-knit community, these two would patently look even stranger when left alone for an inordinate length of time waiting at a deserted station for a return train to Glasgow. You might expect that my performance of pretending to be asleep with a stomach full of tension and pulse racing was worthy of an Oscar. Whether or not it was convincing, it really didn't take much of an effort to fool these goons.

A final quirk was the purchasing of a fraudulent ticket to mitigate these circumstances. All along my destination was going to be Glengarnock. Those ten pence I had cheated *British Rail* out of was a real lifesaver. The escape was pre-planned before the execution could ever materialise: you wonder why anyone could ever indulge in such a practice?!

The day ended when I returned home for dinner, only suffering fatigue as opposed to what could have been inflicted. As always, there sits the blue *Ford Escort* with the large aerial mounted on the roof at the top of the hill near the house, with the driver complete with obligatory blank expression. I retired to bed to consider the day's events and work out who was genuine and who was not. The first situation was the result of deliberate sabotage and resulted in the red car appearing long before the arrival of the requested biker because police bases were not far from the hospital where I had parked the van. The next event was the incident with the small white van, but I remained uncertain about the driver, as I had been caught on the hop while fleeing from the original incident. Was it a subtle, sly attempt at abduction, or was it just a driver who had got lost? He was well off the beaten track where that made him an intriguing prospect. My return home after leaving the damaged van behind entailed the most elaborate set-up with the suspicious involvement of the guard combined with the two stereotypes cast into their positions. You can only be left feeling grateful of being unscathed after such an encounter, which could easily have ended with finding myself on the railway tracks in the path of an oncoming train. Still, there is always tomorrow and more deliberately placed hazards to be endured. After this incident, when I was on the run in Fort William at the time of a political campaign trail, I came across Donald Dewar (Scottish Secretary) with one of his minders being one of the two involved, wearing the same overcoat!

THE EPITAPH

This paragraph should begin with: "Here lies the remains of ...", but instead, it is the story of the one that got away. Not a great one for literature, whereas others write their stories complete with exaggerations and fabrications to enhance their importance or bravery, selling themselves in the process. Here were the exploits of just a single day as they happened devoid of any such manipulation. The day chosen was more exciting than most compared with the mundane existence I was usually restricted to. Here there were plenty of escapades to thrill encumbered with an incident to include the employers of Jill Dando. The affronts and aggression subjected to were a regular occurrence with plenty of other examples, which have not been submitted. Those who remain in awe at my continued survival should remember that these were the details of just a twenty-hour period.

'Why are you still alive?' is the common question that mystifies many. It obviously had an extraordinary answer by continually evading seemingly impossible traps. The lack of success achieved by attempting to curtail one person would slowly demoralise the culprits, raising the profile of the target until it was felt to be pointless to try and launch another attack. In consideration of the very limited injustices sustained, the whole episode, lasting for years on end, could be put into perspective by one word on their behalf - failure.

Then after the newspaper story appeared it may not save my life in the expected way, but it did give me some respite from the continued persecution.

When the numbers deployed that particular day are counted up, plus the ones behind the scenes, you rapidly realize that this exercise to eliminate one civilian must be costing the taxpayer a daily fortune. The multi-million pound expenditure to persecute an innocent man was not a consideration, as those in a position to squander public money freely did so to keep their own pet project of oppression in existence. The other side of this equation is how expensive it would be to them in terms of rightful dismissals and substantial prison sentences. You can surmise that no resource will be spared in this objective. With such a set of manifestly corrupt circumstances, the desperation on their part becomes evident. So determined are they to accomplish the concealment of their atrocities that no measure would be too extreme and the future safety of Jill Dando gave great concern.

The SAS motto: 'Who Dares Wins' was precisely how survival was maintained with a new proponent prepared to exercise this principle,

⸺ when faced with the men in black, whoever they were. Not for glory, only so damned there was nothing left for me to lose.

6. CONUNDRUM AND SIMILES

THE FATAL DAY

On the morning of Monday 26th April 1999, Britain's most popular television personality, Jill Dando was shot dead on her own doorstep. It was a crime that was as inexplicable as it was shocking to the nation when the news emanated from Fulham in London. Everyone was confounded by the apparent lack of any viable motive for the killing in circumstances that were surreal, like the plot of some dreadful television movie. Live news coverage of the crime attempted and failed to convey the tragedy in the context it deserved. Those involved had experienced other settings of this nature. They had covered an even higher profile death, which remains fresh in the memory, when Princess Diana was fatally injured in the Paris car crash. But, this incident was complicated by the fact that Jill Dando shared the same profession and, therefore, was personally known to many of those who now had the terrible duty of publicising her murder. It was a state of affairs so incongruous and encumbered with disbelief that the reality of it could never be sincerely expressed.

She was arguably the best loved television presenter ever to grace our screens. Gone was an icon who bridged the barriers of society and who possessed a universal appeal to men and women alike, regardless of status, wealth, religion, age or race. These are rare attributes in the entertainment industry, which is better known for its offbeat characters, who in their egotistical ways, continually manipulate their own prestige in a pretentious ratings game. The values that Jill Dando exuded were genuinely pleasant to everyone. She was an English rose both on and off the screen. In contrast to this old fashioned portrayal, here was a modern woman at the pinnacle of a successful career who had never lost the schoolgirl charm that endeared her to so many. The missing piece to the social dimension in her life was soon to be fulfilled by her forthcoming marriage to fiancé Alan Farthing, which would now sadly remain an unfulfilled dream. What especially made this crime so much of an affront to moral values was that she was the caricature of an ordinary individual. We assume that such a murder does not happen to decent law-abiding citizens. It was almost as if a nation's code of ethics had died with her. The subsequent investigation could not leave any stone unturned in the hunt for the killer in order to restore a measure of humanity back into society. At the end of the second millennium, how could this murder of a national icon occur with the possibility that the killer would never be convicted? Had standards of public service really deteriorated to such an extent?

Gowan Avenue was a street that, until then, had remained isolated from violent crime in comparison to the ghettos that exist elsewhere in London. Now residing with her boyfriend, the property on Gowan Avenue had been recently sold, with her only making sporadic returns to collect mail. It was with this purpose that she arrived there at 11.30 on that final Monday morning in her *BMW* car, presenting to the world the appearance of someone enjoying a comfortable existence. It was a lifestyle that was bereft of the vulgar excesses of wealth or the need to attract attention, which is all too often exhibited by other celebrities. It was an understated and mundane property that any successful professional could have owned and occupied in identical circumstances, where nothing set her existence apart from any other ordinary person. However, this hitherto tranquil existence was to be destroyed in a horrific manner. The assumption that such a haphazard series of visits would make any planned incident a remote possibility was proven wrong that fatal day by one of the biggest crimes of the century.

Gowan Avenue was busy with parked cars that morning, but she managed to park in a convenient space in front of Number 29, with the distance to the front door only a matter of metres away. A distance never to be accomplished! She was fatally shot through the side of the head by a single bullet on the front doorstep. There were no witnesses to the incident itself and nobody heard the gunshot. The only noise apparent was a shriek let out by Miss Dando. The best eyewitness evidence from initial investigations was that of a tall, heavy-set man wearing a wax cotton jacket seen hastily leaving the murder scene shortly afterwards. Then a second suspicious character was sighted at a nearby bus stop at a time that corresponded with the incident. He was dressed in a suit and was sweating profusely. The third piece of evidence that followed Miss Dando's dying scream was the sighting of a blue *Range Rover* speeding away from the area, but there were a very limited number of actual clues to the murder itself for detectives to work on.

What was eerily disturbing about this murder was that in late morning in a well-populated suburban street in London, Britain's favourite daughter could be slain without any hint of interference from friends, neighbours or passers-by. Where was the executioner's noisy motorcycle or stolen car screeching away after the deed? Why did the sound of the gunshot not ring out along the terrace of houses? The dying scream was heard, so, even with the use of a silencer on the gun, surely a muffled shot and rush of air would have been detectable. Yet, no one ever claimed to have heard such a noise. Why should someone in the prime of a glittering television career be killed for no apparent reason? Where was the distraction that allowed the murderer to operate by stealth? Surprisingly, there were no adverse weather conditions to give him cover, nor were there any momentous occasions commanding a large television audience or any spectacular events taking place in the neighbourhood to captivate people's attention. One could scarcely believe that such a clinical execution could happen where it did, at that particular time to such a likeable person.

It was somewhat ironic that the presenter of *Crimewatch* - a television programme dedicated to solving crime - should herself become the subject of forthcoming appeals on that very programme. Being the host of this production was the second best public screening she was known for after the *Holiday* programme, in which she was shown in exotic locations around the world. To have graduated from being a journalist originally to being the focus of attention after joining the television industry and appearing in an array of popular programmes only to ultimately gain notoriety as a high-profile murder victim, murdered on her own doorstep in the most confusing and tragic manner. The sad ending to this remarkable life gained unprecedented media coverage, and the spotlight being focused upon this personality would not diminish until a presentable answer as to why this murder occurred could be found. The motive and the identity of the suspects created feverish intrigue and speculation in the media.

Jill Dando was laid to rest by her family in the town of Weston-Super-Mare, where she grew up. The funeral ceremony reflected the appeal she held for ordinary people, show-business celebrities and VIPs alike, who turned out to pay their respects and to mourn her loss. Her elderly father, brother and her fiancé were prominent among the many local people who fondly remembered the local girl who captivated television audiences of millions in the nation, and the grief they were experiencing was complicated by the countless questions that remained unanswered. Answers and who the perpetrator was, with background assistance, all existed to make sense of this modern day mystery that surpassed all fictional detective films. Only by unravelling the few clues given could the identity of the guilty party be revealed.

It was strange that in one corner of Scotland that was known for its high death rate and unsolved murders there was someone making allegations about both who the culprits were and the motive. These allegations were in total contrast to a void of evidence that was consuming the rest of the nation. Although it sounds cruel, I was not surprised by the news that had stunned Britain. It was just a predictable final insult that fitted in with the horrific terror campaign that was being conducted. I was beyond caring and failed to express any emotion when the news broke. Afterwards, I was never sober long enough to attach any relevance to the dreadful scenario. One day, I would consider the facts and come to the same conclusion. Once the high profile investigation had released details that corresponded with who I thought to be responsible, an effort would be made to retract what was said. Unable to find any facet to contradict my assumption, the refusal to continue with these allegations was due to the momentous implications concerned, not a conflicting appraisal. Every aspect of the murder of Jill Dando held similarities with the mass murder being inflicted upon the people of the West of Scotland, where she had already played a part in this scandal. The connection was there and her death had certain unique hallmarks.

The problem was always the same as the one illustrated previously, where I, for one, did not believe that the true culprits involved in the murder of Jill Dando would ever receive their rightful life sentences in jail for this crime. Either the case would remain unsolved or an innocent person would have a wrongful custodial sentence imposed upon them to protect the guilty party or parties. Perverting the course of justice is another feature that had consistently appeared throughout this story. Was the same indignity to surface here?

MOTIVELESS

Every crime, from the most trivial to the most severe, has some reason for its happening. Random attacks do occur infrequently where the perpetrator can be venting their anger because of another set of circumstances, or a mentally disturbed person has attacked for their own misguided gratification. The difference between these sporadic random attacks and the attack on the likes of Jill Dando is that they don't have a pre-planned agenda and are not directed at a pre-designated victim. An assailant is certainly not going to be holding the choice weapon to injure their victim. Alternatively, the opportunist assailant stumbles upon a situation intended as a future accomplishment, and capitalises on whatever is presented. This type of crime is exceedingly difficult to solve.

As a general rule, the bigger the crime, the greater is the gain with a motive increasing in parallel, as does the punishment. With the exception of the murder of a member of the Royal Family or the Prime Minister, few were held in greater esteem than Jill Dando, hence the illusive motive had to be substantial. Likewise, the numbers prepared to accept such an assignment are few and far between due to the greater prospect of being caught. The ensuing investigation was always going to be enormous in terms of manpower and resources deployed in a relentless attempt to track down the culprit in comparison to someone less well known.

The basic fact that no realistic motive was established at the outset of the investigation was out of alignment with the magnitude of the crime. A blatant reason was always suspected to give the detectives involved a clear line of inquiry to follow and enable them to eliminate the countless suspects in the process. Without a clear motive, the frustratingly laborious task of considering all the aspects and acquaintances in Jill Dando's life was embarked upon, thereby increasing the investigation team's workload. This anomaly was inconceivable with the circumstances that consistently defied the accepted form.

The dangerous assumption that such a crime does not happen to nice people could not be further from the truth here. But, finding a reason for this execution became a problem. Were any of the three common motives for a murder - money, jealousy or revenge - appropriate? Jill Dando was a successful woman with substantial financial savings from a long and distinguished career, but she had not written a will by which this money could be dispensed in the event of her death. Therefore, there were no direct beneficiaries who could be accused of plotting this murder in order to benefit from this windfall. After the deduction of inheritance tax, the money would be received by her family, who all cherished her existence. Hiring a professional hit-man to carry out a contract killing would have been a particularly expensive business here when you take into consideration the celebrity of the intended target. The price would have been extortionate. Therefore, with no apparent profit to be gained from such enormous expenditure, it seems that personal financial gain was not a viable contender for the motive.

This brings us to consider jealousy in its many forms as a motive. Could it be that Miss Dando's intended marriage to Alan Farthing was the catalyst that drove a jilted former lover to carry out this murder? It was well known that wedding plans were at an advanced stage and this third party, if he was the jealous type, could be so incensed by the news that he would do his best to wreck these plans by any foul means possible. But, surely this possibility would have been noted by the engaged couple and measures taken to prevent him invading their privacy. The fact that Miss Dando's property in Gowan Avenue was now empty because she was living at her fiancé's residence greatly reduces this possibility. Only someone of a seriously deranged personality, who existed in a fantasy world with no personal contact with the lady, could take the announcement of the forthcoming wedding as an affront to his devotion. It is hardly viable that such a person could undertake and accomplish this specialist killing in such a professional manner or that such a mentally deranged person could elude the attentions of the authorities. It is true to say that famous people are despised for their power, wealth and status, but in these cases envious parties are only likely to indulge in minor anti-social acts. It is unlikely that such petty nonsense is going to include murder. Jill Dando was not a person to flaunt her wealth status and power in a manner that would infuriate such small-minded people.

The much heralded other theory concerning jealousy adhered more to inventive journalism than it ever did to it being a realistic motive. The inventive journalism being referring to was the exposure of Jill Dando shortly before her death on the front cover of the *Radio Times* magazine wearing a shiny black jump-suit. One reporter had noticed the lady was wearing a costume that was a departure from the sensible skirts, blouses or trousers she usually wore, and then proceeded to make an issue out of this new dress code. Others jumped on the bandwagon and regurgitated this story in the only way that those members of the gutter Press who are incapable of segregating fiction from reality can. The articles suggested that the new costume was provocative in a sexually explicit way, and were written in such a way that this could provoke the thoughts of an unbalanced mind of a violent psychopath. When we think of black

PVC, or leather, it holds connotations that are, more often than not, associated with pornography and fetishism and it was depicted that Miss Dando was wearing such a jump-suit with this purpose in mind. Only, what was actually shown was a garment of amusement not undone to be sexually stimulating, thereby lowering the tone of the lady's otherwise immaculate credentials. In a day and age when the more outrageous female stars of the entertainment world wear see-through dresses and minimal underwear, Jill Dando's black jump-suit was so subdued in comparison this should never have been made into a prospect. Such desperation on the part of the media to produce articles presenting possible motives summarises the dearth of acceptable proposals that were available.

With money and jealousy shown to be unlikely motives, the third common alternative is revenge. This case cannot be considered in the literal sense as an eye-for-an-eye killing, as Miss Dando had not been directly involved in someone else's murder. However, as presenter of the crime-busting programme *Crimewatch*, she indirectly contributed to the jailing of criminals. The unusual preconception arose after her death, where this obvious setting targeting criminals, was not what gained the immediate focus. It was as if the public's attention was being deliberately diverted. It would take a distraction of substantial proportions to plant the thought that this high profile murder was not related to the crime-solving programme, which regularly featured serious crimes, including murder. This came in the guise of an allegation that Miss Dando had somehow been the victim of a Serbian terrorist reprisal. After all, NATO had been responsible for considerable devastation in the Balkans conflict, which was going on at the time with the RAF playing a full and leading part in these military operations. The television station in Belgrade was heavily bombed and many innocent lives lost. Jill Dando had also fronted a television appeal to raise funds to help Kosovar refugees. But both of these events could only be considered as very oblique reasons for a retaliatory attack on the British television presenter. Something nestled uncomfortably with me about this situation; it was as if you were being told to look this way, not that way. Focus on the war in Eastern Europe, which was being highlighted, and not the feasible connection to the *Crimewatch* programme. There were lingering undertones that suggested that concerted efforts were being made to increase public intrigue and to diminish the *Crimewatch* angle...

There was plenty of scope for revenge in connection to the *Crimewatch* programme. Countless convictions had been achieved by the police in serious criminal cases as a result of appeals featured on this programme. Many crimes that had seemed unlikely to be solved when conventional methods of detection had been exhausted were cleared up as a direct result of evidence raised by reconstructions shown on *Crimewatch*. Fugitives were also targeted, with photographs of people wanted by the police being shown in a Rogues Gallery. This ensured that these individuals were exposed to a vast audience further afield than that of their own locality. Did an arrest arise from the show because Jill Dando was personally involved in broadcasting the case? This is very unlikely because the individual who received the prison sentence would still be detained at the time of her murder, because she had only presented the programme for a period of two years. Accomplices could have acted on behalf of the person who had been imprisoned, but with all the cases documented, those in detentions are well known, as are their associates. So that reduces the probability. Co-presenter, Nick Ross, further played down the theory of retaliation. He commented that such a scenario was unlikely because of past history. Professional judgement of the dangers posed was that the informants who call into the show are in the greatest danger of being caught up in reprisals and not a harmless woman who is simply reciting what is on the auto-cue. A replacement will always be found, but what set Jill Dando apart from the other staff enough to have her killed?

The lack of a motive has always hindered this investigation into an incident where a woman with no apparent enemies was shot dead, again, for no apparent reason. A diversity of motives were presented, including mistaken identity, but once again none seemed to hold that crucial element for a killer to embark upon this assault. Whatever the real reason for the killing was, it certainly surpassed all these incumbent suggestions. The truth would only be revealed once the motive was found. In the meantime, one alternative after another was put forward, considered and then dismissed. This was neither professional, nor reassuring, and it seemed that the real reason would never be disclosed.

A MICKEY MOUSE JOB

From the beginning; here was a killer who was not seen on approach, shooting the woman dead with a technique not divulged in mainstream literature, without any witnesses to the act that late spring morning. The assailant had access to both a handgun and ammunition. The best clue to finding the culprit lay in the single spent cartridge that was found at the scene. Interestingly, the cartridge had unique markings. Jill Dando was shot behind the left ear with a single bullet from a silent gun. After a slight scream, suspects were seen vacating the area on foot and a blue *Range Rover* was also seen hastily leaving the area.

Sometimes an exercise becomes too professional, or too clinical, thus placing it out with the reach of ordinary people no matter how well acquainted they are with the subject. Glasgow's prostitute murders were such an example of this, where few people originally thought it to be anything more than a drunken struggle or an unfortunate clash of personalities culminating in an assault. Once the number of deaths increased with the majority of the victims dying by the specialised technique of strangulation, where the killer(s) can gaily waltz undetected under the gaze of security cameras, plus a multitude of other suspicious deaths in Strathclyde, only then was it considered unbelievable that the perpetrators could be ordinary people acting on aggression.

When the details of Jill Dando's murder were assessed by other underworld gunmen, the only description applied to attempt to belittle what happened was '*a Mickey Mouse job*'. An absence of a fast getaway vehicle, the lack of a disguise on the various suspects seen leaving the vicinity, and the fact that only one shot was fired at the victim didn't match the practised method favoured by gangland hit-men. Contrary to this appraisal, the mission was successful. Asking convicted murderers their opinion of the crime can give an unbiased opinion. However, this does not constitute scientific fact. Was this shooting too professional, that others involved in this type of crime were fooled into thinking that it was the work of an amateur? Drug-related feuds are a present day source of first time would-be assassins, where the incidents are more hit-and-hope and involve firing salvos of bullets in the general direction of the target, rather than examples of precision killing that this case evidently was. Youths participate in violent street clashes: here the suspects were middle-aged men. The difference between the nervous inexperienced hit-man and this particular killer fitted with the next revelation that was disclosed: namely that the gun muzzle was placed against Jill Dando's head before the trigger was pulled. Those who referred to this killing in a derisory manner were completely deluded. Anyone could see that this assassination could be placed in an exceptional category. Further analysis of the few details available will wholeheartedly vindicate this appraisal. When this is accepted, the candidates for this crime are very limited in number.

The absurd circumstances where nobody heard a gunshot had other aspects to be considered apart from the format of the attack and the fact that the bullet used was tampered with. The gun used in the killing was also modified. Gun barrels conventionally have what is called rifling - these take the form of a spiral of grooves running the length of the gun-barrel. These grooves impart rotational forces onto the bullet as it travels along the barrel, which gives it the characteristic spin in flight once it leaves the gun and enables it to fly accurately to the target. The murder weapon was a short-barrelled handgun that had been modified by honing off these grooves, reducing the accuracy of the weapon and, thereby, requiring the assailant to fire the gun at close range. The killer obviously believed these modifications held some advantage. So, what was it? The rifling on the inside of the gun barrel creates drag: an absence of this drag meant that less gunpowder was required to propel the bullet for the same amount of force.

Like the gun, the cartridge was also found on direct inspection of the evidence to have been modified. The bullet casing had no markings left by the rifling because the rifling had been removed, although intriguingly there were also six tiny indentations around the mouth of the cartridge, which some people wrongly speculated to be the signature of the killer. A reduction in the charge used could correspond with the reduction in friction with the gun barrel to propel a bullet with the same force. But these indentations are not compulsory when the shell was separated to remove some of the gunpowder and then have the two pieces pressed back together. So if the reassembled bullet did not require these six tiny punch marks, what relevance did they have?

A highly specialised ballistics technique exists here, which requires an explanation. Whether or not you have watched a cartoon, spaghetti western or any sort of adventure film, the scene where they are about to rob a bank or free a captive from prison is familiar. Picture the scene: a barrel of gunpowder is placed against the wall of the building with a trail of explosive powder leading out from the keg. The characters in the film then light the end of the line and watch it burn along to the supply detonating a massive explosion. This is all fictional and done with special effects, but the principle remains the same. In reality, the gunpowder on the ground would burn at an immensely faster rate along the line creating a trench in the dust, with the time between being lit and the detonation being the blink of an eye. The charge used to fire a bullet is exactly like the fictional trail of gunpowder. When the hammer on the gun detonates the gunpowder inside the cartridge, the amount doesn't light simultaneously. In a process measured in milliseconds, the initial spark at the centre of the cartridge has a flame front radiating outwards to burn all the charge. With a bullet like the one described that has been separated from its cartridge to be reprocessed, the fit of the two pieces will be looser than it was originally. A shell that has not been tampered with is blasted out before the complete charge is burnt. Whereas a shell that has been tampered with leads to a further reduction in the ultimate pressure propelling the bullet, because the bullet leaves the cartridge fractionally earlier than the standard one making the shot less dangerous. However, there is an ingenious method of alleviating this loss of efficiency, which can achieve maximum force from a reduced amount of explosive charge. By crimping the two components together to increase the adhesion you can prevent the early release of the shell until the pressure behind it has reached its optimum force, thereby enabling the shell to be fired off at an abnormal velocity but with the minimum of noise. This is known to be a dangerous procedure because if the securing of the elements is overdone, the user can be injured if the firearm malfunctions. The process allows a further reduction in the amount of charge used to be a bare minimum when combined with the modification of the gun-barrel.

The six tiny indentations on the casing that was found at the murder scene outside Jill Dando's house are an accurate example of this technique. It also suggests that the killing was not carried out by your ordinary gangland hit-man because of the level of professionalism required to doctor the weapon and bullet. The fact that the victim was shot behind the left ear with a unique weapon and doctored ammunition showed the assailant was a ballistics expert. The human skull is a substantial and impenetrable structure designed to deflect blows and protect the brain. However, it does have an area of weakness behind both ears, where it is soft and unprotected, which was ruthlessly exploited in this murder. This implies that the assailant knew about this defenceless area of the anatomy of the head when he was administering the fatal shot. Jill Dando was held by the upper arm as the end of the gun barrel was pressed into the flesh at the exact chosen spot to provide a complete seal, so that no noise was heard. Flesh and brain tissue acted as a silencer for the gun to absorb the remaining reduced noise from the bullet. It sounds morbid in the extreme how such a level of technology could apply itself to the killing of such a pleasant soul. How many times was the final role rehearsed with a mock up of the lady about to enter the house to achieve the immaculate timing and precision required?

Who was involved in the actual conspiracy to conduct this crime? Full access to illegally held firearms was acquired for the selection of what is not a common short barrelled handgun, combined with engineering facilities to carry out the modifications. Knowledge of ballistics was required to alter the weapon to specification. The bullet demanded an even greater degree of expertise to be remanufactured into an unknown quantity unless previous ground trials of this technique had been conducted elsewhere. The craftsmanship on display was exquisite as, unfortunately, was the fatal result. The problem is, only experienced gun enthusiasts, university educated ballistics experts and well trained military personnel are the only categories that would know about and have access to such techniques. But, who had the opportunity to practise such an ill-conceived experiment? The delivery was flawless suggesting that both training and experience in a unique set of circumstances had been brought to bear, with the main suspect being of a suitable age to have committed other such murders. Knowledge of the human anatomy was required to know the exact area to shoot and to know that brain tissue could be utilised as a silencer for the gun. In order to familiarise the assassin with the setting, a person of Jill Dando's build would be required for rehearsing the execution. Finally, the most overlooked aspect was the acoustics involved in this silent kill. The task of estimating the quota of gunpowder left in the cartridge in order to achieve the desired amount of force while reducing the noise to a bare minimum is a science that few could indulge in. Using someone's brain to eliminate the remaining sound becomes a black art unto itself. If this was shown on television as part of an espionage thriller, people would switch off their sets in disbelief.

In addition to a professional killer, here we have a firearms supplier, an engineer, a ballistics expert, a researcher, a technician, a craftsman, a medical expert, an acoustics genius and an acting cast of proxy victims, or failing that, a tailor's dummy. You would be a bigger dummy if you believe all this to be one and the same person. When one of the most intricate crimes ever committed was belittled by describing it as a '*Mickey Mouse job*', you soon realise the magnitude of this was out of the scope of everyone other than the most professional of assassins. The options left in this murder are incredibly scarce when considering realistic suspects. Who were these specialists in killing and where are they hiding? Whose idea was it to confuse the issue by publicising a statement that made it sound as though any thug could have executed this celebrity in a fit of temper, regardless of the detailed planning that was evident?

If both the motive and the method are perceived to be distorted in any way, soon a sceptical public will include the word 'conspiracy' to the eventual outcome. The benefits of never revealing the ingenious compliance had to outweigh the disadvantages, but, who were the beneficiaries of not publicising this?

SUSPECTS INCORPORATED

This momentous crime that offended so many people causing such widespread revulsion was always going to be debated and become the topic of conversation then referred to for comment. Whatever questionable motives were presented could be dismissed with a conflicting opinion or rejected with a general air of anticipation as to the real reason for this untimely death. The enormity of what happened required the obscure motive to be equally as large. On the surface, the blunders of a novice fumbling about on their first assignment was dispersed once the episode came under closer scrutiny, concluding in the masterful accomplishment of a specialist utilising techniques very few knew about, let alone practised or executed. As for suspects, a few, albeit limited in number, did present themselves in the vicinity of this unorthodox crime, although what distinction they came under remains a mystery. The motive may have been concealed, the method of killing was unique, but certain individuals became apparent for consideration.

The first suspicious character became known as the 'sweating man' due to his appearance. In the minutes after Jill Dando made that telling scream, this gentleman was witnessed running through the traffic on the adjacent Fulham Palace Road towards the park. The incident took place on Gowan Avenue, which begins at the junction of this road and finishes at Munster Road. Then a man, who is assumed to be the same person, was sighted talking on a mobile phone by the park railings. The last and close up emergence of this suspect was somebody dressed in a dark suit standing at the bus stop on Fulham Palace Road. He inadvertently attracted attention to himself by the fact that he was sweating profusely. His erratic behaviour was exemplified by the fact that he did not board the first bus that came along, but waited for a second one. Plenty of witnesses had the opportunity to see this perspiring man. The man standing next to him in the queue described him as having the bearing of a policeman due to his manner. On the bus this suspect did take, he is then believed to have disembarked at Putney Bridge tube station, after which his final destination was never determined. A photo-fit was compiled and released four days after the incident to see if anyone recognised this suspect.

One of the most interesting quirks to materialise in this increasingly baffling case was the certain likeness the photo-fit held to Jill Dando's fiancé, Alan Farthing. Only the markings on the brow of the nose differed as if the man at the bus stop that fatal morning normally wore spectacles in everyday life. Whether this was by accident or design or not, this uncomfortable coincidence could only increase or complicate the suffering being experienced by the bereaved partner. To have lost the woman he loved and then, being a close acquaintance, to come under suspicion from the police investigation because of this perceived similarity.

The second suspect was possibly the most important because he is, in all likelihood, the killer seen leaving the murder scene seconds after the dying scream was uttered. But the photo-fit issued for public consumption did not depict this man, believed to be the meticulous assassin, because the descriptions gleaned from the limited sightings of him differed from the description of the man seen sweating at the bus stop, thereby, dispelling this possibility. It was simply another misleading anomaly that was to complement the previous diversions included in the procedures of this high profile investigation.

When Miss Dando arrived at 29 Gowan Avenue, she parked her car outside the house, and then set the distinctive car alarm. In the process of entering the property an assailant caught her by surprise with his assault because, presumably, he was hidden behind the small garden wall or in some other area of concealment. A single shot with an instantaneous scream accomplished the fatal result. The disturbance was reduced by the fact that the victim was held by the upper arm, so that she didn't crash to the ground. The noises heard were the setting of the vehicle alarm, then the scream and finished with the latch on the gate clicking shut. There was no noise of either the gunshot or the victim clattering to the ground. In his complete confidence, the perpetrator even had the audacity to close the garden gate behind him, leaving the lady lying dead on her own doorstep. To the casual observer, the scene outside the house was undisturbed.

In the passing seconds after the scream, two eyewitnesses saw the main suspect leave the area of the crime. Within a few steps, the suspect turned and looked back as if to say goodbye. Was this over-confidence, defiance, arrogance, or was he simply checking to see that the victim had not recovered from the injury inflicted. Another deviation on this theme is a programmed body following orders, making certain that the instructions were carried out, including the unusual action of closing the gate. He was described as being five foot nine inches tall with dark hair and wearing a three-quarter length Barbour type jacket. His heavy powerful build fitted with the lady being overpowered in the swift operation that killed her. A next door neighbour gave a telling account when his judgement said that the bearing of the suspect resembled that of an ex-SAS member rather than a criminal gunman. The military connection, in vague terms, to this crime is inconclusive until a motive is determined where the paymaster's association to the executioner is established. Any terrorist grouping, criminal gang or others unknown could have hired a freelance mercenary to do their dirty work, or failing that, this suspect had his own agenda in killing Jill Dando. Reported as being in possession of a mobile phone, which is becoming a clear mode of communication on the day, therefore, the fact that he was in contact with someone eliminates all the solitary motives and suspects, such as a crazed loner, or a celebrity stalker.

The blue *Range Rover* that was in the vicinity long before the incident, which then left hurriedly after the event, revealingly, had at least one occupant other than the driver. This is not the favoured transport of the criminal fraternity out on a hit, and is also at odds with the working class roots of terrorists. It is more in keeping with members of high society displaying a patriotic allegiance. Aside from who should be the driver of the *Range Rover*, it did however blend into the surroundings in that part of London had it not been illegally parked outside her house. Forty minutes before the murder, a traffic warden attempted to issue a ticket for the offending vehicle only to be surprised by a hidden occupant who tapped the inside of the window to warn off the inspector. It is suspicious behaviour that someone should be hidden inside their own vehicle, especially here, where they could be carrying out reconnaissance for the forthcoming murder. The vehicle was reported after the incident with the traffic warden as travelling at high speed in an erratic manner as though this encounter had agitated the driver. An amount of determination and commitment is observed if a corresponding vehicle was the same one in the previous confrontation now fleeing the scene after the murder. The *Range Rover* seen speeding along Fulham Palace Road was caught on a roadside camera, but it was not possible to discern a registration number from the blurred photograph. It is difficult to believe that this *Range Rover*, with the suspicious actions of its occupants, its positioning and the time it was seen, with the erratic manner it was being driven after the murder, was not directly involved in the crime.

Apart from these two main suspects and a vehicle that was also potentially involved, an abundance of other characters were reported, some of which, rather confusingly, could be duplicates of one another. Before the crime took place, a man resembling an estate agent was seen to be watching the house. The property was recently sold, therefore such a person would not attract attention from the neighbours. Another suspect, who could have been acting as a lookout, was reported at the end of Gowan Avenue on the junction with Munster Road, although the majority of activity reported took place at the other end of the avenue, where other lookouts, possible accomplices and suspects were seen running down Fulham Palace Road. One witness gave an extraordinary account of seeing someone who resembled the suspect on Gowan Avenue jumping over railings into the River Thames. From all this one development in the investigation did lead to a suspect being interviewed. He had hurriedly fled from the park after the threat of being approached by another man for homosexual sex. He was later released once an explanation was heard.

An array of suspicious bodies at or around the crime scene, before and after the incident, had to come under some classification because the list was diverse. Criminals targeted by the *Crimewatch* programme were a favourite with East End of London gangsters in particular being set apart for increased attention. Only, the most professional criminal could not be party to this crime as the subsequent investigation would focus acutely on their activities and associates. Even if they could not be convicted for this crime, their

other wrongdoings would be unearthed, thereby, substantially damaging their illegal empire. A rogue Serbian terrorist had limited reason to be included in the list of suspects, but the possibility of this was dismissed by Serbian community leaders who rightly said that they were also appalled by this crime. Other terrorist groups had little or no reason to attack the celebrity. The bizarre prospect of the killer being a loner, infuriated, having his fixation on Jill Dando destroyed by the celebrity's forthcoming marriage also failed to hold credence with the multiples of suspects apparent on the fatal morning. When all the main suspects were eliminated from the inquiry, another fanciful alternative emerged. A story was reported that a Russian gangster had hired IRA hit-men to execute the entertainment personality. There was something surreal remaining about this that said, 'if you cannot find the culprits, why not just confuse the issue, deliberately mislead the public and, in the process, protect the guilty?'
Who dreams up this nonsense and to whose benefit was it done?

A few days short of the first anniversary of Jill Dando's murder, a second appeal was reconstructed for *Crimewatch*, which, interestingly enough, had a preset agenda to channel people's thoughts to one possibility as to who the perpetrator might be. The theory that was presented was that the murder suspect was a loner wearing a trilby hat who had been seen on two Mondays prior to the crime. A series of sightings had produced the wanted character contrary to the background of conflicting descriptions by various witnesses. Your guess is as good as mine as to how this conclusion was arrived at.

The selective knowledge and highly specialised techniques were never publicly divulged, where it is impossible to imagine these practices had evaded the investigation team with its massive budget and many sources to draw from. It is also too convenient to eliminate the accounts of witnesses, evidence found, the inside information required, the preparation and the unique techniques to give such a streamlined version that this could be the work of one man. On the second appeal, which did lead to the arrest and detention of an individual, why was there a need to dismiss 'wild conspiracy theories'? Then the most unlikely classification of suspect was the one processed conflicting with the situation?!

SANCTIONED OR SACRIFICED

Initially progress was slow in the painstaking investigation to achieve any kind of result. Why then was it not possible to start asking the Glasgow question not about who committed the crime, but who was covering it up? Taking a different perspective could only be helpful in circumnavigating the dearth of options on offer. Why was it also taboo to start considering government agencies and the military for possible involvement? The European Convention for Human Rights gave a greater emphasis on free speech, which can rightfully be exercised.

Here was a massive crime of such national importance that few realistic suspects would ever consider participating in it. It was a crime where the murder weapon was described as a 'James Bond gun' by an eager Press corps determined to provide fitting descriptions to make up for the shortage of subjects to comment on. The obvious connection to a spy thriller was contained in the phrase. It was a scenario where the first suspect, the 'sweating man', possessed the attributes likening him to a policeman, and the second character seen leaving the house at the time of the murder was described as being an ex-SAS man. The specialist ballistics techniques used in doctoring the bullet and modifying the gun with the objective of murder, the stealth with which the lady was executed all aligned themselves to an espionage dimension. The final piece in the jigsaw was the blue *Range Rover* that cried out, 'buy British' by its existence, plus, again, hinted at military involvement.

At face value, here is a patriotic element with a police and/or a military connection, supplied with information and a firearm uniquely associated with spies. All the evidence points one way: towards the British Security Services as suspects, whether they are Special Branch, MI5 or MI6, in association with the armed forces. None of them are above suspicion, where discussing their potential appears to be sidestepped, as though they were above criticism. Then at the second appeal on *Crimewatch*, a concerted effort was made to discount any thoughts in these quarters with the ridiculing phrase of 'wild conspiracy theories'. Why attempt to curtail such speculation in this very deliberate manner unless there was a need to do so? After all, the public was being told which category of suspect was, in their opinion, the most likely candidate. Once primed, an arrest followed in this vein. Maybe it was too convenient, because after all, the women in Strathclyde were the first victims in this gruesome story. Was it time to think the unthinkable?

THE LIE ACCUMULATOR

With reference to the *Crimewatch* programme, the source of contention concerning Jill Dando was the double murder of Lin and Megan Russell. Did serious manipulation of a criminally corrupt nature occur with regards to this crime? Her involvement began with the second reconstruction shown in the BBC studio, when the ridiculous film had the car change colour during the screening. All the implications this crime held in relation to myself, the massacre being committed in Strathclyde, and the further suspicion that the genuine perpetrator was being shielded from justice duly gave reason to conceal any misgivings presented. An arrest did follow which resulted in the conviction of Michael Stone after a key prosecution witness, who was a fellow convict in a marginal case, testified against the accused. The witness, Barry Thomson, later retracted his statement by publicly admitting that he had perjured himself. The awkward confession was broadcast in the national Press (*The Mirror*) at the end of October 1998 to the detriment of the conviction against Stone, increasing the likelihood of a successful appeal. It was hardly a light-hearted decision to freely admit such an offence due to the substantial prison sentence he could receive. Ambiguous to this situation, other witnesses were reported to have been manipulated by other means, and then a couple of months later the final incident was played out in the BBC studios.

From time to time, the programme would reflect on past successes that had been achieved and show excerpts from other featured cases, which had been processed due to this exposure. The Russell case had part of the reconstruction shown in this manner with the questionable red coloured car in the frame. That night the script gave the impression of reaffirming the guilt of Michael Stone, contrary to the previous admission of the witness who had reneged on his testament. A problem arose when Jill Dando was charged with delivering this speech where with hesitance and reticence she finally said the words, spitting them out in an unconvincing manner after some background prompting, making an obvious gesture of defiance. Why should she? The programme is not a propaganda service to formulate opinions of others, but merely staged to try to solve crimes. The process of referring back to previous cases demonstrates the success rate in a self-congratulating way, where it is not a means of convincing the public who is guilty, as in this instance.

There was a final inclusion concerning the Russell murder case that gave a final twist to proceedings. Before the prosecution witness reneged on his statement, a telling rumour circulated with extraordinary allegations of who the culprit was, thereby supporting the suggestion that Michael Stone was innocent of this crime. This suspect, whose description related to the first reconstruction, has broad shoulders and light coloured hair. The suspicion regarding the suspected person and vehicle in the second reconstruction increased its foundation in light of such allegations. All of which hinted that the guilty party was being protected, and that the second appeal was a deliberate method of targeting myself with the buckled stance, the large car seen prior to the crime, the (changable) red *Ford Escort* and a photo-fit with photographic similarities. This, all due to Jill Dando's intervention now required a massive cover-up. Three out of three murder cases now had their shortcomings highlighted with a need to conceal the skulduggery due to all the implications included.

THE CONUNDRUM

To finalize this completely brutal story, an interesting conundrum presents itself as to how and why Jill Dando was murdered. Here it is stressed that the following passages in no way intend to apportion blame onto anyone, only to offer one possible scenario for consideration.

We begin with a motive: this being the key ingredient in any crime. The *Crimewatch* programme is the most likely source of a reason that an otherwise blameless personality should be murdered. It was not done for the conventional reason of some aggrieved person extracting revenge after receiving their comeuppance, but to prevent further exposure concerning the manipulation associated with the second reconstruction of Lin and Megan Russell. The importance of what had already been revealed emphasised the reasons as to why it came about, then was exemplified by later events, in particular, with the name of an alleged assailant known where with it his liberty, due to assisted protection, in a case unlikely ever to be solved. Only public revulsion was strong because two little girls were bludgeoned in a frenzied attack, where a conviction could alleviate these concerns. In Scotland, a mass murder campaign was occurring with government agencies being responsible where a problem arose concerning a would-be victim. Military personnel were despatched to eliminate the target only to be outflanked, then deemed unsuccessful, where after this victim could tell of their involvement. Next, the continued attempt at framing was exposed by revealing one of their specialised tactics, namely the poisoned milk. Why not marry the two problems together?

This could clear up an horrific case where the culprit was never going to be brought to justice, by framing an innocent person, and also in the process dispose of someone who had already partially revealed the ongoing terror campaign in the West of Scotland. Collate all these details together, and then apply them to the case to produce an altered reconstruction. Only after the broadcast, the presenter became perplexed by the unbelievable account, then unintentionally proceeded to underline the discrepancies. Now thanks to Jill Dando's observations and questions, it was no longer feasible to arrest the one who had been deliberately targeted. Potential suspects could be assessed with the purpose of finding another candidate to cover up this revealing state of affairs. An arrest followed where the next unfortunate soul was going to stand trial for this double murder. Meanwhile back in Scotland, someone had attempted to put a public face to the massacre being committed. The incredible answer of who would go on the record to cover up this atrocity surpassed all expectations when both Donald Dewar, the Scottish Secretary of State, and his number two, Henry McLeish became embroiled. From now on Jill Dando could never be allowed to facilitate the configuration of events. After the conviction of someone for the double Russell murder an important witness retracted his statement and cast doubt on the validity of the verdict. A means of reinforcing the perceived guilt of the man convicted for this crime was required due to the gravity of the scenario. Using the *Crimewatch* programme to convey a corresponding message, this once again happened to backfire when Jill Dando was commissioned to relay the words. The second and last time her intervention disrupted the arrangements where the stakes had continued to multiply in an escalating predicament. So how did this translate into the substantial motive required to murder one of Britain's most popular personalities?

The plan was all falling apart and starting to incriminate both government ministers and government agencies, where neither would have a pardon against the charge of murder. They could not, therefore, afford any more complications or exposure, which Jill Dando being in the public eye, broadcasting live, was in a position to do so, unyielding to their demands. The Scottish nation could soon realise how cheated and betrayed they had been by the elected Labour government. Unable to provide a satisfactory cover-up concerning what was already apparent, if justice had prevailed, both Donald Dewar and Henry McLeish would have been removed from office over the Dr Ian Oliver saga.

There is also the question of accountability concerning who is held responsible for what had been going on. Many grievous accusations remained unanswered with the termination of the Grampian Police Chief's career being another affront to justice. An original allegation was the murder of drug addicts, the only group not to be focused on. Glasgow was the source of a mysterious illness killing those who were abusing drugs, which was later reported as being based on Anthrax. The response to the situation was equally telling. First it was dismissed as an ordinary virus: it was as if an agent involved in biological warfare should be on the streets?! Then it was later denied as being Anthrax. In a news report, one woman, from *The Big Issue*, did ask what many were thinking. What was really happening in the city of Glasgow? Only to be followed by a suspicious lack of follow-up coverage. Was the truth being stifled here? Then a second outbreak of a killer virus happened in the city after this. All along, cover-ups and dishonesty were to be expected in accordance with the policy of continuing the campaign of terror hence protecting the guilty parties.

Another example was the promoted insanity I was meant to have, where the last defence in a campaign of oppression is satire, which predictably had no basis. A psychiatrist, Dr Locke, was to admit there was no mental deficiency, where it was only a test of her ability, thereby exposing another lie. However, later on I was to find medical reports had been fabricated to the contrary, but my medical reports have been known to change depending on who is going to read them and for what purpose! Few options remain in concealing the treachery. Could the events that ejected Dr Ian Oliver ever be rehashed into an acceptable account?

The next great insult was cost. The public were paying through taxes for their own murder and those of fellow citizens. One murder, for example, that of Tracey Wilde had a price consistently in the £1 million bracket for the investigation. This is a single cost in the multiples of other cases and their corresponding expenses. Even the basics such as surveillance cameras continue to be installed at great expense and negligible benefit to the public until those monitoring the film are regulated with legal obligation. Furthermore, MI5 today is, in itself, an expensive extravagance with marginal purpose, whereas back in the days of the Cold War, when they had a reason to exist, their effect was minimal. Align this to the next time a government minister claims that there is a shortage of money for the fundamentals such as housing or employment after millions of pounds have been squandered unnecessarily. How could they ever sound convincing? Such a syndrome is more acute in Scotland, which is officially the seventh richest country in the world, where it was economically impossible for Strathclyde to be in such a rundown state unless it was deliberately imposed. Plenty of examples support this view, likewise, this being the district most affected by the deliberate problems inspiring fear into a community, denying opportunities and creating oppression. The principle of manufacturing a problem to solve it is obvious here.

The last dilemma was political. Once people no longer believe the rhetoric being conveyed, as is the case gaining momentum here, or trust the official in public office, how could they possibly vote in their favour? Victims were random where the fear was that they could be next prevailed, or that of family members, friends or children. The results are obvious as Strathclyde is depopulating. People can see the derelict factories, vacant housing schemes and hear the news reports of increasing numbers of deaths to conflict with the hypocrisy of what they try to relay in the media. As individuals, it was easy to victimise people, whereas now one in particular with every incident, attack, slur, injury, insult or act of persecution only verified what was happening. The methods of discrediting him had all failed. The only question was; why was it happening to someone who had saved many lives in direct opposition to Labour and Conservative governments, who both assisted in its configuration? With few alternatives available to them, with people seeing how they had been ritually humiliated in gradual succession, they certainly did not need Jill Dando providing more complications to fracture the infrastructure. Left feeling betrayed and conned as evident by the following. The open secret that Raymond Stevenson was Tracey Wilde's killer failed to have his body exhumed to solve this crime. This was another indictment of how incriminating this really was because with it, every other crime and atrocity had the culprits known and shielded. The sham was no longer convincing, but the guilty remain free and the usual quotes of 'national security' and 'official secrets' were just another lie, like every other facet. Could any person ever vote for this and keep their integrity intact?

Now a motive unlike all those flimsy reasons that have been proposed had materialised with ample repercussions to execute Jill Dando. With a realistic possibility as to why, now it was time to consider how the murder was carried out.

On the Monday morning of the 26th April 1999, the day Jill Dando died, there were three unpredicted elements to her murder that could not be foreseen in any pre-planned attack. She had stopped unexpectedly to do some shopping once she left the new residence of her boyfriend's house. The second was the appearance of the traffic warden and the third was her dying scream. Take these three out of the equation and what have you got?

Jill Dando was, without question, under the surveillance of the Security Services with a massive scandal in Strathclyde to conceal in addition to the allegation of the culprit in the Russell murders living under protection. To portray an idea of how obsessed with secrecy this country really is, as ever a Glasgow story will assist in this perception.

Listening on the local radio one morning, I heard that the drugs counsellor had resigned on a matter of principle. At his house that same morning, I informed his wife that he would become a victim of the 'old boy network'. On my departure, just as her husband arrived home, having only driven the distance of eight houses down the street, two large *BT* vans came up the road together as though they had been pursuing him. Feeling vindicated, I only ever pondered the ludicrous situation that his admirable stance of resignation could offer no threat to the nation, yet there was the predictable harassment only seconds after I had said what would happen. As ever the question of the authenticity of these telecom engineers arises.

Where this is leading is to convey how people come under surveillance for little or no apparent reason, where Jill Dando had a certain amount of provocation to attract their ill conceived attention. They were protecting their own interests over the designated purpose of guarding the national interest with the widely acknowledged Special Branch murders in Strathclyde, plus the alleged culprit in the double murder who had plenty to support his involvement other than just hearsay. This presents an interesting proposal that Alan Farthing was the other unsuspecting victim of their evil attentions solely because Jill Dando now lived at his residence. No outsider would then have the potential to kill the lady having to evade both the couple's observations and that of an unknown protection racket operating incognito. This also throws up the interesting prospect that belies the first unpredicted movements on the fatal morning. Why did all the activity on Gowan Avenue occur thirty to forty minutes before the murder happened with agitated suspects?

Very simply, her fiancé's house was under surveillance. When the lady was seen leaving the house, a message was relayed to those at Gowan Avenue by mobile phone. Thinking that she would drive straight there, the murderer and his accomplices became apprehensive when her arrival was delayed because, unknown to them, she had gone to complete an everyday chore. Of this gaggle, the blue *Range Rover* was included. But, why was such a vehicle used? If you remember, this story begins with a burgundy *Land Rover Discovery* with a woman driver. Even once the blue circle was sighted on her lap, the other occupant wasn't readily recognisable until, with some strained peering, I distinguished his features. Passers-by are unlikely to see anyone hidden inside the blue *Range Rover* as opposed to another type of car. The *Land Rover Discovery* fitted well in the rural community of Ayrshire. The *Range Rover* is recognised as a society vehicle and was equally fitting in the affluent area surrounding Gowan Avenue. An inconspicuous means of transport would have remained so if the traffic warden had not disturbed its position where a secondary purpose was also rumbled by its removal. The large and high vehicle could disguise the sinister attack from them with the best vantage point on the other side of the street, concealing the murder as it occurred. Next door neighbours would have to come out the front door to witness the crime. This concludes in all the thought and expertise of operating professionals supplied with all the relevant information, where even the very basics like the two addresses are a problem to find for average people. The sporadic returns to the property previously owned were monitored (possibly by a bogus estate agent/s) until a pattern of consistency was found. This explains the appearance of the suspect wearing the trilby hat on the consecutive Mondays before the murder.

So now an explanation could be put to the activists seen before the killing happened with a vehicle conveniently placed. Only the unexpected stop made by the victim damaged some of the arrangement. Continuing on after the shopping expedition, both ends of Gowan Avenue had lookouts posted to give prior warning of her arrival, once again by mobile phone. After parking her car outside, Jill was then about to enter her former home when she would be surprised by an assailant.

Then came the intricate assassination with the masterful techniques very few people knew about, had access to, or had the capacity to practice to determine the effectiveness and reverberations. Modern day warfare is no longer about supplying an army with tin hats and guns. The military have turned killing people into a science with laboratories to analyse performance of weapons, diagnosis of techniques and practice operations. All the highly specialised input associated with the murder of Jill Dando corresponds with special operations carried out by the military with extremely rare viable alternatives. The Security Services have full access to the armed forces routinely providing dossiers on targets.

The third and final unpredictable element in this murder was her dying scream. With meticulous preparation reinforced by formidable intelligence, the actions of the victim during an attack can never be fully anticipated. Was this oversight the greatest flaw in the developments causing the most disruption to the detailed instructions? What if this one shriek was subtracted from the scenario? The events would then read as follows.

Jill Dando is acknowledged to have arrived at 29 Gowan Avenue: that was when the distinctive car alarm on her car was heard being set. Without the scream, the next door neighbour would have no cause to look out of his window and, therefore, would not have seen the suspect, and the second witness would only have seen a passing stranger wearing the *Barbour* type jacket, who can be later dismissed as irrelevant. Now the emphasis is on the reckless character seen running through the traffic on Fulham Palace Road. Incidentally, if Jill Dando had arrived forty minutes earlier by not going shopping, the *Range Rover* would have been conveniently parked to obstruct the view of the second eyewitness, and the killer would not have had to leave the scene on foot. These three minor deviations come together to formulate the same conclusion: that the killer operating by stealth was never meant to be seen in any way, thereby placing the full burden of suspicion on the other character making a nuisance of himself on Fulham Palace Road. Why transfer the blame in a regimented procedure? Again a Glasgow tirade could provide the answer. The photo-fit made up from the description of the suspect at the bus stop on Fulham Palace Road was published in a newspaper beside that of a photograph of Alan Farthing. Incredibly, there were such striking similarities between the two that I exclaimed, "This reminds me of Charles McGregor!"

He was the man who was tried for the murder of his wife, who happened to be one of Glasgow's murdered prostitutes, and then found dead three days before I stood trial in Greenock for that infamous minor traffic offence. The importance of this rested with the alleged murderer being a Special Branch agent and the man standing trial for the crime to cover up the real culprit, preoccupied by thoughts of self-preservation, was unable to see why this second injustice was occurring. Someone out there was attempting to not only eliminate Jill Dando, but also her future husband. Someone was trying very hard to frame Alan Farthing for Jill Dando's murder! The crime then would only have one suspect where a motive was already in place to match the circumstances. This came in the configuration of James Dando. This fictitious character, sharing the same surname, had emerged three months before her murder, albeit only existing at the other end of a telephone line, attempting to pay utility company bills on behalf of Jill Dando. Alarmingly he knew intimate details about the lady including her ex-directory telephone number, which was suspected of being tapped by the Secret Service. The question is; why did he materialise displaying bizarre behaviour? Very simply it provided a motive with the potential for Dr Alan Farthing to murder his girlfriend. Not being a known relative, James Dando could be construed as a secret lover using the surname as a pseudonym, paying these bills as a gesture of kindness. Now with two men being rivals in love, this could give the incentive to kill, especially here with the high profile wedding that was planned, leaving Dr Alan Farthing the object of much ridicule if it were to be cancelled because of this intrusion. The devil is in the detail where this fictitious person had to know enough personal details about Jill Dando in order to sound convincing. This is something that is outside the scope of any ordinary member of the public. As for the timing of James Dando emerging, again it corresponded with the second incident exposing the corruption associated with the Russell murders shown on BBC television. His final contact six days before her murder guaranteed this presence would feature in the investigation.

So like Charles McGregor in Glasgow, again disposing of a close confidant who could already know some of the background regarding the incidents that had occurred in the BBC studios. The beneficiaries of such a catastrophe were only those involved in the murder needing both partners eradicated and an obnoxious crime cleared up in the process. This eliminates the possibilities of Jill Dando being killed for financial gain, revenge, jealousy or publicity. As ever, the only suspects with the potential to conduct and gain from the situation are neither criminal related nor terrorist inspired, leaving the Intelligence community as prime suspects. No; you don't think so? However, the more it is examined, the more likely this scenario becomes.

The term 'James Bond gun' was used as a description of the size of the gun, not for the fact that it fired a silent bullet to fulfil the intended purpose. The *Range Rover* did have a hidden occupant, who was disturbed by the traffic warden, and was then reported to have a second passenger, or more, as it finally fled from the vicinity of the murder scene. Whoever became the first suspect masquerading as Alan Farthing at the bus stop drew attention to himself in a subtle manner by sweating profusely then rejecting the first convenient bus to come along. Both Alan Farthing and his girlfriend were highly suspected of being under surveillance by the Secret Service, therefore they would already have his details known to produce this clone. The reason the gate was closed after she was murdered was to leave the murder scene undisturbed, with the potential to have the greatest amount of time between the crime taking place and her body being discovered. This is crucial to leave the time of her execution unknown, in case anyone seen the culprit, so as to place the full burden of suspicion on the clone attracting attention to himself on Fulham Palace Road. A suspect who was released after questioning had left the park after the proposal of gay sex. Like a onetime fugitive leaving a Portuguese beach when two others came along to indulge in such a practice, it is a subtle way of clearing an area. Had the man been physically threatened, this more obvious method of removing him would have alerted further suspicion. With all the activity centred on this area, there was a need to disperse potential witnesses. Then the peculiar sighting of a suspect apparently jumping into the Thames had its reflection as a wanted man returning from the Continent, when on nearing the English coast I considered jumping overboard in sheer desperation. A mixture of intrigue, planning, daring, cunning, ingenuity and thought encapsulate the events in Fulham that fatal morning similar to a good spy novel. Awkward happenings, oblique patterns and telltale signs all conspired to give a chilling conclusion.

Now, if the Security Services had embarked upon this plot to kill Jill Dando only to be foiled in the subsequent cover-up after the deed was committed, where would they then stand afterwards? Apart from cursing the three trivial reasons of a delay in arrival, the unexpected arrival of a traffic warden on the scene, and the victim uttering a small scream, all of which contrived to wreck the second phase of the operation, with the killer seen differing from the positioned charlatan at the bus stop, new viable suspects would have to be found in quick succession. Who, and was there any evidence of this happening?

Nobody had to go scratching the surface to find the answer to fill this void with the heightened menace of Serbian terrorists. British armed forces were involved in the ongoing conflict in the Balkans at the time, therefore, there would be no love lost by accusing this race of people of being responsible – this being a syndrome that is commonly used against current enemies of the British State. This was supported by threats to this effect being made against the BBC, which were received by Tony Hall. Did someone overstep the mark here, as most people had no idea of who this was, never mind issue a threat against him? However, it could guarantee collective silence by means of self-preservation within the corporation. It is scarcely believable that foreigners could single out this gentleman for evil attention, when the majority of the British public never knew of his existence. Once the conflict in Eastern Europe had finished with the reconciliation of both nations, the threat from the Serbian terrorist dimension was predictably dismissed.

Giving ammunition to the *Crimewatch* involvement to this murder concerning the criminal fraternity was a derogatory remark in the Book of Condolence at the funeral. If Serbs could no longer be easy targets to pin the blame onto, this inclusion had the focus revert back to a more compatible alternative. Shot dead in London and buried in her home town of Weston-super-mare, the culprits had the ability to span the country, which was reminiscent of the witnesses being interfered with after Michael Stone's conviction started to look insecure.

If the Security Services had a need to produce deviations to conceal the identity of the culprits, confuse the issue and present different motives other than that of the genuine one, with the inquiry nearing its 100th day without achieving any positive results, it was like clockwork that a new edition appeared. It was timing that was predictable to eradicate the accumulation of suspicion regarding themselves. Intelligence agencies around the world are in contact with each other with the source of this new story being given as the Israeli intelligence service Mossad. It was a fantastic account of a spurned Russian gangster who was infuriated at Jill Dando rejecting his romantic advances and ordered the execution with the assistance of IRA hit-men. This held everything except reality in its telling. It even offered an explanation for the six tiny indentations on the cartridge of the bullet. Why then were the basics omitted, for instance, the interest British Intelligence had in her, or what the purpose those six tiny punch marks in the cartridge really had. It told only what suited their intentions, however fanciful they were, contrary to what was feasible.

Other miscellaneous incidents like a film crew finding another gun on the Thames riverbank could all have been manufactured to increase speculation as to who the suspects were. Only on approach of the anniversary did the investigation team begin to channel people's thoughts into one certain avenue of the killer being a psychotic loner who had a matching profile to that of the man they eventually arrested. Was this the final ultimate cover-up because they declined to reveal the thorough preparation involved? Nothing was said about the surveillance that Jill Dando was most likely to have been living under or the implications the reconstruction of the double murder of the Russell family held, or the motives the Security Services had to murder her. They never revealed the numbers involved contradicting it could be a single person. There was no mention of the massacre in Strathclyde having any bearing on this crime. They didn't say what purpose the issued photo-fit resembling Alan Farthing was meant to achieve, or why the suspects had a need to communicate on mobile phones. As all telephone calls are logged: were the suspects' exchanges not traced? They refused to divulge what the owner of the blue *Range Rover* was really doing that morning once he was found from the limited number of such vehicles in the country. No effort was made to clarify the registration number of the vehicle caught on CCTV. Nor did they suggest the uses such transport could be put to at the crime scene before and after the event. It didn't bode well that so many aspects appeared to be glossed over for the sole objective of making an arrest.

The greatest similarities were remembering the two soldiers rapidly approaching my home two years previously, and then making a calculated decision not to borrow a shotgun to engage in a gun battle that night. This cumbersome weapon was more of a drawback than an advantage, where had the gun used to murder Jill Dando been fitted with a silencer, it would have become equally cumbersome in this close quarter killing. Knowing the military personnel came equipped with legally held firearms, the search for an illegal handgun could well be folly. Faced with dual predators, who were the living embodiment of the SAS in an unfulfilled mission, again the similarity arises with the main suspect in the lady's murder being described like an SAS man. In consideration of that photo-fit that resembled Alan Farthing, with a reserve of manipulated investigation techniques to draw from, the potential treachery was automatically recognised by myself. Furthermore, it was not the first inclusion of a clone to facilitate the developments with one appearing in a blue *Ford Escort* to impersonate a suspect earlier in events. The closing of the gate in the London suburb was like the killer locking the door behind him at Tracey Wilde's flat, or the shared surname of James Dando as suspicious as the policeman called Bob Rae. Together the employers of Jill Dando, by means of threats, and her fiancé with the dubious photo-fit were targeted, where both parties out of fear could become pre-occupied by thoughts of their own self-preservation to be sufficiently aware of all the implications. The solitude of exile in a corner of Portugal allowed a new definition to materialise concerning other women attacked. Would the final similarity be those closest to Jill Dando, in moments of loneliness, applying logic to the murder and coming to a different conclusion?

All the parallels were there: from the *Land Rover* to the *Range Rover*; from mass murder to prolific murder; from hypocrisy to threats; from fantastic revelations to non-disclosure; from persecution to execution; from set-ups to accomplishment; and from betrayal to treason.

Maybe it was all a wild conspiracy theory, or maybe suppression of the truth was where that term originated. What is certain is the loss, the irreplaceable charisma and the unnecessary trail of sorrow, grief and tears.

However, the final word on the subject may change your judgement; Josie Russell was never in court to identify her family's killer, strange how it was claimed she was used to compile the photo-fit that had an immaculate likeness to myself!

7. IN RETROSPECT

Personally, I owed Jill Dando a debt that can never be repaid. Now her friends, family, Dr Alan Farthing and many admirers can have this explanation as to what went on prior to her death. Certainly, her murder was never going to be avenged or justice obtained for the countless victims in Strathclyde. Something had to be done, hence the writing of this book. Watching Barry George being convicted for a murder he had no possibility of committing in his impaired mental condition provoked an outcry that such a travesty of justice could take place. George, at his trial, was defended by Michael Mansfield QC, who is arguably the best in the country at his profession, which calls into question the legal system and asks how this verdict was produced.

So what did go wrong?

Hamish Campbell led the investigation team with the task of solving Jill Dando's murder. On the anniversary of this crime, he was to prime the public by using the media to one category of suspect; a psychotic loner, then shortly afterwards arrest Barry George as fitting the type of suspect being sought. Was this too convenient? Two main suspects were witnessed being involved, plus a handful of other secondary suspects were apparent, contradicting it could be the work of a crazed loner. George was rejected by the Territorial Army due to his mental deficiencies yet convicted here for a murder that had ballistic techniques so unique that the number of common suspects were non-existent. The operation that killed Jill Dando, where she was restrained by one hand of the assailant and shot by the other, then lowered to the ground, required a strong and confident killer. Such a person is not fitting with George, who is not stable enough in his demeanour to carry out this a crime. No motive was ever established for Barry to murder Jill Dando. Likewise, the evidence against him was non-existent. His sister was known to complain afterwards that the video evidence used to convict Barry was not of him.

The use of psychological profiling was heralded as having a great influence on establishing the type of suspect being pursued. This procedure should have had the focus solely directed onto someone with the bearing of a sergeant in the SAS. To explain: if you are to consider these three extraordinary aspects of Jill Dando's murder - she was held by her upper arm when the killer pulled the trigger; once shot Dando was lowered to the ground; and, on departing the murderer closed the gate behind him – you will have a better insight into the character involved.

The level of composure this assassin held was phenomenal. Irrespective that all three acts had designated purposes, when having killed the most popular woman in Britain then retain the ability to follow specific instructions requires unique qualities outside the scope of any ordinary member of the public. The person who carried out this crime has most definitely killed before, not only that, to give them the level of confidence required, they would be guaranteed that they would never be caught upon accepting such an assignment. In light of which, neither the criminal fraternity nor any terrorist carried out this crime. It certainly was not done by anyone suffering from a mental illness. Any psychologist with a decent grasp of the subject will verify these statements. A selective nature to the passages in a psychological profile used for detective work can deliberately mislead an audience...

Before the high profile trial began an unedited version of this story was initially hosted on the internet at an obscure website, where if it could be found it had the potential to change the outcome of the trial. I personally no longer believed in the British justice system having been a constant victim of the most horrific terror campaign conducted in Western Europe since the Second World War, either to find a law that did not exist, or could change in the course of a trial, or, was never there to punish the guilty. The purpose of the law is to establish the truth, not the present abuse of principles. Therefore, I decided to expose the involvement of Henry McLeish by going public with this story knowing it would lead to his downfall. Once again, leaving many to question what really happened behind the scenes. Upon the death of Donald Dewar, the original First Minister of Scotland, I secretly hoped McLeish would get the post only to have him removed leading to greater implications than previously if his position was lesser. As expected, the methods to discredit McLeish began immediately after the internet release of *'Who Killed Jill Dando'*, because the content was so damning. Exposed in this manner, it left the public to question what they had for a First Minister of Scotland - someone who would abuse the death of a young boy for political gain; someone who played a part in a murder that was one of so many that the charge could be one of genocide (this the description given by a Human Rights representative of the United Nations), and then display conduct that was shameful in the extreme to cover up any involvement. I cringed upon his removal when a fellow Labour Party member described him as a *'good man'*. The first public attack on him was a front page news headline in *The Sun* newspaper of McLeish taped in private conversation with Helen Liddell MP calling a fellow minister, *'A Patronizing Bastard'*. Upon knowing the Secret Service are deployed to prevent this type of comment ever seeing print, you can only surmise how this came to be. Likewise, how this conversation was taped. After this occurred a change of tactic was to take place because McLeish was not a lone wolf in the Scottish Labour Party regarding what is going on, where the political fallout on this party could lead to a massive loss of votes at the next election.

Once again I was to come under attack to presumably save the career of Henry McLeish and the reputation of the Scottish Labour Party. This all centred on a court case for an incident that happened on the 2/10/00 - the same day Britain adopted new human rights legislation - involving myself. Where to prevent this trial happening, which could give credence to the ongoing conspiracy against me, resulted in the previously used tactics of attempting to certify myself insane plus another murder attempt on my life. The case against me was when attempting to drive home alone that night I was witnessed being dragged out of my car by the hair, the assailants being two police officers, and then assaulted. For this incident I received six charges although the medical records from doctors and hospital plus the many witnesses confirmed that I was the victim of an assault. Having always maintained Scott Morrison of Central Police to be responsible, where upon his death on the 6/11/00, in order to bring charges against myself, I claimed he was substituted by Strathclyde officers. This was supported by the refusal of the police to provide statements for this trial, which had it continually adjourned. If the law held true, finally after five years of terror, my persecution could be over. That is a very big if knowing how corrupt the system really is. The lawyers I had were intermitting between Allan Kerr, the owner of the practice, and Alan Muir. There was no conceivable way out of this predicament for Strathclyde Police, and I was reiterating that it was imperative all five officers named in the complaint against me should be charged with perverting the course of justice for producing these fictitious charges and that the police are sued for these actions against me. What happened next surpasses all preconceived logic. The judge, on viewing the case, wanted to proceed although the statements required from the police were still not forthcoming, where it was my lawyer, Mr Kerr, who argued psychiatric reports were to be sought again delaying procedures. At this juncture I became alarmed that my own solicitor should provide an opening to change the course of the trial, especially in this manner by deliberately humiliating his client. If your own lawyer argues against the integrity of the judge on mental health grounds then it is perceived there must be a serious problem. Before this lawyer did his client this injustice there had been mention these reports could be sought, where, with this, curiosity had got the better of me that something underhand was occurring, and if I did not act upon it the consequences could be severe. Medical records are accessible, so I consulted my GP to view what had been previously written by Dr Locke. To my surprise everything written there was a complete fabrication, only the exaggerations were completely overdone, which was favourable by demonstrating it was a pack of lies otherwise at this point such nonsense could have me certified insane. Strange how such an over emphasis can act in your favour! With no possibility of being true, even with this utter nonsense, they were still prepared to exploit the situation. All along I had been saying to both these solicitors to report this psychiatrist to the appropriate bodies for her criminal wrongdoing. Both refused with Mr Muir saying, "That is not appropriate in this case."

The source of the perceived insanity was the former girlfriend of my brother, Helen Stewart, and again I asked my solicitors to do their duty and investigate this undercover agent. Again both refused. Even with the change in tact by them behind the scenes supported by the actions of lawyers betraying their paid allegiance to their client, I still allowed the corrupt practice to continue. Scots Law, as I viewed it, is one of worst in the world, but again the abuse of taxpayers' money paying for this extravaganza could end up in my favour.

On the 7/11/01 with the number of legal proceedings here now in double figures, just like that court case four years previously, once again it was to be memorable when I stood trial in Kilmarnock Sheriff Court; only to have it postponed once again. A fortnight beforehand a row had been blown up concerning Henry McLeish with his failure to register expenses on his claims form for the sub-letting of his constituency office in Glenrothes. The timing of this dispute was impeccable. Digging back 14 years to find fault that did climax with the court case, as I stood there that day wearing a large jacket that could contain any number of incriminating documents. Had they known the pockets were empty McLeish did not need to be ejected the next day. Now with a delay I that had instigated, it would have been nearly impossible to keep the dispute going for another month so with it out went who I had targeted. That is justice in Scotland!

An interesting note was the Scottish leader of the Conservative Party, David McLetchie, pursued the issue most vigorously over these two weeks. A smug looking McLetchie was to bask in the glory of Henry McLeish's downfall. I always wondered what plants British Intelligence had in the Scottish Parliament, is David McLetchie one of them? Or, was he briefed prior to the attacks he led? With a reprimand for his behaviour in the days beforehand he suspiciously continued to pursue the subject!

Finally I had the result I required, which again begs the question; is this a democracy? Are elected politicians no longer in control that they can be removed at will by a Secret Service that does not answer to anyone? On the 2/11/01 five days before the trial that never was, Special Branch ran a speeding car at me presumably to murder me and prevent the trial happening. If successful, this could have been another murder the Scottish Labour Party would have had on their hands, as it was to their benefit because it could save the career of the First Minister and the revealing way with which this party was being funded. On one hand I was supposed to be insane yet on the other they still attempted to kill me, which unknown to them had an independent witness. As for the justice system, I did try to report this crime, firstly to the neighbouring force of Central who refused to accept the complaint, to Allan Kerr Solicitors who did nothing about it and, to Strathclyde Police whose only response was to give me other injuries and more fictitious charges. Could any of them afford to have a record of this next crime given the context?

As a bail condition after 7/11/01 psychiatric reports were sought, where, of course, it was specified Dr Locke would be the person to produce these medical documents. I did attend the appointment only to highlight her wrongdoing where in connection with the legal proceedings told her unequivocally to, "Write what you like, as it will be a load of shite anyway going by what you have already written."
The psychiatrist was left squirming as she tried to say people make mistakes, but then I pointed out every sentence written was fabricated to my detriment, also saying the tone of what had been produced was derogatory. Although her guilt was obvious she continued to deny the previous admission that I had a clean bill of mental health, and, at this meeting, the nearest I got to a confession was this woman asking me to speculate why she had falsified the previous writings. If the solicitors I had had acted in my interests months ago this situation was not possible. It was interesting to note Dr Locke had an offer she 'claimed' from the procurator fiscal; accept medication and all six charges against you will be dropped. Once again unequivocally, I told her this was blackmail (you will now have a better indication of how corrupt the Scottish legal system really is). To have in the region of ten million witnesses before Jill Dando was shot dead confirming my story, the United Nations knowing some of the details of the terror the British Establishment are inflicting on the Scottish nation, and, a neighbourhood and beyond that first disbelieved my story to have changed their verdict and were now singing my praises, yet in desperation all that remained to save the reputation of Strathclyde Police and the Scottish Labour Party were a few pathetic lies! After this meeting I went on the run again, not turning up at the next court appearance to

prove beyond doubt how corrupt it all really is, as the six charges and the warrant for my arrest all mysteriously disappeared! I already had what I wanted, the removal of Henry McLeish, where once again the public did question the true motives for his dismissal.

The whole charade was shown up for what it really was when McLeish had no court case to answer. His supposed wrongdoing regarding sub-letting was sufficient to have him removed from Office yet not stand trial. After that happened the propaganda machine was rolled out again by claiming 17000 cases in Scotland were dropped the year before. This has no bearing whatsoever on his situation but acts as a means of mitigation against the corrupt procedure.

.   .   .   .

On return to Scotland in April of the following year, the persecution was in full flow with the failure of not getting all five officers charged with perverting the course of justice, the Special Branch officer charged with attempted murder and perverting the course of justice (where if successful there would have been no trial), and, Strathclyde Police sued for producing fictitious charges against me. I was being relentlessly hunted down by customs officers, police and Special Branch officers immediately upon arrival. The first day back was spent in hiding, then in an attempt to resolve some of the problems I asked Citizens Advice Bureau who sent me to the local constituency office of our MP; a Labour Party member. A daunting prospect knowing my murder five months previous could be to their benefit, as I conformed with the advice given sitting there that day talking with them suspected of being involved through gritted teeth. On leaving this office intent on following their instructions, first I noticed an undercover van with two officers in it then found myself arrested for walking in a public park. At this latest incident they were to abstract a DNA sample with the help of five officers in riot gear contrary to the advice given by the United Nations that a human rights lawyer be present, which was being denied. The suspicions I had regarding the Labour Party all came to fruition again, realising I had been set up to be framed for murder once again. The murder of Tracey Wilde had many implications concerning both them and the

Conservative Party. Thankfully I am now guaranteed political asylum. This murder was used to damage the reputation of the Scottish National Party (SNP) by connecting a prominent member to it. When I contacted the SNP, I commented the telephone was tapped. The man on the other side said it probably was - an insight that tells how bad the oppression in Scotland really is.

. . . .

When this story was written an original allegation was the murder of drug addicts. The tactic killing them abusing heroin was to gradually lower the purity so that an increased dosage was required to give the same level of fix. Addicts would overdose of their own accord by simply supplying them with high purity heroin afterwards. Glasgow, as mentioned earlier in the text, was also the source of several outbreaks of a killer virus in the heroin either being Anthrax or similar. Similar to the speculation that was promoted of pimps being involved in prostitute murders, again, drug dealers do not want to be murdering them that are their market. If a cull of junkies was taking place it had to be done by them putting the heroin on the streets. Two smugglers of this drug were arrested in Estonia who both claimed involvement with MI6, giving some credence to what is being alleged. Upon looking at the annual drug death figures in Strathclyde (Glasgow) compared to Lothian and Borders (Edinburgh) thinking the number would be similar, I was shocked to find it five times higher in Strathclyde!

. . . .

The greatest turning point in this story was ironically the first conviction of Brian Donnolly for the murder of Margo Lafferty when stories emerged from the court that all was not well to secure this conviction, although a spokesman from Strathclyde Police tried to capitalise on his conviction by claiming this proved there was no serial killer operating in Glasgow. After this episode people were left frustrated and angry because the truth was starting to seep out and my newspaper article now had plenty of believers. The conviction of Barry George created more disbelief, further substantiating my story.

. . . .

Many other murders could be included in this story but in the interests of maintaining a coherent storyline the other crimes and names have not been focussed upon. The subject matter is vast indicating how horrific it all really was.

. . . .

Disturbing as it sounds, Henry McLeish with his promotion to First Minister of Scotland was not the only one to be rewarded for his involvement as Donald Dewar after his untimely death had a bronze statue erected in his honour, and others received accolades from the Queen who had been involved. The victims only received the further indignity of criticising their lifestyles once deceased. Maybe, had all the high standing individuals involved done their duty Glasgow would not have been reduced to the humanitarian crisis it is today, and Jill Dando could still be alive.

MISCELLANEOUS DETAILS

The following passages focus on the characters, places and situations mentioned in the text. It is set out in the order they appear with no precedence over one another.

(1. The Wild West)

Jacqueline Gallacher had a third person targeted in connection with her murder. When I was arrested for walking in a public park under false pretences - it was claimed by the police that they had received a telephone call because I was acting suspiciously, this call, if it was made, could only come from the Scottish Labour Party office that I was previously in, who, as we now know, are floating on human blood. On extracting a DNA sample under duress, I realized that I was once again being framed for murder, potentially having been set up by the Scottish Labour Party for a murder they are implicated in, therefore I could only make a fuss about the situation and promptly leave this country with the possibility of receiving political asylum.

At the time, the opposition party in Scotland was the SNP, who were interested in bringing my case up in the Scottish parliament. To prevent this happening, Strathclyde Police went out and arrested another innocent man for Miss Gallacher's murder; legal proceedings were now pending. Even with another concerted effort to rig the jury by featuring related articles in the Press at the time of the man's trial, they still failed to convict him. Articles such as First Minister's, Jack McConnell, changes to the law regarding rape and Margo McDonald's timely inclusion of prostitute related issues (her inclusions, at the time of other trials has happened before) were to demonstrate the vulnerability of women and give the perception members of the public were involved – this tactic, if deliberately done, is more commonly known as perverting the course of justice. The murder of Jackie Gallacher remains unsolved.

Glasgow continues to struggle in an impoverished state with one of the highest rates of heroin abuse in the Western world. Officially it is the worst in Europe.

Bible John was never caught.

The man in charge of operating the CCTV cameras in Glasgow was given an accolade from the Queen. People, who have heard this, in light of what is going on, are said to respond with the reflective sick joke; "It must be for his services to the blind."

The graffiti that claimed Special Branch and the police were responsible for murdering the citizens of Glasgow has all been removed. I once took a spray paint can and wrote, '*Police killed Tracy Wilde*' beside a busy road in Glasgow, again, this was quickly removed. The purpose was to deliberately spell her first name wrong before I went on to produce that incriminating photocopy. The Secret Service knew this graffiti was mine; so that when I produced the photocopy with the correct spelling of the name 'Tracey' they never suspected me of being its author.

Marjorie Roberts was the woman drowned in the River Clyde; who had her cause of death changed from being accidental/suicide to that of murder.

Mrs Wilson (Jacqueline Gallacher's mother) was never again able to so openly criticize the police after making a condescending comment about them on television.

The female police officer, who led the bogus investigation into Jacqueline Gallacher's murder, was rewarded for her services to policing with an accolade from the Queen. Now retired from Strathclyde Police, her position within the force was the highest achieved by any female officer.

My father took ill with gout. Gout is said to be a rich man's disease, I attribute this not to the poisoned milk but to the water supply being poisoned with blue chemicals. On Sunday nights a Special Branch jeep would stop outside the house and drop blue chemicals into our water supply. How many more families were also being poisoned by these evil people?

No answer to the poisoned milk has ever been received after all these years; agents from both chemical and biological warfare are being used on the Scottish population. Is it any wonder they could never reply to the crimes they are suspected of?!

The SAS soldiers who tried to murder me have never been named. From 1996 onwards a lifelong gagging order was placed against all members of the SAS, which is very convenient with them now deployed to murder any innocent civilian in Scotland. Up until the year 1997, I always wore a poppy for Remembrance Sunday. I will never again contribute to what I now consider a 'bleeding hearts club'. What the British Army is doing to innocent civilians is horrific. Stories from the recent war in Iraq (not found in the mainstream media) proved the SAS not to be as invincible as they like to claim, with heavy losses reported.

Sergeant Webster I have never heard about since that one telephone call he made in a panic trying to cover up their crimes.

On exile; Scotland in recent years, has a drastically reduced population. People who know what is going on, leave before they are next to be targeted or their lives are made so miserable by economic means that they give up the struggle. Scotland had for a long time the highest emigration rate of any Western country; paradoxically it remains one of the richest countries in the world with the potential to be the richest, but not under rule from the present dictatorship/s. My persecution continues whatever country I choose to live in due to British influence having being pursued all over Europe and North Africa. They were never happy that someone survived their killing spree. One example was being under house arrest in the Republic of Ireland by the Irish Special Branch and their forced entry of a friend's home because I part-owned a computer with her.

David Wilson, on being removed from his council employment suddenly replaced his wife's old *Volkswagen Golf* with a newer large *Audi* car plus a *Land Rover* jeep similar to what the British Army use. He found new employment as an engineer.

(2. Going Home)

MI5 moved into investigating organized crime in October 1995. They never took on the Glasgow prostitute murders as a case; did they already know that these murders would never be solved or were they already involved?! Intriguingly, after October 1995 there were cases of 'classic gangland hits' that had the military as prime suspects!

Leona McGovern was the girl who was mutilated before finally being strangled. The argument that the victims received 'humane' deaths is invalid. Leona, like the victims who died in the River Clyde, suffered the most horrific death.

The photo-fit in the Russell reconstruction, that had photographic similarities to myself, had an incident where a photograph was taken of myself that could provide the basis for this suspect photo-fit. At Knockhill Race Circuit I was approached by a young woman, who was over-weight and blonde haired, she persistently had to take a photograph of myself; my hair at the time was similar to the photo-fit shown on television. I have no confirmation of this being accurate, therefore left it out of the text.

The *Glasgow Herald* had the photograph and photo-fit together that bore my resemblance and the name Bob Rae, in the corrupt manhunt for Grant McCaskill.

The police officer Bob Rae was based at Maryhill police station. This is further found to be suspect, in the belief that Partick police station should have been used for a manhunt in the West End of Glasgow.

The honey trap in the Mitchell Library was similar in appearance and manner to a girl I had once gone out with.

The spokeswoman from Strathclyde Rape Crisis I have no knowledge about, I only pray for her safety.

(3. Fight The Big War)

The 11th hour of the 11th day of the 11th month is when the War officially ended. Both the First and Second World Wars are commemorated on the Sunday nearest to this date.

The death of Charles McGregor was featured in an article in the *Sunday Mail*. He supposedly died of a drugs overdose. When retired drugs dealer Charles Rae, no relation, was found dead by means of a drugs overdose during the trial of six Strathclyde Police officers for perjury, a newspaper story implied he was murdered. Needless to say all six officers walked free although a judge had previously branded them 'liars' in an open court.

My court appearance was only possible because I was brave enough as attempt to counter-attack the SAS soldiers who tried to murder me. Otherwise, the chances of getting that far were nearly impossible.

The £50 fine was paid on the spot because I had no visible means of income. Whatever donations I received from people who believed in me, were few and far between.

On my return from the court case; later on I intentionally drove passed the house of a Special Branch officer who had been moved into the hamlet of Glenhead, to see a police sergeant entering his house. Special Branch officers in Scotland are not easily visible in society, where never before had I seen such open communication between the two. The panic I had caused was so immense that they were seen to be breaking their own rules. Later that night, two reporters turned up at my home claiming to be from the *Daily Record*. I was too paranoid to trust or assist them, although I went as far as allow them to take some photos of myself, also, my family wanted rid of them. The night finished with Raymond Stevenson later appearing in his blue *Ford Escort* in a new position closer to the house with both visual and audio surveillance from inside his car.

My newspaper article in the *Evening Times* had the journalists make the exaggeration of including the word 'rape', before Grant McCaskill was convicted of such a crime.

Helen Stewart I last seen in Govan beside a Strathclyde Police base. The last I heard of her was as an undercover police witness in a drugs trial. Whether this was true or not, or whether I was being fed false information I really don't know. In an attempt to discredit the whole story of '*Who Killed Jill* Dando' I was once fed a story, direct from British Intelligence, that they had murdered the respected Irish journalist Veronica Guerin. In basic terms, if they had, they would not be so open about it. I always have to be careful never to adopt false information that could destroy my credibility. As part of the cover-up Helen Stewart moved from her home in Maryhill. I do not know where she is hiding now.

My stupid brother remains in a fantasy world. As near to a confession that was ever going to be extracted from him was when he admitted his version of an original story, where I had to fight off six intruders inside the house one night, had been made up from his own insanity. His ludicrous claim that I had broke the house windows and danced on the broken glass with my bare feet was contradicted by witnesses present that night. For that sole reason I extracted this confession, otherwise he would have continued with this piece of stupidity with the mindset he exhibits. It is doubtful he will ever admit Helen Stewart's influence on matters. On a more comical note was him telling someone over the house telephone another of his fantasies; that I had seen an UFO. In the full knowledge that every telephone call was being monitored and their desperation to prove that I was 'insane', it would only be a matter of time before the 'aliens' appeared. One night afterwards, in the fields adjacent to the house, for 30 minutes a thick red glow illuminated the countryside. Later on a neighbour came round to complain/ask about this untoward event. I kept quiet never saying why it had happened or that the aliens were really Special Branch who left in a blue *Ford Escort* (not Raymond Stevenson's). The last fantasy I heard from this brother was, our father was a millionaire. In reality, the poor man could only afford to buy himself a second-hand *Skoda*! I no longer have any contact with this fool.

Tracey Wilde's murder remains unsolved! The reason the flat door was locked after Raymond Stevenson murdered her was to seal up the crime scene so investigating police officers could not be accused of planting my DNA there after she was killed. It also allowed for more time between the crime taking place and her body being discovered in case there was a hitch in their plan. In this event, there was a major problem with Stevenson seen leaving her flat at a time of around 2am that fatal night.

The head of Strathclyde Police quickly and suspiciously retired from this position. After agreeing an extension to his contract as Chief Constable, he suddenly announced his retirement. Such a contradiction was picked up upon by the public. Not only that, it was rumoured that I had removed him. Once again I was forced into silence on the subject because his removal had been a mistake on my behalf. I had been given the telephone number of *Liberty* and asked if I would give them an outline of my story. Initially I ignored this request, and then when I finally did, John Orr announced his retirement within hours of making that call. *Liberty* is a human rights group who, unknown to me at the time, are heavily monitored by MI5. The late Chief Constable was knighted by the Queen to become Sir John Orr. His replacement was the namesake William Rae, chosen in the belief I would be kinder to him; he wasn't kinder to myself as his officers assaulted, wrongfully arrested and imprisoned me, plus of course, the Special Branch evil attention continued. Officer Alan McPhail claimed I kicked him in the balls. In an effort to improve the moronic standard of Strathclyde Police I suggested it was his testicles. To prove it was just a blatant lie to have more fictitious charges placed against me, I told him to take a photograph of his testicles to use in evidence against me!

The parking places beside the golf club and another parking place further along the road, used by Raymond Stevenson and other Special Branch agents, had earth mounds built up on the entrances to prevent any car parking there again. This was done for psychological reasons in an attempt to erase people's memories that cars ever used these resting places.

The murder of Margo Lafferty: When it was disclosed she was well known to the police, seeking 'protection' from their group who provided security for prostitutes, it can also be surmised the police would know much of what she knew. Draw your own conclusions from that!

(4. The Rat Catcher)

Acre, the Special Branch front company, continued to exist in a rural location outside the village of Linwood. It is situated on the road into Linwood when you are travelling from Erskine or Houston, this road, although being in working condition, was made into a dead-end with no access from Linwood. Why the road was cut off from the Linwood side opposed to the other side was because the Special Branch and British Army bases are on the Erskine side, therefore they continue to allow full access to *Acre*. This change to the roads network was done after I started to reveal who Raymond Stevenson was, complete with his employer. The reason for this was to prevent sightseers passing this company and recognising members of Special Branch who made up the death squads that operate in Strathclyde. Under the government of Margaret Thatcher, Bridge of Weir Leather Company was used in a news report about a thriving business economy – blatant propaganda - but in reality Scotland was in recession. This is the same company at which Raymond Stevenson was killed.

Tracey Wilde's adoptive father was outrageously harassed by the police so he would never have the time inclination or breathing space to see what really happened to his step-daughter. As stated; it has been a consistent practice by the police to target those nearest to the victims.

My unemployment benefit claim that was illegally stopped: I was unable to take this case to court because of the actions of different lawyers, and I was also unable to claim the money owed in back-payment because this meant dealing with the Labour Party, who the local MP is a member of, hence the set-up where I was attacked by the police for walking in a public park with the under-cover police officers present to oversee the operation. Maybe that sad offer made by the lawyer to take the case to a tribunal should have been excepted; it was just such an insult at the time, a means of letting the Social Services off the hook, and gave them involved a free reign to continue their persecution if I had accepted it.

Making a mockery of initiatives to create employment: It could be questioned why few talented Scots are allowed to succeed in their own country. Personally, I have regularly proven to be the best in the world with my technologies, yet it is the likes of me they target. Those that have been successful in recent times are all in the service sector. What is government policy of 'inward investment' other than using public money to make foreign companies more competitive? As for the argument used against poor countries that investment will only materialize when a rule of law established – as demonstrated, it does not exist in Scotland!

Henry McLeish MP (the 'good man'): I doubt if I will ever forget a distressed female member of the Scottish Labour Party referring to Henry McLeish, upon his removal, as a 'good man'. To date, he has never been charged with conspiracy to murder. He had no case to answer in relation to his expenses scandal, proving this was never the genuine reason for his removal from Office. Other Scottish Labour Party members are accused of the same crime, but McLeish was the only one targeted, which again supports my prognosis. He was replaced by Jack McConnell, who was once nicknamed 'Dangerous Jack'.

Dr. Ian Oliver found new employment with the United Nations.

Donald Dewar, former Scottish Secretary and the original First Minister of Scotland, was pressured into an early grave. This is the most controversial one listed, and this piece of insight is the one I never wanted to reveal; but in the interests of giving a complete picture here it is. In October 2000 I was told, " Donald Dewar will not be alive at the end of this week."
Two days later the First Minister of Scotland was lying on a hospital bed in intensive care, two days after that he was dead! Reading that, it implies he was murdered. Far from it, he died a traitor's death. The false version as to why this happened, is an attack on democracy, which I refuse to repeat, only going as far as to say, even the reason for his death was distorted for political gain! A bronze statue was erected in his 'honour'!

The *Sunday Mail* was where I read that the murders of Jacqueline Gallacher, Tracey Wilde and Margo Lafferty could be connected, the next day in *The Sun* and in *The Scotsman* this was denied.

The head of Strathclyde Special Branch, Jim Orr, became the head of the SDEA. This was the newly created policing force dealing solely with drugs crimes in Scotland. The SDEA has had little success since it was formed in a blaze of publicity. Drugs deaths in Strathclyde averaged one hundred a year, in 2002 there was a 70 percent increase in the number of such deaths. The British government stands accused of being the biggest supplier of drugs on the streets of Glasgow, especially heroin. In recent years, people have started to question state involvement in illicit drugs. A few years back, most of the major criminal suppliers were in prison but the amount of drugs on the street was increasing. At this point, instead of the usual triangle of drug dealers, drug users and anti-drug campaigners fighting among themselves therefore blind to the obvious, questions were asked as to what was really going on. Needless to say, Jim Orr was also honoured by the Queen. The last time I saw him was in April 2002 at a roundabout two miles from my home driving in that direction, alone in his large light blue *Audi*. No longer being in charge of Strathclyde Special Branch, if he was once again planning to murder me, he would have to do it himself.

Peter Ritchie, the abnormal sized giant, is accused of many murders in Scotland and Northern Ireland. The last time I saw him was beside a *BT* transit van he had been driving, parked outside his home in Saltcoats – yet the police still can't find any prostitute killers!

The Scottish Labour Party: Reading what is written here it is astonishing that anyone in Scotland ever voted for this political party; so why do they? The first reason is the truth is always concealed, as is evident in the case involving Dr Ian Oliver. The next reason is their stranglehold on power in Central Scotland. Promotion of this Party in the media in Scotland is beyond what you would expect in a democracy, and finally, they are well funded by the Trade Unions. In the future people will be left feeling queasy as to what occurred with their support and money. From the hierarchy to the grass roots of the Scottish Labour Party, the involvement of elements within this Party, in the mass slaughter of innocent people is undeniable. Will they campaign under an honest slogan at the next election, 'Vote Labour, lose your life, liberty and livelihood,' so many that voted for this Party did, or will they use their 'scare' tactics again to secure success?

The Law in Scotland shares a large degree of guilt for what is going on. If the Law was reinstated every Prime Minister and Home Secretary from Margaret Thatcher onwards would find themselves charged with crimes against humanity. Scotland has a Justice Minister, who has consistently failed to stop this terror campaign, but again ministers should be held responsible for their actions in a democracy. Personally, I knew never to trust Scots Law, where we have seen it can change during a trial, but the level of corruption even surprised myself when the two lawyers I had invented the syndrome against me to let Strathclyde Police and the Scottish Labour Party off the hook. Just to prove every avenue was exhausted, I reported them to the Law Society in light of the view that 'they are just there to look after their own'.

This opinion proved correct, with ten serious charges all the Society were prepared to do was pick the most trivial, telephone calls were not being returned as a method of humiliating me, and offer to deal with this – I declined.

The Lord Advocate, Frank Mulholland, a Labour Party appointee, who is best described as being a mediocre barrister from outside sources, refused to accept my evidence pointing the finger at the guilty parties, yet he was made a CBE by the Queen!

Once an SNP Lord Advocate was in place I find the *Royal Mail* no longer functions as a post service for they couldn't find the Scottish Parliament and returned my letter?!

(5. Not For Glory)

A gangland shooting: After the attempted murder by the SAS a contract was taken out on my life by a family of police informants. A would-be assassin would drink in my local pub or drive passed my home in a black *BMW* car. It would only be another kill Strathclyde Police would have to their credit if he were successful; nothing ever changes.

Full, undeniable, SAS involvement resumed in Ireland from 2004 onwards when Welshman, Martin Jones, moved in to be my next-door neighbour. He definitely was a member of this regiment for I seen the tattoo of his blood type that members receive upon joining the regiment – covered over with another tattoo as is their practice when SAS members go into counter-terrorism – and a colleague, David Gilles, to partner with, moved into a neighbouring smaller village. Both were unsuccessful in their attempts to murder me, although Gilles was seen on the street gun-in-hand on one occasion. Jones was thrown out the regiment as featured in *The Sun* early October 2004, and, Gilles was taken out to Afghanistan and then executed causing their leader, Sebastian Morley, to resign. In 2006 an upgraded death squad made a more concerted effort to kill me to include SAS Sgt Tom Kennedy, who bears a likeness to Bob Hope, as does Jill Dando's actual killer, until that was misleadingly changed into Bob Mills to confuse the issue.

I was actually shot once! Witnessed being shot in the back, the gun and would-be killer were both seen, but it had been with a silent weapon with a toxin pellet that burned excruciately as it pierced my upper back. There was also a hole in the shirt to prove this but at the time I never knew the hit had happened such was the James Bond deployment of techniques in what was an MI5 assassination attempt. This assassination attempt is more evidence chemical and biological weapons are being deployed by stealth to murder Scots, plus my house taps regularly run with blue chemicals they have deposited into the water supply.

Atrocities in the West of Scotland; the reason they could not kill an unconnected stranger that night, in light of what is going on, is it would alert people to what is happening. This said, they would not be long in framing some innocent person for the crime. The case of the Secret Service informer, Martin McGartland, who was shot in the North of England, had Scots targeted for his attempted murder, where his would-be assassins drove an alleged Special Branch van.

The sabotage went as far as splitting the chain on my bicycle thinking it would come off when I was using the bike.

The double yellow lines outside the Chinese take-away were finally painted over.

Black Hackney Cabs are a favourite undercover vehicle, which are used in most cities. They did look somewhat out of place in the rural community of Ayrshire when Special Branch used them there.

(6. Conundrum and Similes)

The warrants signed: Jack Straw, as Home Secretary, signed most of the warrants in connection with what happened. Will he ever admit that he signed warrants against Jill Dando and the other victims listed?

Michael Stone lost his appeal for double murder; he continues to protest his innocence. Subsequent television news reports on the

BBC were used, with the conviction of Michael Stone, as examples of a mentally ill killer. Jill Dando is no longer there to prevent such abuses.

Dr Shaun Russell moved with Josie Russell to an isolated cottage far away from Kent.

Surveillance cameras: A network of blue roadside cameras sprang up, which were first placed in Scotland before any other part of mainland Britain. These cameras are said to have been developed by NASA and provide facial recognition night or day. One of the first to be installed was at a crossroads just over a mile from my home; this must have been considered a 'sensitive area'. This camera has since been removed.

The Anthrax used to kill drug addicts in Glasgow; the situation never produced corresponding mass arrests of drug dealers and smugglers to prevent it happening again, instead, there were other outbreaks of this mystery agent on the streets of Glasgow. The question remains unanswered; whose Anthrax is it? I was once told, that going by the amount of surveillance and resources available to the police in their present form, that within three months over 70 percent of the drugs could be taken off the streets in a genuine situation. A man was arrested for posting a hoax Anthrax package to Prince William. This crime is extremely difficult to detect. So why were the drugs dealers responsible for killing many of Glasgow's citizens never arrested when it is a far easier crime to detect?

Dr Locke continued to practice: The medical reports which I had previously read were changed when I finally received a written copy of them. After waiting a full year to obtain a copy of these reports, I had to wait a further week for them to be photo-copied. Although the most ridiculous parts were changed or removed what I have still contains, as quoted, 'As you are aware, Robert has a previous history of paranoid ideas…' from the first meeting with Dr Locke for the benefit of Dr McCormack. On what was this based with no previous analysis to base it upon? Further, the reports I received were incomplete. All of which are very serious offences but there is no law to report them to. Again, I had already tried with my lawyers. In the end, I was only left wondering exactly how many different versions of these reports exist. Did a report saying I have a clean bill of mental health, from Dr Locke's own admission, exist?

£1 million spent on investigating Tracey Wilde's murder, where if Strathclyde Police's Special Branch never killed her, this saving, plus all the other savings from their many crimes, could be put to something useful.

The drugs counsellor did find new employment, not only that, he appeared on television talking in opposition to the Labour Party Administration in Scotland on their proposal to promote homosexuality to schoolchildren; this must have annoyed the old boy network no end. Surveillance on him could be necessary only if the government is flooding the streets with drugs?!

The surveillance on Jill Dando: Celebrities and VIPs are routinely targeted by the Secret Service due to their power and influence. Jill Dando had plenty of other reasons to attract their evil attention.

The photo-fit and photograph of Alan Farthing were displayed together in *The Express*.

(7. In Retrospect)

The non-existent evidence against Barry George: A single particle of gunpowder residue was found on his clothing, which was thee most damning piece of evidence against George. This microscopic particle need not have come from a firearm – a firework, nail-gun or starting-pistol could have produced it – and even if it did come from a gun there is nothing to connect it to the weapon that killed Jill Dando. Barry George had a reduced mental age and liked to play around with this sort of thing. There is also his short stint in the Army to consider. The damning particle could have been transported in the wind from another source onto his clothing, or, contaminated in the forensic laboratory where his clothing was examined. Such a possibility was made public in court due to a breach in procedures at the forensic examination. Any member of the public could have a similar particle present on their clothing! George was later freed upon appeal.

At the United Nations it was disturbing to hear the representative describe the syndrome in Strathclyde as genocide. At which, this should have been the end with a full independent investigation instigated, instead the murders continued.

Henry McLeish was not the only Labour Party member accused of the same scandal involving expenses, yet he was the only one targeted for his alleged wrongdoing. From the very beginning of this fabricated dispute a commentator on the television said, "There must be something else behind this!"
For over a year beforehand I had said I was going to remove Henry McLeish. It was imperative for the safety of all who lived in Scotland that this man be removed, likewise the whole Party (and the Conservative Party with them)! Do not forget, they voted for Mcleish to become First Minister when his disgusting behaviour involving a dead schoolboy was public knowledge. Support for the Labour Party has tapered off in Scotland in recent years, yet in the south, new-comers coming up from England, has caused Conservative support to alarming rise!

Scott Morrison was alleged to have been murdered; his official cause of death was suicide. The night of the incident I tried to hint to him that someone would end up murdered for what had happened. He never heeded the warning. I got off very lightly, only left lying in hospital with the injuries received. In the *Daily Record* it did state he was under investigation for an alleged assault. His death was reported on the seventh of November, my birthday. Was I supposed to be drunk that day and not reading any newspapers?

The Conservative Party was in power when the terror campaign began in Strathclyde that continues to the present day. In the 1950s, they were once the most popular political party in Scotland, now it has little support - thankfully.

POSTSCRIPT

The SNP did come to power, but on wanting to demonstrate trust they kept Frank Mulholland in position as Lord Advocate. However, a power struggle took place between the then SNP leader, Alex Salmond, and the British Establishment regarding who should become the first Chief Constable of newly formed Police Scotland, which he lost. The hierarchy of Police Scotland went on to become predominantly staffed by former Met officers – the Met has a reputation for corruption – where Salmond later on found himself facing sexual misconduct charges that are ill-fitting with his character. This situation should never have materialised in a devolved Scotland, but obviously there was a requirement for London control of the Scottish police service. For the murder of Emma Caldwell an 'elite unit' was formed within the Met to investigate this Scottish crime. This is farcical when those responsible are known about in Switzerland (at the U.N.) yet not a single arrest of the accused Home Secretaries, Prime Ministers and members of MI5 in London has ever been made. To the layperson it just looks like a corrupt method to overspend the Police Scotland budget and give funds to friends in London. At the time of the Scottish referendum for independence, Police Scotland produced a smokescreen by arming officers with firearms to divert public attention away from the many vote rigging allegations that took place to keep Scotland illegally within this corrupt Union, for those living there to be murdered at will.

Seven police officers were investigated for allegedly passing information to journalists concerning these prostitute murders, but all were acquitted. Reports also indicate journalists were being spied upon in relation to the mass murder taking place. Circumstances concerning murdered prostitutes was aired in the Scottish Parliament, where, predictably, the police officers present were accused of misleading Parliament. In particular, by R. Nicolson who displayed great arrogance when he did so. Such has been sencored on the internet for it is difficult to find reference to which, indicating a cover-up is still ongoing at a high level, where this incident as a final revealing instalment would allow many to join the dots and see clearly the British government do have a policy of mass murder in Scotland, thereby the slaughter continues unabated...

'They owe their greatness to their country's ruin.' Words by Robert Burns.

ROBERT RAE 2019

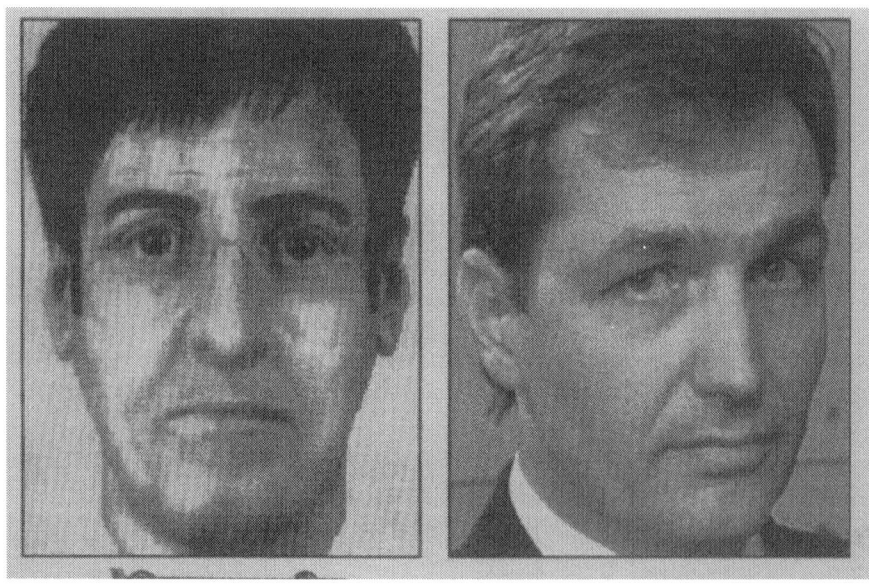

WHO KILLED JILL DANDO   BY ROBERT RAE

EVENING TIMES NEWSPAPER OF THE YEAR Thursday

I'M BEING FRAMED

A MAN has stunned a Scottish court by claiming police are out to frame him for the murder of Glasgow prostitute Jackie Gallagher.

His claims form a tangled web that pull together murder, rape, attempted murder and international intrigue.

Robert Rae ... says he lives "in fear for his life." He made a complex string of allegations to back his claim, including his alleged portrayal by police as a sex fiend behind attacks on 20 women and the killing of six ... including vice girl Jackie Gallagher.

He admits driving a red Renault van in the Glasgow area — cops have linked the driver of such a van to the unsolved Gallagher murder probe.

PHOTO-FIT

The girl was found wrapped in a carpet in a lay-by near Bowling.

Rae also claims the police photo-fit issued prior to the arrest and conviction of Grant McCaskill — who got life earlier this year for stalking Glasgow women after his girlfriend shopped him — bears a striking resemblance to himself.

Jackie (36) was brutally slain and her body dumped in a lay-by on the Glasgow-Dumbarton road last June.

Now Rae ... has put himself firmly in the spotlight.

Yesterday he amazed officials at Inverclyde District Court where he was on trial for a minor motoring offence. He declared: "I am being

Man makes bizarre murder claims in courtroom

EXCLUSIVE By JIM McLEAN Chief Reporter

framed for the murder of prostitute Jackie Gallagher."

Rae (29) was charged with driving his 125cc motorcyle without having a Basic Training Certificate.

When magistrate Ronald McEwan asked what Rae's defence was, the unemployed cabinet maker stormed: "I find my house at 4.30am in fear of my life and to prevent a major scandal breaking.

"The scandal involves the attacking of about 20 women, six of whom were murdered.

"The police are actively framing me for the murder of Jackie Gallagher."

SHOOTING

He claims that a police photo-fit released during the West End manhunt identified him.

He claims that he frequently used his brother's red Renault van — similar to one being sought in connection with the murder — to drive into Glasgow.

He also claims that he is an eyewitness to a sangland shooting in Perth, and this also makes him the subject of police interest.

The two traffic cops who flagged him down in Greenock — Constables Patrick Martin and David Ryan — sat stunned in court.

The magistrate found Rae guilty and fined him £50.

Afterwards Rae said he was "doing a runner" possibly back to Portugal or France where he says he slipped through an Interpol net earlier this year.

A leading detective

working on the Jackie Gallagher murder team, said: "I can categorically deny that Strathclyde Police frame anybody.

"This is a live inquiry and it would be wrong to identify people who we have, or have not, interviewed."

IT WASN'T ME ... Robert Rae claims he is being framed

JACKIE GALLAGHER

TRACEY WILDE WAS MURDERED BY THE MAN IN
BLACK SUIT SEEN LEAVING HER HOME AT 2AM.
STRATHCLYDE POLICE MADE NO EFFORT TO
TRACE THIS MAN BUT PRODUCE FALSE
EVIDENCE TO HAVE HER ALIVE AFTER THIS
AWAY FROM HER FLAT. THIS MAN WAS
SPECIAL BRANCH OFFICER. RAYMOND STEVENSON
FROM HOUSTON HE WORKED FOR ACRE A
SPECIAL BRANCH FRONT COMPANY. AFTER
CRIMEWATCH 24TH MAR 98 THE MAN IN
BLACK SUIT PHONED IN TO ELIMINATE HIMSELF.
NOT ONLY HAD THE KILLER ELIMINATED HIMSELF
BUT A DEAD MAN HAD MADE THE CALL.
RAYMOND STEVENSON WAS MURDERED AT BRIDGE
OF WEIR LEATHER ON 3RD FEB 98 BY
HIS OWN PEOPLE.

Printed in Great Britain
by Amazon